PRAISE FOR *TRUST YOUR LIFE*

Noelle Sterne has written a spiritually practical, sharp and exciting guide to setting free your inner voice and your dreams. She speaks to both the novice and more experienced, and her big heart and quick mind leap off the pages and under your skin.

> —Tama J. Kieves, author, *This Time I Dance! Creating the Work You Love*

In *Trust Your Life,* Sterne shows us that by shifting the direction of our thoughts, we can view life from a new and lofty perspective—to express our God-given potential and ultimately realize our long-held desires and goals.

> —Barbara Van, Unity minister

Noelle Sterne lovingly guides us in an easy-to-read, step-by-step manual to help us believe and achieve our lifelong dreams. This spiritual and grounded book will reach the hearts of people who toil in unhappy circumstances or feel they are victims of God's frivolous will. Noelle addresses these misconceptions with head-on confrontations, insightful and inspired examples and self-bolstering techniques.

> —Aaron Paul Lazar, author of *LeGarde Mysteries,* engineer, KB America

Trust Your Life demonstrates how your past—no matter how dreadful—holds the key to the future you've always dreamed of. This book is for readers of all ages—I am giving a copy to my sharp 87-year-old relative to show her that "getting old" doesn't mean coming to the end of one's "useful" life.

> —Moira Allen, author, *Starting Your Career as a Freelance Writer*

Noelle has created a dynamic, supportive spiritual process if you long to transform your life and fulfill your dreams. Truly a treasure, this book is a masterful, engaging, inspiring piece of heart-work which will undoubtedly prove significant for many readers.

—Sister Brigid McCarthy, RSM, co-foundress of Well of Mercy spiritual retreat

Reading this book, I had the sense that God is ministering to Dr. Sterne to guide you in accomplishing your desires. If you are serious about going after your dreams, I challenge you to read *Trust Your Life*.

—Karen Lewis, MBA, publisher of *Women WIN Journal*

A welcome addition to the self-help bookshelves, *Trust Your Life* shows readers that their future does not have to repeat their past. With very "doable" tools and techniques, readers can create meaningful experiences in accord with their life purpose. The book's humorous, down-to-earth style encourages all who want to make positive changes in their lives.

—Sorah Dubitsky, Ph.D., editor of A *Chorus of Wisdom: Notes on Spiritual Wisdom*

Noelle Sterne's interactive, conversational tone puts readers at ease as she authoritatively guides them through intelligent musings, perceptions and applications to their lives of essential spiritual topics.

—Nicole M. Bouchard, editor-in-chief of *The Write Place at the Write Time*

I wish I had this book 30 years ago. I've been successful in military service and the corporate world, but my life dream was to pursue a career in the motion picture industry. After reading *Trust Your Life*, I intend to take a film class at a nearby university.

—Richard E. Talley, Ed.D., Colonel, Ret., U.S. Army, and vice president, National Electrical Manufacturers Association

Creative people often need two things: permission to follow their dreams and directions for getting out of their own way. Noelle Sterne delivers both in a clear, positive, compassionate guide. I'm sure this book will be life-changing for many people.

—Laura Backes, editor and publisher of *Children's Book Insider: The Newsletter for Children's Writers*

This book helps you get to know your inner self and make new discoveries through seeing and believing the truthfulness of your dreams. You will realize it is never too late to listen to yourself and your inner spirit.

—Rev. Patricia A. Wilson-Cone, Ph.D., director, Pastoral Care Services and Clinical Pastoral Education at Jackson Health System

Noelle Sterne is a gifted writer whose heart touches those of her readers. Her words supply wisdom for the creative soul!

—Simran Singh, founder and publisher of *11:11 Magazine*

Trust Your Life is a great contribution to releasing the creative wonders that remain untapped in the souls of so many people. Reading Noelle's book, I found myself, even after years of a successful career, looking at "bottled up" desires within myself, and I was inspired not to miss the joy of expressing them in this lifetime. For probably 90 percent of the human race this is a must read!

—Rev. Phillip M. Pierson, former vice president, Unity Institute® and Seminary

TRUST YOUR LIFE

Forgive Yourself and Go After Your Dreams

Noelle Sterne, Ph.D.

TRUST YOUR LIFE

Forgive Yourself and Go After Your Dreams

Noelle Sterne, Ph.D.

Unity Village, MO 64065-0001

Trust Your Life

First Edition 2010
Third printing 2012

Unity Books are available at special discounts for bulk purchases for study groups, book clubs, sales promotions, book signings or fundraising. To place an order, call the Unity Customer Care Department at 1-866-236-3571 or email *wholesaleaccts@unityonline.org*.

Cover design: Jenny Hahn, Senior Multimedia Artist, Unity
Author photo: Jeffrey Berson
Interior design: The Covington Group, Kansas City, Missouri

Library of Congress Control Number: 2010940552

ISBN: 978-0-87159-351-1

Canada BN 13252 0933 RT

To God, the Encompassing Source—
All for Your glory.

To Tx—
my God-given gift, my rock, whose unshakable, faith-filled,
relentless positive conviction and life exemplify his trust.

To each of you—
you have the inherent, divinely implanted ability to trust.

Do not settle for little dreams.
God meant you for more.
Listen, be still, can you hear?
The waves of God's thought
Roll, roll in your mind.
The winds of God's will
Blow, blow through your heart—
Where will they carry you?
The winds and the waves of God's sea
Are high and have no end,
But they carry you to a fulfillment
And a consummation greater even
Than your loveliest dream.
Do not settle for little dreams.
Listen, be still, can you hear?
God meant you for more.

—James Dillet Freeman
"God Meant You for More"

In repentance and rest is your salvation,
in quietness and trust is your strength.

—Isaiah 30:15

CONTENTS

PART I
ADMITTING: WHAT'S REALLY BOTHERING YOU?

PART II
CHANGING: HOW DO YOU CHANGE WHAT'S BOTHERING YOU?

PART III
ACTIVATING: GETTING TO YOUR DREAM

FOREWORD

My own life has been a progression of dreams and their fulfillment, for which I am very grateful. Yet realizing my dreams was
sometimes challenging because I did not always have a clear
process for best following my path of dreams, including letting go
of some false ideas about my past.

Now Dr. Noelle Sterne gives us a practical and effective
process that I would like to have had along my life path.
Fortunately, it is not too late because I do continue to have more
dreams in my continuing course. Her accomplished mind, her
work as a counselor, her time as a teacher, and her busy pen as an
excellent writer are blended into this distinctly useful book, *Trust
Your Life: Forgive Yourself and Go After Your Dreams*.

Spiritually based, and with an applied set of tools that work,
this book teaches us how to turn every perceived botching of our
past into a greater bonus for our future—and how to manage our
inner impressions into the successful outer expressions of our
greatest dreams.

Noelle often notes how she has been influenced by different
authors in her own work. She clearly has embraced Dr. Steven
Covey's principle of beginning with the end in mind. *Trust Your
Life* leads us to the end of reaching our dreams by beginning with
learning to forgive ourselves, trust ourselves, and live our dreams
today.

Each of us holds our dreams—our inner insights into our
unique higher possibilities. I have mine, you have yours, and this
book is a realized dream of Noelle's. *Trust Your Life* is the

outpouring of her many years of working with thousands to assist us in reaching our dreams. Now we have the perfect process to move our dreams beyond the past, through the present, and into the joy of unfolding reality.

Thank you, Noelle, for trusting yourself to write this great book for all of us!

—Tom Zender
President Emeritus, Unity
founding member, Evolutionary Leaders
chairman, board of directors, VillageEDOCS, Inc.
author, *God Goes to Work: New Thought Paths to Prosperity and Profits*

PREFACE

Trusting my life has taken a long time. Always a good student, I've found the course outside the classroom a much more challenging campus. Still no expert (if ever), I've learned to trust the inner promptings of mind and heart, the gut feelings, the immediate responses. In sum: Stop, look inside, listen and let the messages come.

Of course, I don't have all the answers, but now I know Who does. When I listen and trust Life within, the answers always come. Showing you how to believe them, practice them, and act on them is what this book is about. Or rather, it's about my growing urge to share with you what could not be denied. You don't need an advanced degree or even any schooling (was Jesus a high school graduate?) to trust-believe-practice-act. You need only desire and openness to what may be unfamiliar, radical ideas.

I was open to these ideas—wavering, leery, inconsistent, letting logic interfere, but finally succumbing to the glorious Promise. *Trust Your Life* evolved from my school after graduate school—a not-easy and uneasy course in trusting my own life. My good studenthood had me obediently climbing the degree ladder, even before I knew what the letters stood for. Now I know, with a Ph.D. in English and Comparative Literature from Columbia University, that Ph.D. really stands for Phenomenon of Divinity. We've all achieved it. Here I want to help you accept your own Ph.D.

How and Why This Book

I've proved that we *can* reach our Dreams, whatever form they take and whatever sphere they occupy. (I capitalize this word and its variations to refer to that very special heartfelt, precious, tucked-away, yearning, craving, aching, hungering, thirsting THING you've always wanted to do more than anything else.) My Dream has been writing. The likely apocryphal story my mother always told had me standing in the crib at 4 months old crying not "Momma, Momma" but "Book-a! Book-a!" Wanting to write my whole life, I nevertheless pursued all those degrees, supported myself with office jobs, and right after the last graduation taught college English and literature. Two years later I retired (or got fired, depending on one's perspective and title), weary of too many committee meetings and too much letterhead.

A friend brilliantly suggested that I become self-employed so I could devote more time to writing. So, being also a good secretarial student, I advertised dissertation typing in my university community. Clients appeared quickly. Maybe it was my hand-typed card, "Intelligent Typing," with the phone number.

As I typed, I often became engrossed in clients' dissertation material, and when they next visited to pick up the work, I started asking questions: "Do you think Keats was heavily influenced by *Paradise Regained*?" "How did Heidegger reconcile his sense of Being and his Nazism?" "Does Kotter believe managers can really become leaders?"

My clients, nascent doctors, began suspecting I wasn't your average office drone and then started asking me questions: "Does this follow logically?" "Does that make sense?" "Am I stretching it?" "Do I have enough substantiation?" "Am I sticking to a scholarly tone?"

From these questions about their work, they spilled their troubles about impossible deadlines, menopausal committee members and drafts of chapters endlessly thrown back dripping with blood-red pen critiques. Just before they left my office, most clients would wail, "I'll *never* get this degree!"

I found myself unable to ignore their draft troubles and outbursts (when the teacher is ready, the student bares all). I began giving advice, suggesting changes, scribbling sample stuffy scholarly phrases (after all, I'd come through the doctoral ordeal), and bolstering them. Often, just wanting to ease their misery, I hardly knew where my guidance came from. The clients' faces relaxed and their small smiles of hope showed me I'd reached them. I felt wonderful.

I graduated again—from typing to editing and advising. I developed a business that became, eventually, one of helping adults pursue their Dreams. Resuming writing, I eventually wrote this book about helping adults pursue their Dreams.

Why Me

Trust Your Life derives from a now 28-year editorial and coaching practice assisting adults who return to universities for graduate degrees. As it and I have evolved, the work encompasses editing, consulting and counseling in the professional, personal and spiritual aspects of life.

Most clients are already professionals in a wide range of fields—education, administration, health care, business, social services, law, even a few in the military. Many are extremely experienced and accomplished, with multiple awards and impressive titles.

Whatever their professional expertise, though, clients often voice doubts and regrets about lost time, fears of finishing, and destructive perspectives that impede their progress. Some have blossomed and developed beyond their degrees. Not content to sit on their newly-granted doctorates, they've allowed their next Dreams to materialize. They've dared to envision higher and more ambitious ones in many venues, some not even requiring an advanced degree. As might easily be predicted, new fears and anxieties pop up, and clients again call (or, more universally now, email).

In assisting them through their trepidations and struggles at every stage, I developed many of the spiritually based and practical methods in this book. Of course, I, too, have learned much more, not only in writing, editing and human relationships (a BIG one), but, more important, in spiritual application to all of it.

Happily, I had a grounding. Metaphysical disciplines have continued as a major thread, passion, interest and necessity in my life. I've practiced the principles of Unity for more than 25 years, with the abundant Unity publications a mainstay and an always-growing part of my library. I also participated in many Unity retreats, courses, lectures and Sunday services, especially those led by the marvelous Eric Butterworth—founder and pastor of the Unity Center of New York City, who effortlessly combined the intellectual and the spiritual—and his unparalleled, calming and inspired wife Olga Butterworth.

I've also studied yoga for a long time, starting with the physical *hatha* and seduced into meditation and chanting. My searching has branched out into *A Course in Miracles* and other spiritual teachers, including Wayne Dyer, Louise Hay and the teachings of Abraham Hicks. With deeper study of these complementary spiritual perspectives and application to my professional and personal spheres, I discovered the strong desire to share the lessons learned from my business (and fights with my husband) more widely than with clients and friends. *Trust Your Life* has become the blessed vehicle for this sharing.

Trust stems from my conviction and personal practice that sharing and teaching the theme of trusting oneself and one's inner guidance is vital in the current climate of uncertainty, fear and conflicting messages from would-be authorities. In our perplexing age of incompatible advice to follow one's bliss or amass everything that can fit in a decorator-designed warehouse, maybe you feel, as many others do, that you cannot trust yourself to pursue what you truly desire or secretly feel called to do. Maybe you lament your past decisions and chafe with discontent in your job, career, relationships and life. You are not alone.

Many of us, having reached a certain stage or age, are admitting that the culturally touted goals of acquisition and status don't satisfy. In this century—with the new consciousness, massive spiritual renaissance, spiritual rediscovery, time of awakening, worldview paradigm shift, or whatever other term you feel comfortable using—increasing numbers of us are recognizing our hunger for greater fulfillment, especially with long-repressed Dreams. Higher spiritual currents are stirring in our postmodern secular culture. We're daring to see, or at least to give a chance to, the messages that emerge from our quietest selves. Thank God!

INTRODUCTION:

What's It All About?

- Do you wake up regretting what you did yesterday?
- Do you dread today, seeing nothing but the same old, same old?
- Are you depressed about tomorrow, convinced that nothing will change?
- Do you spend too much time condemning yourself about what you could have, should have done differently?
- Do you feel stuck in your job, your activities, your life?
- Do you yearn for more, even if you don't know what it is?
- Do you suspect you've got something to give, even if you can't identify it?
- Are you sure it's somewhere inside you, but you can't seem to find it or let it out?

If your answer to any or all of these questions is "Yes, yes, yes, Lord, help me," within these pages the Lord and I will help you reach many of the answers you've been searching for, even if you didn't quite know you were asking.

What's Here?

In the emerging tradition of books on spiritual principles applied to all aspects of life, *Trust Your Life* is a manual of practical spirituality. *Trust* buoys you if your imagined failures are stopping you from reaching for your buried Dreams and living more fully. *Trust* encourages you to forgive your self-judgments, overcome your guilt, step beyond self-imposed "shoulds" and deep dissatisfactions, develop yourself more courageously, embrace your creative strength and power, and learn how to rely on your always-trustworthy, knowing and peace-producing Source (whew!).

Trust Your Life is based on three Universal principles:

- **First, there are no mistakes.** Miles Davis, the great and enlightened jazz musician, said, "Do not fear mistakes. There are none."[1]

Your self-judged "wrong" turns were nothing less than perfect. Your life experiences prepared you perfectly for where you are now.

- **Second, we can reframe our pasts.** When we realize there are no mistakes, we can free ourselves from branding past experiences as negative or wasted. Instead we can view our mistakes as inevitable steps toward the future we want to create. I guide you to awareness of these steps so you can finally forgive yourself for those mislabeled mistakes and take active steps toward building your Dream.

- **Third, the outer reflects the inner.** "Out there" *is* "in here."

Trust Your Life will help you, at whatever age or stage you're at, to find another way of looking at your world, yourself and your life. Here you'll learn how:

- To forgive yourself for what you see as lost time.
- To see the events and turns of your life in a different, perhaps startling way.
- To review, relabel and understand your past differently—as the perfect foundation for reaching your long-cherished desires.

- To recognize that all your experiences have been perfect, nothing less than manifestations of the Divine Order of your life.

In the Bible, Old Testament teachers and Jesus promised and instructed us that when we wholly believe and speak the words of what we desire, we experience it. (Look at Job 22:28; Mt. 9:29; Mk. 11:23.) Later teachings, in newer bindings and flashier covers, reiterate these principles: Napoleon Hill's Conceive-Believe-Achieve, Neale Donald Walsch's Thought-Word-Action, Eckhart Tolle's Power of Now, the ancient-new Law of Attraction. Applying these magnificent teachings, you will learn to name, visualize, deserve, expect and act on your God-planted greatest desires.

You'll gain insights into why you've been stuck on the treadmill of self-condemnation and discover methods for reversing your patterns of negative thinking. You'll burst through your inertia. You'll gain courage from the examples of other people like you (myself included, Lord knows). You'll feel inspired by much practical and spiritual wisdom from venerable and contemporary sources. You'll learn many simple and concrete ways to jump off your seemingly endless treadmill, stop your procrastination, and get a running start onto the path that takes you where you crave to go.

There's more ... You'll see your life differently—maybe differently from the way you've ever seen it—and become freer from the self-defeating thoughts and labels that have kept you down. You'll start to shed your old habits of negating yourself and ease gently into the splendid clothes of deserving. In these new clothes, which are much more than zipper-deep, you'll begin to blossom and develop your talents and abilities as you've always secretly known you could.

You'll start to act with anticipation and excitement.

You'll feel a wonderful sense of rightness and will *know* you're really on the way to your Dream.

As you take in these lessons, you'll feel a new and possibly foreign sense of peace, satisfaction and hope. You'll gain a new grounding:

- Not one of dissatisfaction but of certainty.
- Not one of suspicion, frustration and guilt but of fullness.
- Not one of constant anxiety but of confidence.
- Not one of self-deprecation and denial but of absolute deserving.

You'll notice, too, an unaccustomed sense of buoyancy, even if it's only occasional. You'll have more energy and will come to know, with a certainty you never had before, what you really want to do. You'll be open to, and will start thinking of, the perfect sequence of steps to take you there.

In the process, you'll go from doubting your abilities, your power, your spiritual heritage, and God to trusting yourself, your divine nature and the certainty of God's goodness for you. You'll learn how to discover, develop and trust your innate spirituality and inner direction. You'll see how trusting yourself, and knowing you are master of your choices, can indeed lead to fulfillment of your most cherished desires and goals. You'll find, too, with a shock of joy, that you're enjoying more of the moments that make up your days.

Most important, you'll learn that you're *not* a victim of life or a victim of God—a God who puts us through all manner of tribulation for some perverse, eccentric, mysterious, divine reason.

Contrary to the hard-luck stories that supposedly prove widespread (and contagious) victimitis, you'll learn that you *can* take charge. In Deepak Chopra's often-quoted words, "You and I are essentially infinite choice-makers. In every moment of our existence, we are in that field of all possibilities where we have access to an infinity of choices."[2]

Still Skeptical?

Maybe you're shaking your head and saying, "Sure, sure. I've tried this, that and those. I've spent money, time and tears and got nowhere." Maybe, whatever you've invested, you feel you'll never get out of this dark place. Maybe you've already dismissed the likelihood that any of those wonderful things above can happen to you.

You may have a lot of reasons for this reaction. Other than low blood sugar, one big reason is that you probably don't credit yourself with what you've already done. A lot of us don't even remember our accomplishments. The rest of us dismiss them and say, "Big deal." How can we give ourselves credit and applause and build on them?

I'm reminded of a client. Lilette knew she needed a change of career. For too long, in her view, she'd been a bank teller and, at 36, couldn't see herself behind the glass cage for the rest of her working life. As we worked together, and I asked squirm-producing questions, Lilette realized she'd always wanted to help children. She decided to go for the master's degree in childhood education, dreaming of becoming an elementary school teacher.

When we started filling out the application, Lilette stopped cold. She shook her head, almost crying. "It asks for previous teacher experience! I don't have any!" She threw her hands in the air. "I can't go!"

"Easy, now," I reassured her. "Just take a deep breath. Think back. What have you done with kids? Not teaching, but anything else?"

Lilette shrugged. "Babysat my cousins, almost every week while my aunt went to her weekend job."

"Okay, good. What else?"

Her brow furrowed. Then she lit up. "Oh, a neighbor. My aunt asked me if I wanted to do her friend a favor. So I stayed with the neighbor's boy and read to him." She started smiling as she recalled. "We watched *Dora the Explorer,* and I taught him letters and numbers. He was going to start preschool."

I nodded.

"And then," Lilette grew more animated, "I taught Sunday School! Kindergarten kids. We read stories and did drawings and games." She laughed, finally realizing that she certainly did have "teaching" experience.

We completed the application with little effort, and Lilette looked forward with excitement to enrolling. She'd taken the first step toward her Dream.

Like Lilette, most of us are often the last to give ourselves credit for our positive or valuable experiences. It's hard for us to step outside ourselves and see how far we've already come, to recognize our own potential and promise. Like Lilette, you may feel stuck in a job, or a life, that offers little. You may not quite know what you really want to do. Or reaching your goal seems impossible, you think, because you lack experience, training, education or a truckful of other things. Well, here you'll learn how to reverse this deficient image of yourself, no matter how many deficiencies you think you have, and to take the steps needed to achieve your Dream.

Maybe you're not like Lilette, who needed prompting to uncover her real interests and career desires. Maybe you've always known what you most wanted to do, but by choices and circumstances (and often a feeling of helplessness), you've denied or buried your desire. This was the case with Tom.

Tom had been an important man with an impressive title. Director of the premier art museum in a large Eastern city for 38 years, he handled and acquired the most treasured works. Part of his job was to discover, develop and showcase stellar new artists.

Tom had always secretly wanted to be a painter himself. He'd begun painting in his early twenties but abandoned it as family and responsibilities grew. His Dream receded and almost disappeared as he became busier, kept up with the art world, and graciously accepted promotions, which of course meant more work and more time in his profession.

At 64, with his wife's gently insistent urging, they retired to a quiet, elegant South Florida community. After Tom's decades of living with the best paintings in existence and encouraging and nurturing the next generation of artists, he longed to resume his own painting, which he'd put aside so long ago.

He felt, as he said, "way behind." He feared he'd lost his early promise and daily condemned himself for not having plunged into painting earlier, whatever the sacrifice. He kept reeling off the names of successful artists his age who had "made it" and told me he wished he'd had someone like himself to encourage and guide him, as he had done with so many young artists in the past.

Now, though, with his time his own, Tom was really terrified of starting. He watched too much television, went out and ate too much at trendy restaurants with friends, played cards in the afternoon with other retirees, and struggled with guilt, conflicting desires and fears. Finally, the anxiety in his stomach propelled him to think about applying to community colleges to teach art part-time.

We met at a local art exhibit, exchanging pithy critiques of the paintings and photographs. I told Tom a little about my work, and he asked if we could get together. At our first meeting, he pulled out his yellowed résumé and said he wanted it revised so he could teach art criticism part-time in an adult education program. He admitted in that first meeting, almost with tears, that he knew teaching was a ploy to still avoid painting. As we kept meeting, he made a series of embarrassed confessions, shouted that it was "too late," and recriminated himself with amazing bursts of anger.

Slowly, I helped Tom see that no talent is wasted. His "interminable detour," as he called it, had helped him refine his critical skills and discerning eye. With a great light in his face, he finally realized and accepted that his desire to paint was God-given and he deserved to pursue it.

I told Tom about many artists, writers and world figures who came to their calling in their later years (I keep a list to shore myself up). Look at some of these "late bloomers": Anna Mary "Grandma" Moses; the Dutch painter Piet Mondrian; Miguel Cervantes; *Robinson Crusoe* author Daniel Defoe; President Harry S. Truman; and Pope John XXIII.[3]

In his 70s, gerontologist Dr. Charles Oakes started his third career as an exercise therapist for older adults. Then he wrote a book. In his *Working the Gray Zone*, he chronicles his clients' remarkable sense of purpose, expansion and spirituality.[4]

In 2009 Arlene Arneson won the Boston Marathon in the 70-74 age class. She was 74 at the time.[5] In 2010 Myrrha Stanford-Smith landed her first book deal—at 82—and the publisher, admirably forward-thinking and age-unbound, signed her to a three-book deal. Stanford-Smith never retired and continues to write and direct for a repertory theater.[6]

With this barrage (I showed no mercy), Tom began to see that there's no limit or cut-off point to creativity. More important, our creative desires don't recede with age, like people's hairlines. Tom realized his talent hadn't evaporated. Instead of ignoring it or pretending it didn't matter, he saw he should honor it. He did.

Like Tom, you may have secret desires to do more and be more, whether you long to paint, write, sculpt, make pots, create your own business, or devote more time to anything else that's always interested you. I bet you've pushed these yearnings into the back of your life, like secret photos in the back of a sock drawer.

Are you like too many people who live for the weekends or retirement? Do you promise yourself that then—finally—you'll do what you really want to? Too often, as you may have noticed with others, these envisioned golden times never materialize. Why? Partly because of that mindset of "later," of lifelong habits of feeling nondeserving, and because the steps you need to take first seem mysterious, bewildering or unattainable.

There's no one around to show you how. Like Tom and many others, you spend years that go too fast in self-blame, frustration, illness and a growing sense of failure.

Together we can stop this self-defeating and wasteful cycle. I'll take you by the figurative hand, one logical, reasonable and practical step at a time. Each of the book's three major parts, and each chapter, builds to the next.

In Part I, "Admitting," Chapters 1 and 2, I show you how to uncover and identify the problems interfering with your Dream. You may find it uncomfortable to look squarely at what's hindering you, but it's the way through.

In Part II, "Changing," Chapters 3 through 8, I offer you many methods for correction and change. As you sincerely and thoughtfully consider the suggestions and do the exercises, you'll grow emotionally and spiritually.

In Part III, "Activating," Chapters 9 through 12, I lead you to specific and nonoverwhelming ways to activate your Dream. Then ... to celebrate it!

To reach this point, you'll be asked—I'm warning you early— to examine, 'fess up, and reflect on where you are now. I'll steer and support you with questions, discussions, journaling exercises, affirmations, lists, resonating wise words from ancient to current spiritual authors, prayers, anecdotes, case studies and illustrations from the experiences of all kinds of people. These include my own humiliating stumblings and victorious risings.

The names of clients, friends and intimates have been changed to respect their privacy. Exceptions are individuals who have become publicly known.

I'm honored to be your coach, confidante and fellow confessor. What we embark on here applies to anything you dream of doing, whether it's showing paintings or shoeing horses, wiring a house or writing a novel, winnowing hay or weaving tapestries, making mousses or shooting movies, conducting traffic or composing symphonies, starting a business or sailing a boat. And anything I left out.

It is my pleasure and love to journey with you and help you reach your most cherished Dream.

PART I
ADMITTING: WHAT'S REALLY BOTHERING YOU?

CHAPTER 1
What's Your Secret Rating of Your Life?

━━◦◦◦━━

When I answered the phone, the voice on the other end was strained, uncomfortable and concerned. "Oh, Dr. Sterne, I haven't called you all this time! I've been afraid to!"

It had been about three years, but I instantly recognized Lilette's melodious accent. She'd made great progress since coming to the United States from Haiti, and, as I mentioned earlier, I'd helped her apply to a master's program in childhood education. She had planned to enroll right away so she could finally leave the dead-end bank teller's job she'd held for so long.

"Dr. Sterne, I'm so ashamed," she continued. "I'm still here, in the bank. I don't know how I can move out. Maybe I could do something special, but I feel so stuck. I don't want to stay here for another 30 years. I didn't call all this time because I didn't want you to know."

Lilette's confession touched me. She was judging herself for where she was, and her self-condemnation kept her stuck. She couldn't "move out" and so did nothing different. Yet she couldn't deny her inner yearning for something better.

I told Lilette that phoning me was her first important step in "moving out." Then I asked her one question: "If you didn't feel stuck, what would you like to do?"

Her reply was instant. "Go back to school for the master's. I still want to teach young children."

We then arranged a visit to explore the programs available and see whether she could reactivate her application to the university and, given her work schedule, what beginning courses she could register for. As we concluded, she sounded visibly relieved. "Thank you, Dr. Sterne. I feel like I can move again."

Lilette was like so many others I'd helped, and so many of us. We see only our immediate circumstances and actions—or non-action—and unhesitatingly judge ourselves for them.

Yes, we're responsible for where we are in life, but if we don't like where we are, does that mean we're condemned to stay there? Are we also condemned to constantly do penance for where we are?

Absolutely not. There's no limit to the options, opportunities and actions we can take. If we really want something enough, we'll find ways—comfortable, usual or astoundingly daring—to move toward what we really want. For example, have you ever noticed what a teenager does to get hold of a car?

The Price of Not Moving

Often what keeps us stuck and continually doing penance is the very feeling that we must pay for our lack of action. We become caught in a circle of self-blame, condemn ourselves, feel hopeless, and feed the fire—or slow burn—by reciting like a mantra our history of inertia and self-judged wrong choices.

Well, let's break that dead-end cycle of waste and regret. Like Lilette, you may crave to accomplish and contribute in some area, whether you've identified it or not, way beyond the dullness of your daily routine. Maybe you're at the other end of the spectrum: you've achieved what the world calls "success"—a solid career, an advanced degree, a big title, a stable of people to boss, a secure and ample income, three bookcases of trophies and awards, a 20-room house and 10-car garage. Great.

In spite of such worldly success, are you still judging yourself? Do you catch yourself too often sighing, staring out the cracked glass or gigantic picture window, barely seeing the alley below the fire escape or your endless sculptured gardens, and replaying and regretting your wrong choices?

Maybe it's our nature as humans—whether we've accomplished a lot or little in the eyes of the world (and our parents)—to desire to be constantly better, to strive and surpass ourselves. When we dare to turn off and unplug all our distractions, we hear an insistent whisper. It tells us we really are more than what we challenge ourselves to, more than what we take on, more than what we let ourselves feel contented with.

I'm certain that every artist of every kind feels this way. Between the vision that inspired the first word, brushstroke or note and what's finally on paper, canvas or music sheets yawns a poignant, unbridgeable gap that takes more than a lifetime to fill. The wonderful short story writer Isaac Bashevis Singer put it well: "Every creator painfully experiences the chasm between his inner vision and its ultimate expression."[1]

Even those who have achieved great heights feel this way. At 83, the renowned photographer Gordon Parks said, "My goal every day is to stretch my horizons."[2] The summer before he died, the magnificent American conductor and composer Leonard Bernstein said, "There's so much music I still have to write."

These feelings aren't restricted to writers or artists. They're exactly what Lilette was expressing to me, and what many of us feel, whatever we have or haven't achieved. Most of the time we cover our secret gap with all the daily necessities and fill-ups of our lives.

Every so often, with a sigh deeper than we want to admit, we remember. Like Christian author Bruce Wilkinson's character named Ordinary in his fable *The Dream Giver*, we may discover our Dream "in a small corner of [our] heart."[3] Then we crave, regret, get angry at, hate ourselves for, and mourn for that Something we refused to get serious about. We know in our most solitary moments that if we'd watched television less, surfed the Internet less, and made up our minds more, we really could have attained what still stubbornly loiters in our hearts to do.

We live with pockets of regret, even though most of the time we manage to drown them out. The hard themes echo throughout our years, refusing to disappear, and darken all our celebrations: "If only ...," "Why didn't I ...," "I wish I'd ...."

Maybe buried, these choruses can't be ignored. They color everything we do and surface when we least want them to. If we try to ignore them completely, they burrow deeper, like slugs, and erupt at wrong moments as depression, unfounded flashes of anger, sarcasm, inexplicable rejections of loved ones, too much sleep or food, illnesses of all kinds, and dutifully mouthing "yes" when we ache with "no."

Many of us feel powerless to reverse these negative feelings, or even control them. We continue to live with hovering self-recriminations, at a two-pronged, paralyzing price. Our regrets tie us to the past, keeping us from living fully in the present. They slam the gates on any future Dreams we may still dare to hold.

You Can Break Out

I recently experienced the always astounding disparity between how poorly we usually think of ourselves and how differently others see us. This was a very personal experience that helped me turn a crucial corner in my own life. I recount it here to help you reflect on the possible gaps in your self-evaluation and what you may hear from others.

Two Viewpoints

Two days after my last birthday, I realized with shock I'd never forgiven myself for my life. All my bright dreams of young adulthood had long faded to gnawing shadows in the glare of life's duties, demands and diversions.

My mother and I used to reflect together on our lives. In the too-few years before she died, we managed to resolve all the rages, battles and judgments of each other's every move.

Finally friends, we were rewarded by expansive, delicious and newly intimate talks. During one of these, I admitted something I'd long hoarded with shame. In the metaphor of my academic career, in which A's were the only acceptable option, I confessed that I had a B+ life.

She was shocked. "I never saw your life like that," she said. Then she, too, confessed. "I always kept this to myself, but whatever you did, no matter what you did," she took a breath, "I admired you." She added, her voice breaking, "More than that—I idolized you."

"My God," I said, "Why?"

"You were smart and pretty. You were more gifted in the piano than I ever was. You were talented in writing, more than I was in art. You went to college and graduate school, which I never did. You mastered technology, which I never could. You had a good marriage, which I never had. More than anything, where I struggled just to keep going, you always did everything so easily."

Hearing each new point, I was more astounded. Not only did she see her own life with gloom, but to her, mine was an unequivocal A!

My mother didn't see my mountains of mistakes, evasions, escapes. She didn't care about my countless decisions not faced, innumerable opportunities not seized, irredeemable moments not commanded.

It didn't matter to her that I hadn't reached my long-cherished Dream of writing full-time, that I wasn't a famous writer, or even a consistently publishing one. Only I kept the disgraceful list of apparently innocuous instants of choosing contentment, ease and satiation over discipline and discomfort toward the all-defining life goal.

Today, many years after she's gone, I still see her sitting across from me in her living room, sipping tea and smiling in her gentle way. How different was her perspective from my own!

As I watched her, my heart wrenched at her weakened, trembling hands. Her illness was taking over, and the deep sadness in her eyes told me she knew she would never achieve her own life ambition as an artist.

Her lesson lingers. Would I, too, give up? Continue to damn my life as B+? Or horrifically lower? Succumb to that seemingly invincible gross being who lives deep inside? Like a polluted river, it pours out foul self-denunciations of stupidities and waste of life. That fiend, I knew from many agonized years, is not fooled by avoidances, placated by rationales, or quieted by substitutions.

Thinking of my mother and her stabbing regret, I saw I now had a choice. I could keep flogging myself and plod through the rest of my days with hollow resignation and surface satisfactions, rejecting joy and deservingness.

Or I could choose to see my life differently.

I offer this choice to you.

Divine Order

What's the choice? It's to stop the incessant self-judgments and accept ourselves on a new basis—to accept that every moment of our lives has been part of an all-encompassing Purpose, and that this Purpose proceeds by divine order.

When you acknowledge the workings of divine order, you see your life not as a consummate failure but as an evolving, orderly progression.

Even though we may not see the purpose of each event, meeting or happening at a given moment, each piece fits. When we acknowledge divine order in our lives, we see the pieces anew, and let go of our secret low, and plunging, self-ratings.

What does divine order teach us? We learn that our lives are not the perverse exception to the rest of the universe, as we so often lament. We discover that, rather like the steadfast movements of the planets, the annual renewal of leaves on the commonest trees, and the casually assumed daily workings of our bodies, all our experiences are part of the whole, in divine order.

At the risk of sounding pedantic, let me delve deeper into these two words (can't deny my Ph.D.-ism).

Divine is generally defined as something above us, but it's also something inside us. We may not even be aware of the divine in us, but it is our God-given, inner knowing.

Order indicates not only sequence, but the *right* sequence, succession, progression. That is, every step we take matters—and is flawlessly connected. When we look into ourselves and listen, we recognize and acknowledge this connection.

All of this means that at every stage, each of our experiences is exactly what we've needed. So how can we possibly condemn our lives?

If you're humphing in disgust or disbelief, or mumbling about Fate, Destiny, God's Will, or any other knotty theological enigma, please suspend all such judgments for a moment. I used to raise a thousand objections too, but my doubt only got me exasperation, deepening frustration and indigestion.

One day I discovered the perfect tonic. It wasn't a pill or potion but a poem by Martha Smock, aptly called "No Other Way":

> Could we but see the pattern of our days,
> We should discern how devious were the ways
> By which we came to this, the present time,
> This place in life; and we should see the climb
> Our soul has made up through the years.
> We should forget the hurts, the wanderings, the fears,
> The wastelands of our life, and know
> That we could come no other way or grow
> Into our good without these steps our feet
> Found hard to take, our faith found hard to meet.
> The road of life winds on, and we like travelers go
> From turn to turn until we come to know
> The truth that life is endless and that we
> Forever are inhabitants of all eternity.[4]

This poem has much to tell us. First, divine order is actual. Our habitual mental vision is so narrowly focused that we can rarely step back to see "the pattern of our days" and lives.

Second, the poem advises us to simply accept the many, apparently haphazard, winding roads we've taken. Too often, we hang onto our stubborn, head-shaking guilt and aching regret and continue to label our choices as irreversible catastrophes.

The way out of such self-abasement is to see that every experience has come to us because, as I said earlier, we have needed it. At the time, we may not have comprehended or appreciated the need, but this is nevertheless the truth.

One of the things we do too much is ask, "Why?" You know the riff: "Why me, Lord? I'm a mostly good person. What did I do to deserve this, Lord?" Hugh Prather, the insightful author and minister, makes an unsettling observation: "Asking why is the honored and ancient form of procrastination."[5]

How right he is. Why does *Why* matter? It just gets in the way of our learning from and resolving whatever's in front of us.

Of course, it's in front of us for a reason. Facing this can be difficult and embarrassing. We'll live with ourselves much more easily when we realize that we've chosen each event in our lives, consciously or not, for our growth and our good. As James Allen reassures us, each of us is "a progressive and evolving being," and we are where we are to learn and thus grow. When we learn the spiritual lesson brought us through any situation, Allen comforts us, "it passes away and gives place to other circumstances."[6]

Finally, without these experiences—the "wastelands" that seem so random, unfair and incomprehensible—we couldn't be where we are now. Nor would we be ready to take in the next good thing that's before us.

Hard to swallow? Maybe, but look more closely at the odysseys people have taken to do what's meaningful to them. An industrialist develops a life-threatening illness, the result of excesses of diet, work and pressure. His condition impels him to seek alternative cures, and with these and medical treatment, his body is healed. Deep gratitude leads him to found a cancer center in the major hospital at which he received treatment. The center, by now nationally known, has become a groundbreaking model of combined traditional and alternative therapies.

A woman dreams of a career in business, but she's detoured by marriage and raising a large family. When her children are grown, she returns to school for a master's in business, not quite knowing what area she wants to specialize in. Then she realizes that, during her housebound years, she developed many innovative techniques, activities and games to keep her kids busy and learning. Bolstered by her new MBA, she launches out to create and market educational toys and resources. She runs a rapidly growing company, with two of her now-adult sons as indispensable aides.

"Doing Nothing": Divine Order at Work

These people may have thought they were doing nothing early on. As they doggedly followed their Dreams, their water-treading became the foundations for their later accomplishments.

They remind me, too, of a client who asked me to coach her in writing a self-help book. Nine years earlier, Dot, an energetic, exuberant, easily laughing middle-aged woman, had engaged me to help her complete her Ph.D. in psychology. Now she had a thriving practice, specializing in family therapy. She'd always dreamed of, and said often, that she wanted to write a book based on her practice, but during the throes of the dissertation, Dot's Dream receded to the far shadows.

Immediately after graduation, she set her mind on rebuilding her practice, which had shrunk dangerously because of her long concentration on the doctorate. Dot poured her energy into networking, giving workshops, and even appearing a few times on local radio talk shows. As her practice became more stable, her Dream of the book began to peek out of the shadows.

One day, Dot called, and with no preamble, she announced, "I'm ready."

"Great to hear you, Dot," I said, recognizing her voice. "For what? A yacht, a ranch, a world cruise?"

"A book!" she shouted, laughing. "I told you I'd do it. I'm ready."

I congratulated her, and we arranged for the first coaching session and a schedule for the work. After our visit, in which we generated a detailed outline of her book, Dot promised with fire in her eye that she'd have the first two chapters to me in exactly three weeks.

The day came, but the manuscript didn't. I waited a week. No manuscript. She's busy with her practice, I thought. Then I received an email from her saying that her elderly father, who lived out of town, was seriously ill, and there was no one else to care for him. Dot had to go.

Two months passed, and I heard nothing from Dot. Three months passed, and then four. Finally, I received another email. In this one she begged my forgiveness, apologized five times for not sending even part of a chapter, and thoroughly condemned herself for "doing nothing."

I phoned her. Barely greeting me, Dot poured out the story of her last several months: the heartaches she'd experienced nursing her father; the mountain of tasks she'd taken care of dismantling his home; the challenges of attending to numerous business completions for him; the greater challenges dealing with other relatives and their attempts to dictate how she should handle things; her father's many shocking admissions about his less-than-idyllic relationship with her mother; and eventually, mercifully, his peaceful passing.

As she finished, Dot sobbed for several minutes. When she regained her breath, she said, "I never knew all those things about him and my mother! And the relatives were impossible. Now I understand so much better why the couples and families I see have such trouble!" Then she changed subjects and echoed her emails, repeating her litany of self-blame for doing nothing on her book.

I was truly impressed with how much Dot had handled successfully, but I saw, too, she was so caught up in guilt and self-blame that nothing at that moment could contradict her self-judgment. Many things came to me as she spoke, but I felt she wouldn't be able to hear them in her state of agitation. After a few soothing words, I told her to expect an email from me later that day. When she calmed down, I knew she would be able to take it in.

After we said goodbye, I jotted some notes and asked my Inner Self for guidance, knowing that what would be said could make or break Dot's next moves. I asked silently to be the right channel and for the right words. Here's what I sent:

Dear Dot—

You are so close to yourself that you've understand-ably lost perspective. Look at what you've dealt with and come through the last several months. Give your-self credit for these victories and the tremendous energy that had to go to them.

During this time, you've been attending to what absolutely needed to be given attention to, and because you always do things all out, you've been giving them your all. I'm sure you were a perfect blessing to your father, and even the difficult relatives. I believe they all felt your comfort, love and care.

Know that the material in your head—which you've now added valuably to—is brewing, gestating, growing and will emerge at the right time.

Often when we feel blocked for a period, the subcon-scious is chugging along, working on it anyway. You may be surprised to find later that you're incorporating into your practice things you just learned.

If you had forced yourself to write earlier, you wouldn't have had the experience or outlook to include what happened during your time away, either the expe-riences or insights. Don't exacerbate or cut off this ges-tation period by additional guilt.

Instead of all the self-flagellating labels (yeah, you're good at them), call this time a period of "fruitful inconclusiveness." Know that everything is in divine order; everything is happening in its perfect season.

Call on Wednesday to talk about our next steps.

Love, Noelle

Dot told me later that she wept reading this letter. As she took in the messages, she let go of her guilt and regained her customary enormous energy and enthusiasm for her book. We went on to complete it, and some of her most lively and insightful chapters drew on those months when she was, as she said, "doing nothing."

Many other examples of doing nothing can be cited, from Famous Amos to unfamous but highly successful people of all kinds. They've all got one thing in common: their delays, mistakes and wrong turns turned out to be precisely the right preparation for what they later needed and wanted to do.

My own life is ample proof. I told you a little about how this book came about. Next I'll reveal more succulent details to lure you into seeing the great divine order of it all.

A Personal Testimony

From the earliest age, I craved two things: to earn the highest academic degree and to become a writer. With uninterrupted schooling, I attained the first and watched a college classmate achieve the second. I plodded through the Ph.D.; she stopped at the master's and devoted herself to writing.

Still in her twenties, she rose to dazzle the literary world. In my reactionary state, I was certain that every journal, magazine and bookstore trumpeted her name. As her triumphs escalated, my depression deepened, jealousy bloated, and self-condemnation threatened to engulf me. All I saw was my gutless decision to continue graduate school instead of diving into full-time writing.

Finally completing my degree, I got a job teaching. Consciously avoiding all bookstores, I began to write in spurts. But teaching and its attendant obligations left little time or energy for much else. After two years, with the doctorate securely framed, I felt pulled toward more consistent writing and searched for another income-producing occupation.

One day, as I complained (yet again) to a friend, she pointed out that the university was only a few blocks from my apartment. With my now-considerable knowledge of the graduate school "ropes," she pointed out, I could offer graduate students a valuable service. Her words made sense. I stopped teaching and established a typing business, specializing in the intricacies of master's theses and doctoral dissertations.

My friend probably still doesn't know the value of her idea, although I've told her in more or less maudlin expressions over too many glasses of wine. I'll always be grateful to her. The self-employment gave me greater autonomy, flexibility and freedom. I could now make my own hours for seeing clients and completing their projects, and I was able to write more. I even published sporadically.

As clients shared concerns about their work, they began to ask for advice. I found myself asking pointed questions, giving suggestions about their premises and methods, critiquing their conclusions, and suggesting ways to revise their chapters. From these informal discussions, and clients' enthusiastic responses, my knowledge and critical abilities grew. Clients welcomed my feedback and interest like lifelines in a tidal wave. I gradually phased out of typing and into academic coaching and consulting.

For many years now, I've guided clients to focus, plan, outline, write, edit, and deal with the many vicissitudes and unpleasant, often unforeseen, events of university life. (Only if you've experienced it, or lived with someone who has, can you have any notion of the drama, disappointments, defeats, discouragements, disasters, dashed hopes, despair and eviscerated egos a graduate candidate goes through—next book.)

Anyway, as clients have finally obtained their degrees, picked up their egos from the subbasement, and aim for their next life-longings, their needs have multiplied. I've expanded to meet them and now counsel, too, on career moves, grant writing, academic publishing and more. Some clients dare even to test another Dream, and I shepherd them to publication of fiction and nonfiction.

Like Lilette, whom you met earlier, these people have reached what at first seemed like impossible goals. They've not only achieved a treasured Dream but have grown personally and professionally along the way. With great gratification, I've watched them develop certainty that they do deserve to achieve their Dreams. I see their growth in expression—verbal, written and body language—and their solid self-confidence in inviting their formerly sadistic doctoral committee members for beer and pizza.

I've gained immeasurably too—in self-assurance, the ability to master many subjects quickly, greater organizing skills, and—what a surprise!—greater facility as editor and writer. I've stretched in ways never before attempted or imagined, meeting apparently unthinkable deadlines, putting in longer hours than ever in my life, taking shorter naps, and tapping depths of creativity never suspected.

Falling over at the second wind, I've rallied to the third, fourth and fifth. In completing assignments, what seemed like concrete walls of resistance, inertia and even panic have repeatedly cracked and then crumbled to reveal the perfect answers or questions.

Have all these capabilities developed, or been thrust on me, in a vacuum? Of course not. Each has been absolutely essential for my own writing. Each has enabled me to keep at it, stick to it, and ceaselessly refine it. In the bargain I've learned volumes (another book) about interpersonal relationships—more of what I need for successful writing and publishing. Doesn't this progression show that I had to learn these lessons first?

Here, now, I sit at my computer, another flawless step in the sequence, writing this book and recounting this very "climb." Yes, I'm surrounded by client projects and hovering deadlines, but now I can more equitably divide my time and attention, with neither clients nor writing neglected too much, and both flowering.

We rarely, if ever, see where the path is leading. That's why we fear, shudder, regret and rage at its turns. Was my degree-chasing a mistake? Was my descending a notch in the world's eyes and starting a typing business a professional blunder?

The irony is that what we so fervently crave right now we may be nowhere near ready for. Can you look at yourself honestly and admit this may be true for you? It certainly was for me. During the long period of depressive agonizing over my writing, or more accurately, not writing, I wasn't ready by any means for recognition, much less to write well or interact decently with other people. What I needed was a rigorous apprenticeship to learn discipline, practice skills, hone talents, and simply keep at it.

A Waste?

Was any of this time wasted? Absolutely not. The only misuse of time and energy was my incessant self-deprecation that I hadn't "made it" as early and in the same way as my college nemesis. That very indulgence probably stopped me from moving faster.

Ken Keyes helped: "Your world is perfect from the point of view of continually providing you with precisely the life experiences that you need for your overall development as a conscious being."[7] For me, each experience provided just what I needed to learn, grow and be ready for the dual career that now offers so much fulfillment.

Here's how a Unity *Daily Word* devotional message puts it:

> If we are open to the lessons, everything that happens in our lives helps us learn. ... As we keep a positive attitude, we put each situation into its proper perspective. We realize that the divine pattern for our unfoldment includes learning in ways that will challenge us to move forward.[8]

Spiritual teacher Catherine Ponder, in prose echoing Martha Smock's poem I quoted earlier, gives us additional resolve and renewed comfort:

> Everything moves in cycles, both in time and space. Regardless of the number of breaks that appear in the lines of your life, growth is taking place. Never fight the darkness because through it, growth takes place. The more light you turn on in your life, the quicker will be your growth.[9]

Notice that last sentence. See your life not in dark despair but in light. However you've denounced yourself for your past, know that there was truly no other way. Your experiences have *not* been wasted—they've been no less than perfect.

Our self-judging keeps us depressed, fatigued and illness-prone. Once we scrape away the guilt and self-blame, we're free to shake out our dusty Dreams and release our energy. Only then can we express that shimmering, childlike excitement that propels us to our life's vision.

See Your Own Divine Order

Instead of rejecting your past, thank it. I know it's hard. *Thank* that rat ex-husband, that rat ex-wife? *Thank* that lazy bum former business partner? *Thank* that phony-smile betraying friend? Thank that *mother*? Yes, thank them all. They appeared—and passed through your experience—for one or many reasons.

Look squarely at your secret low rating of your life. Can you see the lessons you've learned and divine order behind them all?

We rarely stop to reflect on the divine order in each of our lives, and that's why it might have escaped you. To get in touch with it, do this exercise.

Your Divine Order List

1. Give yourself 10 to 15 minutes before, after or between the many activities that undoubtedly preoccupy you and the diversions that constantly beckon. Sit in a quiet spot with paper and pen. If you feel more comfortable at the computer, use it (I'm not one of those who swears that electronic advances inhibit creativity).

2. Jot down or type out the events in your life that you consider major. For example, a childhood move to a new town, the birth of your sister, your parents' divorce or remarriage, your marriage, divorce or remarriage, departure for college, getting a certain job, winning something, losing something, finishing something, risking something, going to a certain event, meeting a certain person, missing a great opportunity, making what you've always thought of as a giant mistake.

What you put down doesn't have to be momentous or meaningful to anyone else, or chronological, or even completely accurate. Sometimes the most seemingly trivial moment, even slightly skewed through our memory and emotions, can be a stupendous turning point.

When I tried out this exercise on a friend, she wrote, "Craving a Mounds bar." Huh? She explained that as she ran to a local newsstand to buy a quick pick-up, she literally bumped into the man who propelled her to law school. After the apologies, she discovered he was a lawyer. His encouragement and referral to a colleague started her on the road to becoming a corporate attorney, a desire she'd craved since early adolescence.

A cousin of mine always thought of the apartment she lived in with her first husband as a tiny hellhole; it was 2,500 square feet. She later realized this label was her *emotional* memory, and it propelled her to go after her Dream of becoming a designer of light and airy spaces overlooking the mountains of Colorado. I counted as one of my major events grousing to the friend who suggested I start the academic typing business.

3. When you've got a good list down, look at it. It doesn't have to include everything. You can always add to it later. You've opened the door, and you'll probably think of more things later.

4. Take a deep breath and really look at your list. Ask your mind to reveal the connections. Sometimes it works to look at a relatively recent event or outcome and ask yourself, How did I get there?

5. Study, reflect more, free associate. Let the connections reveal themselves. As you quietly listen to yourself and let your mind run free, you'll start to see things: "If I hadn't done this, I wouldn't have encountered that. If I hadn't missed the train, I wouldn't have met Ann. If I'd taken that job, I wouldn't have had to develop my speaking skills, and I wouldn't be addressing groups now. If I hadn't blurted out to my barber how I couldn't stand my wife's cooking, and pot-rattling, I wouldn't be happily single now."

6. Start numbering the items in their connective sequences. For some, the connections will be instantly obvious, such as my going

from typing dissertations to editing them. For others, you may not immediately see the line, but as you keep studying your list, your mind will give you more links. You'll also start to see obvious groupings of events, such as those that led to your finding the perfect course to take that led to your professional certificate that led to that specific job that led to meeting the person you married.

7. Put your list away in a private place. That list is yours, and no one else has to see it to question, deride, laugh or pull it apart.

8. In a day or two, revisit your list. More insights will come, and you'll uncover more relationships.

9. Acknowledge them. Even if you're not yet ready to stop blaming yourself for some of your "mistakes" and "wastelands," at least you'll have recognized their connections.

Starting to see what each event has given you? If not, take heart. As you keep thinking about your list, and the truth of divine order, more associations will spring up.

A word of caution. Something else may spring up: the nagging, persistent fiendish thought "So what?" This may be followed by another troll: "Big deal. I see the divine order. But I'll never get to where I want to go. I'm too old, tired, poor, bogged down, busy, unfocused, overwhelmed, uneducated, stubborn, stupid, timid, fat, thin, ugly, uncertain, afraid ... "

If any of these little devils or others pop up, it's okay. Notice what they're bombarding you with. We'll zap them in the next chapter.

CHAPTER 2

Could You Feel It's Too Late?

If you're already complaining it's too late, do I really need to remind you otherwise? Now more than ever, the horizons of longevity, health and vibrant activity increase daily, even with the medically orthodox. Almost daily, reports in the newspapers and on the Internet boast of people in their 70s, 80s and 90s who are doing great things.

A Bushel of Examples

Many more examples could be mentioned than those in Chapter 1. The consummate comedian Jerry Lewis was a star in his 20s and only reached his lifelong goal of appearing on Broadway (in *Damn Yankees*) at 69. Despite a debilitating illness, he's going strong with his annual telethons and irrepressible spirit at 84. The late actress Janet Leigh published her first novel at age 68. At 65, Maggie Kuhn was forced to retire from her long-time church administrative job. Within a few years, she founded one of the first organizations to combat ageism and ignore chronological limits, the Gray Panthers.[1]

Michelangelo was 74 when he began painting the ceiling of the Sistine Chapel, and he was carving the Rondanini Pietà six days before he died at age 89. At 81, Benjamin Franklin created the compromise that led to adoption of the U.S. Constitution.[2] Picasso drew a bearded man and woman in erotic play less than two months before he died at 91. Even then, as an art critic comments, "his hand was quick and sure."[3]

More? The excellent actor and comedian Tony Randall at 81 continued to involve himself in serious Broadway projects. He made headlines in 1995, when at 77 he married a woman 50 years younger than he. They had two children together. Yes, he fathered them![4]

Photographer Gordon Parks, who was on the staff of *Life* magazine for many years, said at 83, "I'm a better writer, a better photographer, a better musician—a better everything."[5] At 85, Parks told a television interviewer that he felt like he was just beginning.[6]

He proved it: In 1999, when Parks was 87, he launched a four-year national traveling retrospective of his photographs. The show included works with completely new media in completely different styles. As if this wasn't enough, he was also working on his seventeenth book.[7]

Martha Graham performed until she was 75 and choreographed her 180th work at age 95. Grandma Moses had her first one-woman show when she was 80. Marion Hart, the sportswoman and author, learned to fly at age 54 and made seven nonstop solo flights across the Atlantic. Her last flight was in 1975 when she was 83.[8]

Do you need a breath? Take a big one, because here I go again. Abraham was 75 when God told him to journey to Canaan. Moses was 80 when he was called to lead the Israelites out of Egypt to the Promised Land.

A little more current look at the long-reigning and resuscitated rock groups and singers in their 60s and 70s—Mick Jagger, Paul McCartney, Leonard Cohen, and many more whose group names sound to me like bad novel titles. Elsewhere in the arts, in 2010

Eleanor Ross Taylor, a lifelong poet, won the American Poetry Foundation's prestigious $100,000 Ruth Lilly Award—at age 90.[9] Janet Wolfe founded the New York City Housing Authority Symphony Orchestra in 1971. The jazz drummer and composer Max Roach once said of her that she provided "more work for Black, Hispanic and Asian players than anyone in New York."[10] In 2010, at 95, Wolfe was still tuning the strings of the orchestra and vows she will continue bringing music to the city's housing developments.

In painting, Adele Lerner in Long Island, New York, earned her bachelor's degree in fine art at 85. In 2008, at the age of 101, she produced her first art show, and in 2010, at 103, continued to paint and mastered the computer, including email. The contemporary painter Will Barnett, who at this writing is 99 (in 2010), has had more than 80 one-man shows, including one at the Metropolitan Museum of Art in the spring of 2010, and whose works sell for up to $400,000. Having lost the use of his left leg in a fall, he cannot stand but nevertheless paints three to four hours a day and continues to mix his own paints. His zest for life and art remains intense: "I've seen it all but I want to see more.... I didn't compromise, ever.... The old masters are still alive after 400 years, and that's what I want to be."[11]

On the athletic front, a recent book called *Second Wind: The Rise of the Ageless Athlete* inspires us to pry ourselves out of the Barcalounger and use our bodies to their full potential. Author Lee Berquist recounts the stories of no-limits athletes. After the age of 80, Don McNelly completed more than 150 marathons; Clarence Bass has the physique of a man 50 years younger—he's 70.[12] Other athletes smash limited-thinking body stereotypes. Bodybuilding legend Ed Corney, who appeared with Arnold

Schwarzenegger in the documentary *Pumping Iron*, still trained ferociously in 2010 at age 75—and his muscles looked it.[13]

Even life as an invalid in a nursing home doesn't have to limit your activity and creativity. At 87, Stewart Elliot lived in a nursing home in Evansville, Indiana. Confined to a wheelchair, he survived two heart attacks and suffers from severe osteoporosis and acute digestive problems.[14]

Nevertheless, on a manual typewriter that must now be a collector's item, he wrote a weekly column beginning in 2002 for the *Evansville Courier & Press*. Elliot wrote especially about life in a nursing home and the problems of many residents. Throughout his columns, and despite the concurrent ailments of his wife, who also resided in the home with him, he stressed the importance of worthwhile contributions and had a relentless positive attitude.[15] Elliot's words, and the emphasis on giving, are mightily inspirational, are they not?

Late Bloomers

These individuals show that we can, with enough interest, passion and desire, continue enacting our dreams for a long, long time. Some people, though, don't get to them until rather late, if not in God's then in the world's eyes. Connie Goldman and Richard Mahler wrote a wonderful book titled *Secrets of Becoming a Late Bloomer*, and the 14 secrets include those of attitude, forgiveness, work, health, humor, creativity and spirituality. In the Foreword, Ken Dychtwald called for a shift in our perspective:

> The antiquated view of maturity as a period of stagnation and decline must be replaced once and for all with the reality that the latter part of life is an exciting time of growth, productivity and newfound pleasures—if we know the secrets of becoming a Late Bloomer.[16]

One of my most cherished volumes is a board book for young children. I discovered it in adulthood and, given my history, identify mightily with the main character. *Leo the Late Bloomer* is a tiger who couldn't do anything right. His animal friends could all read, write, draw, speak and eat neatly. Not Leo. His father grew impatient and angry, but his mother gently advocated patience. Through winter and summer, Leo didn't bloom. Then "one day, in his own good time, Leo bloomed!" He could now read, write, draw, eat decently and speak. He exclaimed, "I made it!"[17]

In the grown-person part of my library, another favorite book is called, aptly enough, *Late Bloomers*. It's by the *New Yorker* writer Brendan Gill, and in the Introduction earlier I listed some of his 74 well-known and history-changing people from every area of life. They all made great contributions, as Gill shows in his profiles of their lives. And they all had one thing in common: they "bloomed" late.

Here are more of the people in Gill's book, and I bet you had no idea: Harry Truman, Paul Cezanne, R. Buckminster Fuller, Julia Child, Ed Sullivan, Charles Darwin, Colonel Harland Sanders, Pope John XXIII, Edward VII, Mary Baker Eddy, O. Henry, Mother Teresa, Miguel Cervantes, Jonathan Swift, Charles Ives, Edith Wharton, Sir Alexander Fleming.[18]

Gill is unfazed by their lateness. In fact, he applauds it and even maintains why it's needed:

> The lateness is every bit as significant as the blooming.... [I]t has to do with the moment in time at which we discover, whether through an event dictated by forces outside ourselves or by a seemingly spontaneous personal insight, some worthy means of fulfilling ourselves.[19]

Gill makes a startling assertion: The age at which we make this discovery is an irrelevance.[20]

In other words, a particular age, despite our culture's constraints and judgments, doesn't affect our desire for fulfillment, the means we choose and must have, or our talent for accomplishing what we desire.

Late bloomers, as Gill's profiles show, may be in their 40s, 50s, 60s, 70s or 80s. Who are they?

> They are people who at whatever cost and under whatever circumstances have succeeded in finding themselves…. If the hour happens to be later than we may have wished, take heart! So much more to be cherished is the bloom.[21]

Could it be that late bloomers flower bigger?

You protest: These are famous people, exceptionally talented people, not ordinary like us. Okay, a few others.

At 64, when many people are ready to throw in the towel, spread it on their couch, and plunk down, Bill Weinacht began running. He had run as a youngster but stopped for 50 years. When he resumed, he started amassing state medals and went on to world events. In Japan, he finished first place in the 100 and 200 meters and set a world record. He was 76.

Three weeks after these accomplishments, Bill had triple bypass heart surgery. After four months (would you believe?), he was running again and racking up the medals. At 84 he competed in the South Florida Senior Games, doubtless winning more medals.

What's Bill's secret? "The first thing I do in the morning … is read an inspirational passage from *Daily Word*. It sets the mind thinking right. I get eight hours of sleep every night. I like to think of myself as being overly enthusiastic, an optimistic person."[22] A

50-year hiatus, the length of some people's entire lifetimes, did not hold Bill back, nor did his serious illness. He refused to see time, age or his physical condition as restricting or blocking him.

In a professional networking group I belonged to, a woman who had a going Internet business selling handmade crafts and jewelry shared something none of the group had suspected. Terry said:

> Only in my 30s did I realize I could achieve anything. Before then, I plodded along haphazardly. When I was 32, I started tennis lessons. This is definitely not an early age to start any sport. Well, soon I got the competition bug, and I started practicing six to seven hours a day. In spite of those teenage stars, somehow my age didn't interfere, or my idea of what old was.
>
> As I got better, I started believing I could achieve, and I competed in the circuit. Within several years, I kept beating all those nymphs. When I finally retired, I had three shelves of trophies and prizes, a scrapbook of clippings, and a name in the Western circuit.

Several of my clients began doctoral programs in their 60s. One, Stan, after a successful career as a salesman of office equipment, started at 77. Another client, whose attitude is very much like octogenarian columnist Stewart Elliott's, began—hard to believe—when she was 84. A particularly demanding program, it was largely self-directed, in which you're required to design your own courses and attend many seminars in different geographical areas. Evelyn completed most of her seminars and some of the courses and lined up her research subjects for her dissertation. Not only that, she had a very ill husband at home and took the bus an hour each way for our visits.

I was impressed with Evelyn from the outset, and not just because she chose to go back to school when she did. Like Elliott, she put to shame the prevalent belief that to get old is to lose your mind. Her writing was excellent and thoughtful, her understanding of difficult concepts remarkable, and her questions and observations piercing. She followed through with our work, doing research, writing new material, and sending me emails (yes, she mastered the tech-marvels too), more thoroughly than other clients with half her problems.

Even more—she volunteered at a nearby hospital, working with preschool children, and continued to volunteer at the voting board in her neighborhood. When I walked her to the bus stop, she moved so briskly I could hardly keep up with her.

Can you stand two more examples? These are of writers, buoyant reminders of principles that apply to us all.

Prompted by her children's questions about family roots, a grandmother in New Jersey started writing at age 59. She based her first novel, and most of the succeeding ones, on the experiences of Jewish immigrant families in the United States. For 25 years, Belva Plain, the prolific and popular romance writer, steadily produced best-sellers, about a book a year, and she wrote everything by hand. Born in 1915, she passed in 2010 at age 95. Twenty of her novels were on the *New York Times* best-seller lists, and 30 million copies of her books are in print, with translations in 22 languages. Her most recent work appeared in hardcover in 2008 and was followed by audio, e-book and paperback editions.[23]

Another woman writer has an equally impressive, although different, story. A Kansas native, Jessie Foveaux attended a writing class at age 80 at an adult learning center. For class assignments she wrote memoirs of her childhood and life in Middle America. The memoirs circulated among her friends for nearly 20 years. Then, in 1997, Foveaux's creative writing teacher at the learning center sent an excerpt to a *Wall Street Journal* reporter.

Foveaux's story was featured on the front page, and the publicity immediately attracted several New York City publishers, resulting in a contract for $1 million from Warner Books. Both hard and softcover editions came out later that year. Foveaux began her second book almost immediately and was working on it when she passed at 100 two years later.[24]

A startling example was J. L. Hunter "Red" Rountree, who began a successful career at age 86—as a bank robber. He gained a fortune through his Houston, Texas, Rountree Machinery Company and eventually lost the company and his fortune, citing these as his motivation for his second and new career. Unfortunately, he wasn't that good at it, because he was caught and served time for all three robberies and died in prison at 92. When asked why he robbed banks—and maybe this is the point—he replied, "It's fun. I feel good, awful good."[25]

I'm not suggesting you follow Ol' Red's trail. But he sure proves that it's never too late to follow your daring Dreams. In Red's case, he had to live with the dubious fruits, or I should say consequences, of his Dreams.

Since 1970, the number of people who live to 100 or over has doubled every decade.[26] A newspaper article in 1996 featured several of these remarkable people across the country. A 100-year-old woman in Missouri worked 40 hours a week as a columnist and proofreader on an Independence newspaper. Another woman, 102, who lived in California, maintained a mountaintop studio where she created artwork and pottery displayed in galleries and museums around the world. A Los Angeles businessman built a multimillion-dollar business and has given $5 million to charity. At 102, handsome and dapper in a suit and tie, he said, "With my sharp mind, I knew I should go into contracting. Ever since, I've had a reputation as Numero Uno."[27]

A more recent national study of centenarians shows they are active, socially involved, surprisingly healthy, and interested in many activities. At 105, one woman wrote her memoirs and continues to write, and at 106 another holds the world record for shot put and competes in the Senior Games.[28]

As the director of the Alliance for Aging Research commented, "The centenarians are helping to stretch our sense of human potential. If people live to 100, how can you think of a person as 'used up' at 65?"[29]

I bombard you with all this information and legions of astounding people to show you that "too late" is only a state of mind. We mark and dread "the big This-0, the big That-0," as if each turn is a milestone of dread. When I was about 12, a neighbor's daughter turned 19. I looked at her and thought, Disgusting! I *never* want to be that old! Here I am, at a decades-later 0, and more active, healthy, productive (and publishing), if I do say so, than ever. I expect no reason in the world to stop.

For every terminal couch potato, there's another person, probably older than you, who has cast off a mislabeled past history and is living life wholly, vibrantly, victoriously. Each of the people I've talked about had one thing in common: They didn't accept that it was "too late" to do what they wanted to do.

You've Got Time

Stan, whom I mentioned earlier, was 77 when he came to me for help with his doctoral coursework and looked forward to our working together on his dissertation. Stan didn't let his age deter his lifelong goal of getting a Ph.D. "I've had this Dream," he said, "all my life. No one in my family ever even went to college, and I told myself I was going to get the highest degree they gave."

He'd been a successful businessman, but the Dream never left him. When he retired from business, he began graduate school.

Stan said he'd like to complete it in a year, and if he didn't, it was all right.

"After all," he chuckled, "I've got time." He meant it.

Stan saw no barriers or boundaries of age, limitation or energy. Apparently the university that accepted him didn't either.

A former client, whom I worked with on his master's degree, has become a good friend and role model to many. When David Johnson at age 71 was awarded the master's in social work, he decided not to continue to the doctorate but to return to a passion he'd had from his early teens. After practicing social work for several years on the East Coast, he moved back to California, where, at age 21, he'd been the first African American to study with Ansel Adams at the California School of Fine Arts.

David never stopped photographing, and after several detours (although not mistakes, as we know), he resumed his boyhood Dream. Johnson's photographic career spans more than 60 years, and he has become increasingly well-known as a premier photographic historian of the many aspects of African American culture. His work documents the vibrancy and joy of the music and nightlife of San Francisco's Fillmore District. This was the American jazz "Harlem of the West" in the 1940s and 1950s, which attracted such stars as Ella Fitzgerald, Louis Armstrong, Duke Ellington and Billie Holiday. Johnson always loved jazz, and he started visiting the clubs and photographing what he saw.

His images include the civil rights movement of the 1960s and 1970s and individuals in politics and culture—Supreme Court Justice Thurgood Marshall, A. Philip Randolph, Paul Robeson, Jackie Robinson, the poet Langston Hughes, Nat "King" Cole,

Eartha Kitt. Poignant and powerful are Johnson's images of ordinary African Americans—a young boy sitting pensively on a fence; weary civil rights marchers in Washington, D.C.; a father watching his daughter on a carousel; a man lounging in a rundown shop doorway; proud deacons at a storefront Baptist church; and children of two races delighted to pose together, oblivious of their different skin colors.[30]

Having acquired gallery representation in 2008, David has been featured in several books on the Fillmore District and Ansel Adams, has had many shows, is the subject of newspaper articles and a documentary on his life, and continues exhibiting photographs. Five of his photographs are in the Library of Congress in Washington, D.C. In 2009, on his 83rd birthday, David got married. He and his wife, an author, are extremely happy and working on his autobiography together.

This bio is not a commercial for David (although he certainly deserves it). His story is meant to show you an octogenarian who's broken the senior ceiling. A little while ago, he came East to arrange several shows. When we met for lunch, he looked at least 20 years younger than his age, walked straight and tall with a lively step, and carried a large portfolio like it was a single negative.

Ignoring chronology, David Johnson continues his drive to expand and create (his latest project is learning Spanish). He not only excels at his profession but also shares his expertise and wisdom with younger artists. He proves that expansion of learning, enhancement of craft, and the drive to create and contribute know no age boundaries. Johnson clearly articulates and continues his legacy of the African-American experience. He may not have envisioned his additional legacy—as an inspiration to others of every race, age and creative field.

David Johnson, the doctoral clients, and others I've told you about prove that our Dreams don't vanish with the years. Julia Cameron, the creativity expert and coach, says that if at 20 you want to write a novel, you'll still want to write it at 80.[31]

Your Dreams don't go away.

They just go underground and keep resurfacing until you're ready.

For Everyone Who Has Will Be Given More ...

David and the others also prove another point. It's related to a controversial biblical verse that holds many lessons: "For everyone who has will be given more, and he will have an abundance. Whoever does not have, even what he has will be taken from him" (Mt. 25:29).

These words by Jesus are often interpreted, with grumbling that can be heard for miles, as "the rich get richer." What it really applies to is not material things but consciousness. When we believe we already have whatever it is we want, we will have, and when we believe we don't have, we not only don't get, but what we have disappears.

Skeptical? Think of love. When people feel loved and act loving, they experience pleasantness, cooperation, gratitude and love from others. When people feel isolated and act grouchy, they experience unpleasantness, stubbornness, conflict and grouchiness from others, and the few friends they have tend to drift away.

As we believe, so we have and experience. Stan believed, and acted on, the premise that he had all the time, energy, motivation and enthusiasm he needed to reach his goal. David Johnson did, and does, the same. They experienced in kind.

So "For everyone who has" is a self-fulfilling prophecy. If you have faith and believe and feel (even manufacture) that you *already* have what you desire, you will act like you do. You'll be shown the steps to take and eventually will really feel and experience what you dream of.

What's Age Got to Do With It?

Stan, David and many others didn't let age hamper them or get in the way. The limits of what constitutes "old" are stretching remarkably. As you've seen by all the examples here, at later, traditional retirement ages and beyond, people embark with relish on second and third careers or all kinds of things they've always wanted to do.

Maybe the "Baby Boomers" should be "Baby Bloomers."

Maybe retirement should be "refire-ment."

The supposed and sanctioned prohibitions, barriers and blocks to many activities at certain ages are being smashed daily. The authors of *Living to 100*, Perls and Silver, run the New England Centenarian Study in Boston, which started in 1994. They tell us that, contrary to earlier prevailing thought, many way-beyond-Boomer older people continue active engagement in business, volunteerism and family life. Centenarians, say Perls and Silver, "paint a stunning picture of the potential of aging. They demonstrate that long life can mean a healthy, enjoyable life … a life of satisfaction."[32]

Age is indeed a state of mind. The "too late" lament seems to have no lower limit. When a man of about 45 told me he'd always wanted to take piano lessons, and I suggested he start, he cried, "Oh, no, it's too late! I couldn't learn now!" In the park, I saw a 30-year-old mother wheeling two babies and telling her friend she wished she'd gotten into the pastry-catering business she'd always craved. She added, "I couldn't begin now. It's too late."

The great English poet John Milton, author of *Paradise Lost*, wasn't immune to the "too late" chorus. In one of his more famous sonnets (pardon the rearing up of my English lit background), he mourned the passing of opportunity: "When I consider how my light is spent / Ere half my days in this dark world and wide …"[33] Translation: Milton felt his life was half over and he'd done nothing with his "light" or talent. How old was he? Although scholars differ as to when wrote this poem, they agree he was between 32 and 47. In either case, relatively young. Incidentally, having become blind at 43, he began *Paradise Lost* when he was age 52 and finished it at 57.[34]

I recall my own lament when the college classmate (read: nemesis) I spoke of before attained such instant fame. Because of her success, I thought everything was over for me, that I'd never have any chances at publishing, and it was indeed way too late. My age at the time? 21.

The "too-late" bug can bite at any age. It can burrow and get under your skin as depression and fester with its insidious bedfellow, jealousy. When you compare yourself with others, of course, you always come out wanting. That train of thought only leads to more depression and paralysis, the opposite of Bill Weinacht's self-professed attitude of being "overly enthusiastic."

An Ageless Principle

When you trust your life, and God's timetable, you'll realize, with relief, joy and enthusiasm, that there's no such thing as too late. A time-honored quote by the novelist George Eliot should be tattooed on the forehead of everyone over the age of 5: "It is never too late to be what you might have been."

Martha Smock, whose poem "No Other Way" I quoted in Chapter 1, also wrote an essay, "It Is Never Too Late." She counsels us with comfort about our "too late" convictions:

> Those who condemn themselves for past actions or failures need to know that it is never too late to be forgiven,

to be set free. It is never too late to let go of old ways and begin again.... It is never too late to begin. What has gone before—age, years, doubts, or self-condemnation—none of these things can deter or dismay us when we live and act on faith.[35]

Herman Cain, the successful businessman, founder of Godfather's Pizza, speaker and author, never accepted any too-late ideas. Coming from a background of poverty, he rose to executive positions in several companies (his first vice-presidency was at age 34 at the Pillsbury Company), gained national success in business and speaking, and published three books. But Cain felt destined for greater contributions. He looked inside himself for his "new purpose," as he said, and his answer came.

As he held his 15-minute-old first granddaughter, he thought, What do I do to make this a better world? So at age 51, Cain entered the ministry, and four years later founded and continues to oversee centers throughout the country to help at-risk young people in academics, social skills and spiritual development. At 58, he ran for the Senate in Georgia.[36]

Cain demonstrates that we never need to accept conventions of age, notions of impossibility, or even satisfaction with accomplishments. He completely resisted and rejected the stealthy, apparently incontrovertible beliefs that so many people catch like the flu. They all begin with "You get to be a certain age and ...

- You're supposed to think only of retirement.
- You're supposed to start getting all kinds of ailments.
- You're not supposed to entertain the idea of doing all kinds of things, much less break new ground.
- You're supposed to give up your Dream and wail, "It's too late!"

Who says? Don't the people in this chapter, and I'm sure others you can think of, prove the opposite? Age may be a chronological fact, but that doesn't mean we have to accept all the usual labels, constraints, restrictions and limiting beliefs and assumptions that our society has enshrined. They are powerless—if we make up our minds that they are.

There's more hope. In her book *The Age of Miracles*, Marianne Williamson, the spiritual teacher and illuminator of *A Course in Miracles*, discusses the growing new attitudes toward middle age, and, as we saw earlier, her words apply as well to more-than-middle age:

> What is new is how many of us are reaching for something outside [middle age's] culturally prescribed norms…. We can forge a new vision, a new conversation, to take us beyond the limited thought-forms that have defined its parameters for generations.[37]

In support, Deepak Chopra expands on these ideas in a wonderful book whose title can serve as a mantra for all of us. In *Ageless Body, Timeless Mind*, he writes:

> You are much more than your limited body, ego, and personality. The rules of cause and effect as you accept them have squeezed you into the volume of a body and the span of a lifetime. In reality, the field of human life is open and unbounded…. Once you identify with that reality … aging will fundamentally change.[38]

Think about these words. They are true to the degree that you accept them. The examples in this chapter show how "open and unbounded" life can be. I've often heard older people—and you may feel this way yourself—proclaim that they may look a certain age but they feel like 30. A 76-year-old neighbor has a boyfriend 15 years her junior. She told me, slightly blushing, "I'm really a teenager."

If you feel this young, how can it ever be too late?

Maybe you still feel it's too late, thinking about choices and changes you had. Read Martha Smock again:

> The old saying that opportunity knocks only once has been disproved again and again by people who have risen to make a new life, a new start. The opportunity that passed them by or that they passed by was not the only one.
>
> There are always undreamed-of opportunities before us. There are always new paths and new doors opening before us.[39]

Smock suggests how we can activate this new conviction:

> Rather than sitting back and thinking, "It is too late for me now; it is too late for my life to change; it is too late for me to be the successful person I dreamed of being," say to yourself: "It is never too late for God. There is always a way, there is always the power in me to begin again."[40]

Choices: Your Past Again

We've all made wrong choices. Admit them. I only recently stopped kicking myself for choosing an agent among several who showed interest in an early nonfiction book of mine. The one I chose was about to retire, and she couldn't or didn't want to put her best efforts into my book. Her head and heart were already out the door. I had to remember that I was acting out of my best knowledge and capability at the time, not to mention receiving the great ego boost I needed.

Similarly for you, whatever the situations you've been in. You made the best choices you could, given where you were. Accept this. Reaffirm also that your choices during those times *were* in divine order. Review your "Divine Order List" from Chapter 1 and think about it again. You may want to write a new list from a larger perspective and greater understanding. As Eckhart Tolle says in *The Power of Now,* "I have little use for the past and rarely think about it."[41] Good advice.

Look at when Belva Plain and Jessie Foveaux started their novels. Look at Bill Weinacht, and the many others who used their experiences, difficult as they may have been, toward their life's Dream. Instead of rejecting your past, forgive yourself, thank yourself for having your past, and embrace it.

Your *But* List

"Sure, sure," I can hear you saying. Are you just trying to please me? Are you really intoning any of these excuses or similar ones?

But I couldn't! I'm too …

- Old
- Tired
- Sick
- Weak
- Set in my ways
- Busy
- Overwhelmed
- Disorganized
- Undisciplined
- Overobligated
- Hopeless
- Rusty, mentally and physically
- Lazy
- Uneducated
- Stupid
- Timid
- Fat
- Thin

- Ugly
- Afraid
- Poor
- Far behind …

Look at all the "late bloomers" in this chapter. Choose again. Think again.

Tiptoe into a couple of your Dream choices, or maybe the one big one you've kept buried or hidden all this time. Maybe you know your choices already or need to stop and think a little. That's fine.

The internationally known pastor Robert Schuller, who originated "possibility thinking," asks, "What Dreams would you be setting for yourself if you knew you could not fail?"[42]

Schuller doesn't stop you from answering this question by asking about your age, your physical condition, what's in your bank account, or how gray your hair is.

Focus on your choices. Calm down and reconnect with yourself. If you need to, go back to your childhood or adolescent self, the one who felt, and knew, that life is endless and exciting, and that all possibilities exist.

Make a list of your Dreams now.

No one has to see this list but you. No one else will laugh or dismiss your ideas or say, "At *your* age? Get out!"

Dreams at Which I Cannot Fail

1. I would like to begin _____.
2. I would like to resume/continue _____.
3. I would like to complete _____.
4. I've always wanted to _____.
5. I've always wanted to _____.
6. I've always wanted to _____.

Maybe this list doesn't cover everything you want to say. No reason to feel limited by it. Once you start writing, you may find that many more ideas, thoughts and buried Dreams start floating up. Get down as many possibilities as you wish.

Because you're recording these Dreams doesn't mean you will, or must, carry them out or complete everything. Rather, writing the list opens you up to the unrestrained, unbound, limitless choices you do have.

The list may reawaken interests and passions you've forgotten or long hidden and pretended they don't matter to you anymore. Still, I bet they've festered under the surface of your daily life, satisfaction and even accomplishments. They hang onto you like a low-grade cold, which you can't quite rid yourself of, even if you think you want to.

There's a corner in our minds, dark and dim and dusty. We cordon it off because we don't want to visit it. This is the dungeonlike place where most of us have locked away that early Dream or desire. It's well-guarded by wardens who never seem to retire, named Shouldn't, Can't, and Would Never.

This dungeon place is hardy, a place that buries your desires and magnifies your self-disparagements. Your Dream has survived all the tortures you've subjected it to, the mental deprivation, starvation of interest and attention, attempts at suffocation, lack of the sunlight of motivation, and denial of its very reality.

In spite of every torture devised to break your Dream, it has survived. No matter how we try to destroy it, the Dream doesn't vanish; from that mind-dungeon, it nags and nags at you.

Tom, whom you met earlier, finally faced his emaciated Dream after his retirement as director of a large museum. He asked me to help him restore it to perfect health, and as we cleared out his self-condemnations, we worked out his daily painting schedule.

Recently, with great pride, he showed me a painting he'd just completed.

"Only took me 40 years," he beamed.

Don't be afraid to unlock your Dreams. They're with you and in you. The sooner you let them out of that dank dungeon, the sooner they'll be ready to give you what you've wanted all this lifelong time.

Do I hear another set of "Buts" surfacing? "I'll never catch up. There's too much to learn. Too much has happened. I can't master everything I need in the time left."

Well, sorry to undercut all those excuses. They're only fear cropping up, masquerading as rationality. Swallow hard and ignore the fear. The great and surprisingly good news is this: as you muster the courage to unleash and enunciate the Dreams you've been harboring, your Inner Self responds instantly.

In his book aptly titled *Do It! Let's Get Off Our Buts*, which I quoted from earlier, Peter McWilliams wisely tells us, "Your goal-fulfillment system is working all the time—pulling experiences, lessons, information and people to help you fulfill your Dream."[43]

Sounds suspiciously like divine order, right?

Right. Well, trust it. And trust yourself. In later chapters, I'll lead you step by step toward making your Dream a reality. Command those barking fears to silence. Stop them from permeating your mind and outlook. Start repeating the real truth about yourself and your life. Follow these Divine Orders.

Divine Orders

- A divine order is at work, enabling my life to unfold in ways that are beyond my greatest expectations.
- I know what to do to meet my responsibilities to family, friends and my job and still pursue my own special interests.

- God is preparing my way as divine order moves through my life and circumstances.
- Order is restored where there seemed to be chaos.
- Hope is revealed where there seemed to be none.
- Because the order of God is always active, I am blessed by divine order every day.[44]
- If you need more bolstering, read—and believe—what *A Course in Miracles* tells us: "Your passage through time and space is not at random. You cannot but be in the right place at the right time."[45]

Think again of Belva Plain starting out at age 59. Were her children's questions not divine order? Did she need to master the wild, intimidating and endless gadgetry of the electronic revolution to write her 20-some novels? No. All she needed was the decision, her lifetime of experiences—which she already had—and a case of yellow pads and pens that her granddaughter could buy at the local Office Depot.

Is it too late? You know the answer. It's never too late to rewrite, revise and reframe your life.

PART II
CHANGING:
HOW DO YOU CHANGE WHAT'S BOTHERING YOU?

CHAPTER 3
Listen to Yourself:
Get to Know Your Inner Guide

When you talk to yourself, what do you hear? Who's really talking?

Inside our heads, we're always talking to ourselves. We hear many voices, and most of the time they're far from friendly: "Hey, stupid, use the big bowl for all that pasta!" "The Phillips screwdriver, idiot!" "You want to do that? You must be kidding! You're too old, tired, fat, lazy."

Voices like these whirl around all the time, endlessly. Psychologists call them the superego, inner judge, censor, internalized parent, and many other fancy names. A friend dubbed them "the bad priests."

As you no doubt already know, these harsh, negative voices pound us. They're insistent, tenacious and stubborn. They easily dominate our minds. The more we try to ignore or quiet them, the more they clamor for attention. The East Indians name this part of the mind a "drunken monkey," always chattering and condemning.[1] If we're ever going to get beneath these raucous thoughts to really listen to ourselves, we must show them who's boss.

You may not believe it yet, but you *can* ignore that unruly creature, shut it out, starve it, and listen to something else instead that's much more on your side. You reasonably ask, "Who the heck is this?" Beneath the frenzied surface of our daily trivia, endless judgments, catalogues of chores, and swirling wisps of past regrets and future fears, it's our Inner Guide, our Voice, who lives quiet, untouched, inviolate.

The Voice has many names: inner knowing, intuition, right brain, soul, higher power, inner self, true voice, Jesus, Holy Spirit, God, your heart, your gut. Over the centuries, many have acknowledged and developed it—artists, scientists, great leaders, enlightened beings, philosophers and countless people like you and me. Most of the time, though, the Voice has been talked of or written about largely by mystics, and it's been reserved for saints or schizophrenics.

With the exciting reawakening of spiritual consciousness throughout our culture, the Voice has again become respectable. It's being rediscovered as a quality we all have and can develop. Marianne Williamson describes it beautifully:

> We are graced with a greater capacity for direct contact with our own higher power than most of us are in the habit of using. When we stay close to the wisdom of our own knowing, seeking solutions to our problems in the sanctuary of the heart and not in the vanity of the mind, then we can pretty much trust in the unfolding, mysterious wisdom of life.[2]

As we lose our society's embarrassment about drawing on resources other than the material and palpable, we gain the strength in recognizing the value and virtue of our Inner Voice. It's resurfacing (have you noticed?) not only in inspirational writings like Williamson's, but even in the popular media, a testament to our society's hunger for spiritual content.

Inner listening is recommended in everything from diet advice ("Hear your body's cravings for broccoli") to clothes ("That purple shirt is crying out to you") to dating ("Your stomach does flip-flops when you study his eyebrows, and it's not indigestion") to daily living ("Do you know when the phone will ring before it does?") to major decision-making ("Something's prodding you to take that job offer").

All this acknowledgment doesn't mean the Inner Voice is easy to find or listen to. We may read about it or hear dramatic accounts of how other people found theirs. I think especially of the dramatic account of the irreverent and candid Elizabeth Gilbert in *Eat, Pray, Love* the first time she heard her Voice—in the middle of the night as she sobbed on the bathroom floor about her unbearable marriage.[3] No one else's experience, though, can substitute for our own. Like life, each of us must go through the stages ourselves.

Why Bother?

Why should you care about finding your Inner Guide? Why is it so important? Like a kid pushed to violin lessons, you may be whining, "Aw, do I have to?"

No, you don't. Here's a good reason to take the lessons: If you don't cultivate your Guide, you'll never get to trust yourself—or your life. You won't be able to succeed at the forgiving self-dialogues that help you see your past in a newer, more wholesome light.

If you're no longer fighting the idea, it's time. Let me help you locate your Inner Voice, separate it from all the others, and then foster it. In our sophisticated know-it-all or know-where-to-get-it-all culture, unlike our teaching about manners and the pursuit of money and ever more information, we haven't valued this Guide or taught its importance. Despite the increasing and encouraging openness about spiritual matters, most of us find the concept of the Voice strange and slightly suspect. We need strong intent, determination and some courage to recognize it.

Recognize

Of the many voices that drown out our Inner Voice, the most insidious is the Inner Judge. This is the master negator and torpe-doer, the ultimate disapproving and demeaning parent, the ever-demanding, never-sated god to which we've all sacrificed too much psychic energy and too many years.

I'm sure you know it well. Every time you do something good, solve something, or get a great idea, this is the voice that instantly trumpets, "Ridiculous! Who do you think you are? It will never work. Are you crazy? Don't you know all the things that will go wrong? Let me count the ways."

Replace

How, then, to turn off this endless doomsaying loop? I've learned, through much mind-gnashing, that to try to suppress it is almost impossible. It's as stubborn as weeds. If you try to grind it into the ground, it will spring up again the minute you lift your foot. If you try to reason it to sleep, it will stay awake forever and stare at you with hollow glee.

The better line of attack is to replace that ominous voice with more productive messages—following some principle we were supposed to learn in middle school science class, something about two things unable to exist at the same time. The replace-ment principle can be triggered with many techniques.

Inner Judge Replacements

1. Talk back.

Shout that monkey down. Give it some of its own medicine. Tell it, with all the force you can muster, "Shut up! You're wrong! I am *not* crazy! I've never been saner, and you're not gonna stop me!" Even if you don't quite believe your own retorts, shout them anyway. Bellow as if you believe.

2. Do affirmations.

Affirmations are wonderful, elevating replacements that quiet the Inner Judge. A version of verbal prayer, they have been used for centuries. Catherine Ponder reminds us of the powerful visceral connection affirmations tap between our thoughts and spoken words. Repeated aloud or in our minds, affirmations "make firm" our positive thoughts.[4]

Many books contain excellent affirmations. Louise Hay's *You Can Heal Your Life* is one of my favorites. At the end of every chapter, she prints a meditation that sends you to the ceiling. Although specific to the subject, each begins with this: "In the infinity of life where I am, all is perfect, whole and complete."[5]

You can also create your own affirmation for any event, circumstance, person or quality you want to feel better about. There's only one rule: Always decree your affirmations in the present tense. Here are some broad-spectrum ones to get you started:

- I am worthy of all good in my life.
- I deserve to love and be loved.
- I forgive myself and I am forgiven.
- I lack nothing. All I need is here now.
- I hear my true Voice now.
- I am guided to the right words, decisions and actions in this situation.

3. Pray.

It's okay. Praying doesn't commit you to going to church on Sunday or major holidays, or joining committees. If you need reassurance, prayer has made it into the mainstream media. A few years ago, an article in *Family Circle* recommended prayer for stress and told about people who prayed for guidance in conquering, among other things, marital discord, fears and even to-do lists.[6] Current magazines and Internet features almost daily report on prayer as a force in solving problems, either in how-to articles or summaries of studies with 4,256 people in the Republic of AwGoOn.

If you think you don't know how to pray, take a verse or hymn from childhood, a psalm, or even a Christmas carol, and repeat it to yourself. Or try a contemporary prayer, like one from Marianne Williamson's *Illuminata* or Thomas Moore's *Care of the Soul*.[7] Or any work of James Dillet Freeman, who is always lyrical and moving. I often use this statement from *A Course in Miracles*: "Let every voice but God's be still in me."[8]

Silently or aloud, as you say a sentence like this or passage of your choice, focus on what it means. Let it saturate your attention. Keep repeating it and feel yourself lifting and lightening, yielding to the Higher Power. That's prayer.

4. Meditate.

Although it's close to prayer, meditation doesn't need to have a religious connotation or mysterious quality. You don't have to join an East Indian monastery or never lose your temper. Like prayer, meditation is now routinely written about and advised in magazines and online along with diets, relationships, kid-raising and certainly stress. If you still don't get it, you can buy *Meditation for Dummies*.[9]

Despite the many books and articles about how to meditate, it's basically simple: In a quiet place, with no distractions, take a few deep breaths. Choose a word, phrase or sentence, or one of your affirmations if you wish. The important thing is to pick something that grabs you or has special meaning. Repeat it steadily, without pressing or hurry. It doesn't have to be an esoteric mantra, or right according to any authority. It only has to be right for you.

Here are some examples:

- Peace
- One
- Love
- Ahhhh
- Joy
- I am whole
- I have all I need
- I like myself
- "Divine order is established in my mind and body"[10]
- God is with me
- "In quiet I receive God's Word today"[11]

A warning, though: When you meditate, your Inner Judge, that old drunken monkey outraged at your audacity, will do its utmost to get your attention. It will succeed more than a few times, with all manner of ridicule, condemnation and barrages of random thoughts, scenes, lists and worries.

Recognize its antics and just keep coming back to your chosen meditative words. Like a good parent to yourself, be patient, steadfast and forgiving, shepherding your child-mind to the sidewalk out of traffic. You're steering your mind out of negativity to determination, self-confidence and the good you deserve.

Emmet Fox in *The Golden Key* counsels wisely. Every time a negative thought comes up, he says, "Stop thinking about the difficulty, whatever it is, and think about God instead."[12]

By such means, you'll not only feel better but will—miraculously—quiet the Inner Judge enough to begin to hear your Inner Guide.

Cultivate

Cultivating your Voice takes desire and practice. Expect to hear it and make room for it. With one of the methods above, you can schedule special undisturbed times for practice.

You don't have to limit yourself to these times. Give your Voice a chance in any situation. As you're getting dressed, having lunch, or driving, consciously tone down the automatic background noises we're so accustomed to. This may mean resisting the instant flip of the stereo or news the moment you get up, or tearing your eyes away from the TV in the lunchroom, or flipping off your iPhone earbuds the minute you start the ignition.

Cultivating your Voice may mean not grabbing the latest *People* magazine in the dentist's office and devouring as much juicy pseudo-news as possible before your name is called. Not grousing to the person next to you while you wait a full 30 minutes on the ATM line. Not showing off your baseball stats while you wait in the car wash.

Cultivating your Voice may mean—watch out—reacquainting with what's in your mind, in a foreign, almost unheard-of, revolutionary state of ... quiet.

Afraid?

Are you getting nervous? Good. Edgy? Great. Really anxious? Terrific. The more any of these emotions are churning, the more you need this lesson. Your terror—is this too strong a word?—is in direct proportion to how much you need to reconnect with yourself.

You don't have to go cold turkey. Try silence a few times. When you do, simply observe the thoughts that stream through your head—and they will. See how many you can identify that are undeniably negative—condemnations of the past, worries about the future, or criticisms of the very thing you're doing now.

Are you afraid of quiet? It's probably been so long since you've experienced it that you hardly know what it's like. The unknown can be frightening. Don't be afraid. Your Inner Guide is your friend. If you give it a chance and a hearing, it will support you. That's why it was placed inside you.

Your Voice is given to you to be developed and used. How? For anything you want or need to know. In all the ways that the Inner Judge condemns you, the Inner Voice—in reverse—helps you see the past more wholesomely, gain insights into present events, and make moves that will benefit you in the future.

Are you afraid you've got nothing inside? It may seem that way because you've been smothering your Guide for so long with so much noise. It hasn't had much chance to peek out and chirp hello. Like every fledgling, all it needs is a patient, accepting environment.

Your fear is natural. There's a simple way to meet it.

The Remedy for Fear of the Voice

I discovered this remedy in graduate school many years ago, and I'll tell you the whole story, because it illustrates several things we've been talking about. Researching materials for a literature paper, I discovered a poem that was probably the first seed for this book. Little did I know then, in this seemingly unrelated event, how important an anchor and mainstay this poem would become to me.

Maybe you've spotted a few times like this in your own experience. You may have already uncovered one or two on your Divine Order list. That moment may have been commonplace, even unpleasant, one you hardly noticed at the time. Later, thinking back, you realized what a turning point it was. Even if you're still having trouble with the concept of Divine Order, that apparently insignificant event showed its truth in your life.

There I was in the stacks of the Columbia University Library—multiple levels of vast, dimly lit, cement rooms buried deep in the core of the building. Each room holds endless rows of crammed bookshelves wedged tightly between the yellowed floors and ceilings.

It was hard to believe anyone ever ventured into this underworld, much less wanted to stay. No windows, no natural light, a pervading stale-sweet smell of crumbling bindings, and doorways too low and narrow. Those doorways were like bomb shelters, where you had to stoop not to bang your head. Yet sleeping here were the glories of civilization, ready to yield their treasures to anyone with the fortitude to find them.

Coughing a little in the dank air, I dutifully traced the confusing numbers of the Dewey Decimal system and tiptoed down the narrow aisles. As I finally reached the right section, from a dusty shelf my eye lit on a slim volume. It wasn't the book I was looking for, but I couldn't resist pulling it out.

With this small, casual action, I discovered a poem, and especially two lines, that would influence me profoundly and contribute to my lifelong growth. I've shared them with clients and friends, written about them often, and repeated them to myself countless times. From "Walking to Sleep" by the American poet Richard Wilbur, these lines have never failed to reassure and sustain me: "Step off assuredly into the blank of your mind. / Something will come to you."[13]

Wilbur's words aren't for writers alone. They apply to any blank canvas, lump of clay, empty stage, question, quandary or new endeavor. We panic at meeting a new client or prospective mother-in-law. We hyperventilate at creating the all-important plan for a project or presentation. We freeze at addressing a group or composing the perfect menu for important guests. Wilbur knows that when we let go, this "blank" of our minds—which I take as our Inner Guide—will give us what we need.

Accept

You, like the rest of us, *do* have this Inner Resource. How do I know? Not only because so many, including myself, have proved it innumerable times, but also because it was guaranteed us. Read this unmistakable command and promise in Psalm 81:10: "Open wide your mouth and I will fill it."

This command is a thrilling, invigorating, supremely comforting assurance—but with a condition. Like Wilbur's startling instruction to "Step off," the psalm instructs us to action: "Open ... your mouth."

As Wilbur directs us to step off "assuredly," the psalm similarly commands us to show our faith by first opening our mouths. When we obey, what are we doing? We're expecting, anticipating, getting ready to receive. We're making room to receive a lot: We're told to open our mouths *wide*.

When we do, we're given a glorious promise: "I will fill it." Like Wilbur's rather understated declaration, "Something will come to you," the psalm plainly tells us the good we can expect.

Another Old Testament verse promises similar abundance and commands us to be ready to receive. Isaiah calls us to anticipatory action for the blessings to come:

> Enlarge the place of your tent,
> stretch your tent curtains wide,
> do not hold back;
> lengthen your stakes.
> For you will spread out to the right and to the left.
> —Isaiah 54:2-3

This message again commands us to act first—"Enlarge ... stretch," that is, expect. How often have we felt an answer is "too good to be true" and have held back, rejected or dismissed it? Isaiah's (God's) directive insists: enlarge, stretch, lengthen. Like Wilbur's "assuredly," God is again telling us to accept fully deliverance of the supply we need, and more.

Many centuries later, *A Course in Miracles* puts it simply: "I need but call and You will answer me."[14]

First we've got to pick up the phone. This means exercising our courage—jumping off, opening, enlarging, stretching, taking action. By these things, we're showing ourselves (and the Universe) we've got the faith, strength of mind, and character to meet the unknown without the material evidence we think we need and usually rely on.

Our daily, habitual world encourages us to operate on the principle "I see, therefore I know." To experience the wondrous promises, we must step off, leap, open, stretch *before* the material assurances: "I know, or at least want to know ... and therefore I will see."

In traditional Christian terms, I think we're asked to relive the progression from Thomas, who doubted, to Peter, who knew. When the resurrected Jesus appeared to the apostles, Peter immediately knew—and bowed down. Thomas, though, needed material proof and asked to see the wounds.

Whose faith was greater? Who accomplished more and gave more to humanity? Do we hear about Thomas as the builder of the Church? As performer and consummate role model of countless miracles? As tireless spreader of the Christian doctrine? As magnificent proselytizer throughout the entire Mediterranean, traveling with great hardships?

No, but two millennia ago, Peter knew how to listen to his Inner Voice. Even in the face of many threats on his life, it trumpeted inside him so loudly he couldn't deny it. He knew the requirement: take that first step in faith, and he fulfilled what he came to do.

It's the same with us today. However great or humble appears our life's mission, we will fulfill it if we take the risk of ignoring our material senses, unhooking from the world's logic, and looking beyond so-called reality. We will fulfill our purpose as we courageously step off into what appears "the blank," in Wilbur's words, open wide our mouths, enlarge, lengthen, and don't hold back.

We will be filled.

Test

Go ahead. Test your Inner Guide. Find an undistracted spot, mentally and physically. Quiet down. Stop reasoning and figuring. Ask something simple: What should I cook for dinner tonight? Who should I phone next? Should I do this task or that?

Listen. If 26 things are whirling in your head, you're not quite ready. Let them stream until they run out. Ask again. As your mind echoes the question you've asked, you may notice it comes up with some "good reasons" for choosing one over the others. Somehow these don't convince you, and the whirling continues.

Ask again.

If there's no clear-cut answer, just wait. Take a breath. Ask again.

Then you'll hear it. Or maybe feel it, or see the image of it in your mind's eye. You'll know. And you'll act.

Testing: An Example

Recently, I had vivid proof of the Voice. A coaching assignment for a client required that I prepare him for a major examination. His career with his medical consulting company hinged on his passing this exam, as did my future assignments with him. Exam preparation was something I'd done little of and didn't particularly like. I was angry at myself for even having agreed to it.

He kept sending fat overnight packages of materials for me to work from. With a groan, I'd throw each envelope under my desk in a pile, untouched, unopened, unorganized.

Every time my foot hit the pile, I had one instant response: to worry about how I'd ever begin. I couldn't figure out a way that would be easy and comprehensible for him and at the same time give me an organized blueprint to follow. Continuing to ignore the propagating pile, I knew, wouldn't solve anything, but that didn't stop me from avoiding it, even though it startled me awake many nights.

Finally, one day when the exam date hovered even closer, I could stall no longer. Clearing a space on my desk, I hauled up all the envelopes, ripped them open, and spread everything out. I pushed the manuals around, glanced at the supplementary booklets, straightened the loose pages, inserted a paper clip here and there, and heaved a great sigh of anguish.

It was worse than I'd thought. My only options were to refer the client to a respected tutorial service or jump off the balcony.

Then, probably out of panic, I ran to the bathroom, shouting out loud, "I don't know what to do!"

My lament barely over, I heard It. Who? The Voice. In three simple words, It told me exactly where to begin. How this first step would lead to the rest of the materials or what I would do next, I didn't yet know. Hearing the Voice, I knew that what It told me was the perfect first move.

Shaken but calmer, I went back to my desk. Without hesitating, I began to sort through all the materials. The organizing came naturally and flowed quickly.

This was the start of a successful coaching plan that ended with the client passing his examination brilliantly. Because of his performance, he was singled out for a special training program that would lead to further excellent career opportunities for him and assignments for me.

Of course he did his part and followed my guidance. For my part, I credit my Inner Guide. Once I stopped complaining, opened my mouth (remember?), and called, I heard the answer and my need was filled.

Practice

Before this dramatic episode, I'd heeded the Guide occasionally, but now I started deliberately finding ways to use It. After all, for most of us, it's been dormant so long that, like someone who's overslept, it needs to stretch and rev up. Essayist and journalist Barbara Graham (who wrote the provocatively titled *Women Who Run With the Poodles*) calls the Inner Voice a "muscle."[15] Like its physical counterpart, it strengthens with practice. If it's not used, it grows weak and unrecognizable.

From early childhood, we've learned to ignore the Guide. Our culture brooks no such nonsense, and we learned this lesson well. Those who mattered, and on which our survival depended, consistently told us not to follow It, and we were censured for any attempts. Instead, we were instructed in other voices.

Other Voices We Were Taught to Listen To

- Listen to your mother.
- Your father won't like that!
- Follow the teacher's instructions.
- Obey the church rules.
- What will the neighbors think?
- You know, dear, you really shouldn't do that.
- Oh my, that's not a wise move.
- How dare you do that!

Recognize these? Is it any surprise you've been faithfully practicing how *not* to listen to the Voice? It's always been there. The challenge is to keep practicing so you let it come through. Practice to trust it enough so you get under the crust of surface reality, past those many other voices, and down to your internal, nourishing core.

Sometimes you won't have to ask a formal question. Intention will be enough, or a heartfelt and humbled admission that you haven't a clue, like my cry about the client's exam preparation. You'll hear, or sense, what you need.

Other times, as Psalm 81 promises, you'll hardly be finished asking when the answer comes. The key is to quiet down.

Once you do, and stop trying to figure everything out, the Guide responds unconditionally. You don't have to be anywhere special or in a holy, religious or even pleasant place. You don't have to be in a good mood or act happy, loving or saintly. The Voice doesn't withhold because you snapped at your husband, growled at another driver, or ate the fourth piece of supersize pizza.

How Does It Feel?

To find out whether we're truly in touch with our Inner Guide, I've looked to our bodies as the key. Learning to listen to your body is an art in itself—eating when we're hungry rather than because it's clock-time for lunch, resting when we need to and not pushing ourselves to one more to-do. As our body tells us what's physically good for us, it also tells us when to listen to our Voice—if we pay attention.

Your Body Is Telling You What's Wrong

First, if you're having trouble hearing the Voice above all the daily, disapproving chatter, try "tuning in" to your body.

Your body knows. Mine certainly told me by waking me at night about those neglected exam materials for my client. My body told me again by my sudden bathroom urge that something was wrong about my approach to the coaching assignment.

Our collective wisdom is often wiser than we are. Look at our language. It reflects our body's messages, even if we don't admit them consciously. We've all had "a gut feeling," "butterflies in my stomach," "a sinking feeling," "a lump in my throat," "cold feet." In fact, our stomach and related organs give us amazing messages, and I don't mean those annoying fried-dumpling cravings. "The brain-gut connection," an article in *Elle* tells us,

> has led to a new field of science, neurogastroenterology, whose experts reverentially refer to the gut (comprised of the esophagus, intestines and stomach) as the "second brain." Unglamorous as it may sound, the gut is a physical and emotional powerhouse: It's estimated to contain more than 200 million neurons, more than the spinal cord has.[16]

So there. Your body is monumentally equipped and craving to tell you. Pay attention and listen to it.

Listen to Your Body

Here's an exercise to help you begin:

1. Sit quietly, close your eyes, and tune in to your body. Become aware of yourself sitting there.
2. Scan your body mentally, from toes to head.
3. Notice where you feel tense: jaw, hands, stomach? Is there a little throb over your eyes? Are your shoulders high? Is your chest tight? Does your stomach feel a little achy?
4. Focus on the tense area. Ask it to tell you what's bothering it.
5. Allow images, feelings, words to float in. What comes to you?
6. Chances are you've been hiding from something—information, feelings, realizations, action—and this is what's tightening you up.
7. Listen.
8. Act on what you hear or see mentally. This may mean taking a step, not taking one, accepting or rejecting something. You'll know.
9. Thank your body for talking to you.
10. Take a few deep breaths, stretch, open your eyes, and go do what the Guide has told you.

You can practice in many ways as you become more aware. Your body knows before you do. For example, when someone asks you to do something and you really don't want to do it, does an involuntary moan escape? A soft curse? Do you physically cringe, furrow your brows, roll your eyes, or clench your fists? Now you know where headaches and indigestion come from.

With practice, I've learned to identify the emotions my body is signaling. Whatever I'm pretending, my real response is tightness in my chest or hollowness in my stomach, as in that looming client exam coaching project. These sensations color every action and decision, and I'm not fully present for anything else until I confront them—ask, listen, act.

Notice how you feel after you tell a friend he looks good when he looks more tired than you've ever seen him, after you cheerily agree to bake 12 dozen cookies for the fundraiser, or after you accept a weekend invitation when you really want to stay home with the mystery-movie marathon. The body, as life coach Martha Beck says in one of her excellent articles, is our built-in, infallible "lie detector."[17] In another article, she expands: "The body is an organic polygraph machine. When you lie, even unwittingly, it responds by producing reactions that range from dryness of mouth to increased blood pressure to red, blotchy skin."[18]

Maybe such symptoms are relatively minor. But denial of our real feelings and desires isn't at all good for us, not only in the actions we're forcing ourselves into, but also in our bodies themselves. Barbara Graham says, "each time we ignore our inner voice, we shrink a little inside ourselves."[19]

Even the conservative medical community has (grudgingly) come to recognize that stress, anxiety and repressed anger all contribute not only to bodily tension, but also to a host of physical diseases. By now, increasing research shows the connections between our emotions and physiological changes in our immune systems, enzymes and hormones (see, for example, the many books and articles by physician and National Institutes of Health researcher Esther Sternberg).[20]

On the more ethereal plane, I've found invaluable Louise Hay's list of relationships of body, mind and soul. Her extensive chart of correspondences between negative emotions and physical maladies has been reprinted, enlarged and refined continuously since 1976 and translated into many languages throughout the world.

Derived from years of listening to clients and to her own Inner Voice, Hay's equations have been gradually supported by mainstream medical and scientific research (see, among many, books by doctors Benson, Dossey, Seigel, Simonton and Simonton, and Weil[21]). For example, in Hay, stomach problems indicate "Dread. Fear of the new. Inability to assimilate the new."[22] Such emotions produce excess stomach acids and precipitate heartburn, ulcers and other digestive problems.

The remedy? Not chugging a bottle of antacid or grabbing a little purple pill but affirming, "Life agrees with me. I assimilate the new every moment of every day. All is well."[23]

When we yield to negative emotions, our bodies tense and protest. When we act against what we really know is right for us, our bodies signal their rebellion.

Your Body Is Telling You What's Right

When we think and act in ways that support and harmonize with our true feelings, our bodies relax. We feel a well-being, or better—we're not even aware of our bodies. In that rocky start of my client's exam project, the instant I got the answer, my chest opened and shoulders relaxed. The stomach hollowness disappeared, and I stopped unconsciously biting the inside of my cheek.

There's more—along with the bodily symptoms, all mental torments vanished. My head no longer whirled with frantic possibilities, weak attempts, frustrated trial-and-error shots, and self-denunciations that I'd taken on something I shouldn't have.

Even more dramatic than these effects, and the most important of all, was the Guide's response. It was instant, unhurried and totally certain. In the moment I'd enunciated my need, the Voice was there. My mind and body, finally ready to listen, instantly responded.

I felt a lightness in my chest, a sense of completion, of everything dropping into place, like a toddler at play finally getting the round block into the round hole. My body, like the child, breathed "AH!"

This is one of the real touchstones and tests of the Voice's message. Do you still feel anxious? Do you still wonder, "Well, maybe if I said this, did that, tried the other thing"? Or do you feel a peaceful certainty in the rightness of the answer you've just heard that eradicates any further questions?

Other touchstones: Between smart-chick observations, Elizabeth Gilbert in *Eat, Pray, Love* realizes, "Even during the worst of suffering, that calm, compassionate, affectionate and infinitely wise voice ... is always available."[24] In a wonderful article, Unity minister, author and speaker Ellen Debenport tells us how we know the Voice: "We finally stop asking whether we truly heard God's voice."[25]

As you keep turning to your Inner Guide, It becomes stronger and surfaces more easily. Finally getting past all the other voices and pulls of conditioning, you get into the habit of asking, hearing and listening. You get used to its calm, certainty, love.

With practice, you'll gain more confidence in It and turn to It more often. In the next chapter, I'll answer some questions that may have popped up. You'll be able to keep practicing, so you get into the habit of relying daily on the Guide, your Guide. Consistent practice will enable you to trust yourself through all the days that mold your years, and to continue to trust your life.

CHAPTER 4

Keep Listening:
Your Inner Guide Wants to Talk to You

You're somewhat acquainted with your Voice at this point, and I want to answer some of the questions everyone asks and tell you more about the many ways the Voice can come to you. My desire is to help you strengthen your conviction that you can indeed rely on the Voice in every situation, and especially those involving the manifestation of your Dream.

What Happens When We Don't Act on Our Inner Voice

Of course, you're free not to listen to your Voice or act on it. I certainly don't mean to scare you but simply inform you about the consequences of not listening to your Voice. Besides, you've likely already experienced some of these.

If we stop a minute and observe ourselves, we can always tell when we haven't listened. Something inside tells us when we've ignored the Voice, attempted to bypass it, or tried to get around it. Have you ever known what to do and then not done it? What happens? For me, everything generally becomes more of an effort and at some point goes plain wrong.

One example: I ran out shopping when my Inner Voice trumpeted like Joshua that it was time to stay in and work. What happened?

- I didn't find a parking space.

- I parked too far away and had to walk to the mall entrance, sweating through my blouse.
- Whatever I came out for, I didn't find in my size or the right color.
- They just sold the last one.
- I snapped at the saleswoman.
- The saleswoman responded rudely.
- I snapped back.
- I forgot my wallet.
- The sale begins tomorrow.
- I rushed around angrily.
- I bumped into other shoppers, who gave me dirty looks.
- I ended up having a miserable time.
- I didn't accomplish my mission.
- I lost two hours.

When I got home, I felt guiltier than ever for taking all that time. At this late hour, I still had to face the work I left to avoid.

The effects of ignoring the Inner Voice may take other forms. When we engage a plumber we don't really like because of a low bid, when we buy a car that doesn't really turn us on because it's practical, when we agree to a project at work that we know we'll never be able to complete fully, and a thousand other things we can all think of that don't feel right, you know what happens. The same thing as I experienced dashing out to the mall—inevitable failure.

More intimately, when your partner or another important person in your life says something that really ticks you off, do you pretend you haven't heard, change the subject, or agree, for the sake of (so-called) peace? Are you cursing inside, or telling yourself how stupid he/she is? Your Inner Voice is shouting so loudly you can hardly hear yourself denying it.

When you respond like this, do you think your anger has dissipated, or that you've conquered it? Sorry.

This is the stuff breakups and breakdowns are made of: swallowing feelings, covering them over with surface conversation or entertainment, substituting supposed harmony or feigned satisfaction for courageous confrontation. Negative feelings, like deeply held desires, don't go away if they're ignored. They go underground, bide their time, multiply like termites, and surface days, months or years later to chew your life into dust.

Repressed feelings also appear as illnesses. They may range from mild to devastating. A sore throat, Louise Hay tells us, can often be traced to unexpressed rage at someone or something.[1] The cancer-prone person hasn't been able to deal effectively with a major loss, feels unworthy, represses anger, lives by an army of "shoulds," and is often consumed with daily resentment.[2]

The unadmitted, unexpressed bundle of negatives may appear suddenly, terribly as apparently irrational behavior. We hear about the sedate businessman who opens fire in his club at lunchtime. The wife in a 20-year marriage who tucks the children into bed, straightens the living room newspapers, and drives away, not looking back, in the middle of the night. The brilliant and popular student discovered clutching a suicide note in the garage with the car motor running.

Such examples may sound extreme, but they happen more than we like to admit, and sometimes to people we know. Such tragic acts all signal that people ignored or minimized what their Inner Voice was telling them and tried to shut it off.

When we have the courage to listen, and then act, we can overcome our fears. We can follow what the Voice is telling us, even when it seems contrary to all logic or everything we've been planning, have succeeded at, or think we want. We then see by how we feel and what happens next in our lives that the Voice, as always, was right.

A Personal Lesson

At a time when I was certain I'd gotten what I wanted, I learned a difficult lesson involving the Voice. This lesson was unsettling, even devastating, but it showed me the Voice's unerring strength and accuracy.

In January of my junior year in college I met Chad. We instantly discovered much in common—classical music, architecture, walking in Riverside Park in any weather, getting huge hot fudge sundaes at the local Greek diner. Chad looked like Clark Kent, had a great apartment near the campus, and was rising quickly to a bright and secure future in the Columbia University administration.

As we shared more of ourselves in the long, delicious talks of early dates, I told him I wanted to go on for the master's in English literature, and then the doctorate. Lifting a spoonful of hot fudge to his mouth, he stopped. His face clouded. "A doctorate? I have only a master's."

I smiled and tried to attribute the flush of cold in my stomach to the ice cream disappearing from my tulip glass.

We spent most of our free time together and stopped seeing other people. As spring came, we took longer walks in the park and marveled together at the trees sprouting new leaves and daffodils popping up near the rain gutters and dumpsters. I don't know how I got any schoolwork done.

One evening in the diner, as the waiter set down my hot fudge sundae, I saw something sticking out of the top scoop where the cherry should have been. It was a delicate, beautiful diamond ring.

That was exactly one of the things I adored about Chad—despite his sober and responsible administrative position, he was so quirkily creative. That night we became engaged.

The next morning I awoke with a terrible headache. When we met for lunch, Chad embraced me, checked my left-hand ring finger, and asked if I'd told anyone yet. I shook my head no. He said he wanted to shout it from the rooftops. I smiled weakly.

Over the next weeks, we started planning. The best time, we agreed, would be at the end of the spring semester, or maybe at the start of summer. Late at night, I completed my applications for graduate school. We continued our walks and kept ordering our sundaes. My headaches persisted.

One day, as we sat on a favorite bench overlooking the river, Chad sighed heavily. He turned to me and said, "Do you want to say it?"

My eyes filled with tears. Neither of us had to speak because we both knew.

A few days later I gave him back the ring.

It took me a long time to get over Chad. Walking to graduate school classes, I'd see him from a distance across the campus. My heart would race, I'd notice how handsome he was, and I'd want to run up and take him out for a sundae. Every time I had this response, my Inner Voice—even though I hardly knew what it was at the time—told me, just as at that first headache, that it wouldn't work.

I was accepted into the master's program. After a moment of excitement, still mourning Chad, I dragged around for the first two semesters. Then, in a course on Renaissance literature, I met David. We laughed easily and argued over interpretations of *Paradise Lost*. He was a few courses ahead of me and fully supported my academic aspirations. We spun scenarios of how we'd both become professors at a small, elite New England college.

As we got to know each other, we discovered other commonalities (metaphysics, classical music, puns, mutual writing critiques). When, in the library over the *Oxford English Dictionary,* he proposed, I instantly said "Yes!" My feelings of soaring and excitement continued, without a single headache or any other telltale symptoms that this was the wrong direction. My Inner Voice was cheering.

Seven months later we had a simple wedding ceremony and a weekend honeymoon between semesters. We both completed the master's and got into the Ph.D. program. At one point, having received some searing comments from his professors on two major papers, David became discouraged about his progress and considered dropping out. He supported me nevertheless in my continued studies and joked about my being a professor at our mythical New England college and him being a student advisor. With my support, though, he weathered the graduate school storms and got his doctorate the year before I did. We both obtained teaching jobs at colleges in the city and for a long time had a solid, nurturing marriage.

Despite all Chad's appearances of rightness, my Inner Voice knew that he wasn't for me. I had to go as far as engagement before I couldn't ignore the Voice's promptings.

Another woman might have recognized the signs sooner and acted on them.

I berated myself for a long time for not seeing them earlier. Mostly I felt gratitude for not making the mistake of ignoring my Inner Voice and marrying the wrong man.

How Does the Voice Sound?

Most often for me it's a voice, unmistakably male and authoritative, probably a vestige of patriarchal childhood images of
God. It may sound like a nagging mother or a soft-voiced angel,
or anything else, depending on what you need at a given
moment. There are no proscriptions or limits to its expression.

God does have a sense of whimsy, though. Your answer may
come through a song lyric, a commercial, a graffiti scrawl, a newspaper headline, a friend's comment on the phone, a phrase over-
heard in the video store, or a chatroom memo.

Once a message came to me during a heart-wrenching time,
precisely at the right moment, in a most unique and appropriate
way. It was almost dawn, and David and I had been up all night.
Our beloved cat had had an accident, and we couldn't locate a
vet. We tried everything but finally had to face the horrible realization and gave up. Still unbelieving, we wrapped our pet's
body in a towel, got in the car, and drove to the local ASPCA.

David parked and asked if I wanted to come in. He said it
might be good to see the homeless kittens, maybe even bring one
home. Unable to speak, and in dry-eyed anguish, I shook my
head and sat like a stone in the car.

My mind whirled with agonized questions and self-recriminations. If I had only watched him ... not turned my back to check
the TV at that instant ... called a vet sooner ... why, Lord, why?

Tears finally flowing, I felt in my handbag for a tissue. The
morning light was emerging. As I blew my nose, something made
me look up. A car had parked in front of ours. My eyes riveted on
its license plate. It was an unmistakable message: "I AM."

This perfection made me sob all the more. My grief became
tempered by gratitude. That license plate gave me exactly what I

needed at that awful moment. It told me that God was always here, wherever I was, in every situation.

A neighbor in AA once remarked, "God is in the gutter too." That sorrowful, early morning, God was at the curb, in the street, and at my side. The Voice gave me the message I needed most.

Forgive Yourself and Keep Listening

Of course, we don't always pay immediate attention to the Voice. What's asked of us may not be easy or obvious. We're so conditioned to acting from "shoulds," others' approval, and supposed appropriateness that obeying our Voice may be difficult. As you keep listening, though, you become better at identifying its messages and following it more consistently. You gain confidence in yourself and your ability to recognize the many ways the Voice has of reaching you. For the times you sidestep it, or fail to act on it, you can forgive yourself more easily.

We often expect and demand much more of ourselves than we do of others. Expanding self-forgiveness, let's give ourselves the leeway to begin again. A better way of seeing our "sins" of avoidance, denial and willful ignoring may be to recognize they're not irredeemable catastrophes. Instead maybe we need to reframe them as simply mistakes.

When a child knocks over a glass or bumps into a chair, do we condemn her and say she's sinned? No. She's simply made a mistake. When a child spells or pronounces a word wrong, do we punish him for sinning? No, we simply show him the right way. As Louise Hay says, honor the child within you—no guilt, no recrimination, only forgiveness, learning and love.[3]

A good way to start practicing is with small things. Listen to the Voice when It tells you to say *No* to the second helping of ice cream or the fifth straight hour of television. Obey the signals— those vague feelings of discomfort, restlessness, boredom or outright shame. Say *Yes*, even if you think it's silly, extravagant or unproductive, when your Voice prompts you in ways It's been trying to nurture you with all this time.

In a wonderful book, *The Journey With the Master*, Eva Bell Werber helps us become better acquainted with the Voice:

> My Beloved, I am ever by your side talking to you…. To keep tuned takes constant practice of the Presence, which is ever with you…. As you go about your daily work, learn to feel the Spirit Presence in all that you do…. Often pause for a moment and incline your ear, and gently and sweetly you will know of a guiding, a cautioning, or a blessing, according to the circumstance which exists at the moment.[4]

Neale Donald Walsch, author of the penetrating and best-selling *Conversations With God*, explains in the first *Conversation* how He speaks through the many avenues of the Voice:

> You do not need the form of this book. This is not the only way I speak to you. Listen to Me in the truth of your soul. Listen to Me in the feelings of your heart. Listen to Me in the quiet of your mind. Hear Me, every-where. Whenever you have a question, simply *know* that I have answered it *already.* Then open your eyes to your world. My response could be in an article already published. In the sermon already written and about to be delivered. In the movie now being made. In the song just yesterday composed. In the words about to be said by a loved one. In the heart of a new friend about to be made.[5]

Part of listening to the Voice is listening for what you yourself need. Listening and acting aren't completely about giving to others. Giving is good, yes, but we can't give from our hearts if we don't feel given to. Incline your ear, and listen now so you can give to yourself.

Give Yourself a Self-Nurturing Date

Often we're not good to ourselves. We feel completely natural inflicting on ourselves the kind of deprivation we'd never inflict on our children, partners, pets or even plants Somehow we feel there's virtue in the self-denial of basic human pleasures, and even necessities. This denial may have worked for medieval monks and martyrs (and I wonder about that), but it doesn't work for most of us. We usually have to find ways to square pleasure with ourselves, as if to pay it off. Some people take a day off or a vacation only after they've worked themselves to the edge of exploding blood pressure or a heart attack. Some people take time off only when they can rationalize to family and friends that they haven't had any days off in six months. Some people never do it.

Do you think you'll get a prize for all this denial? You're right. The prizes are resentment, depression, constant criticism of others, and a host of illnesses (so you can feel more martyred). Oh, yes, you can congratulate yourself on creating a rotten life.

Think of some of the things you've wanted to do for ages and have never given yourself permission or time to do them. The Voice knows what they are and has probably suggested them many times. You've always said inside, "Oh, I couldn't. Costs too much. I've got too much work. I'm too tired. I can't be away from x for that long. Should clean out the garage instead."

It's time to stop cleaning and start living. We all have these desires to do what we firmly think we shouldn't do. We may think they're self-indulgent or—that dread condemnation—selfish. However, they're not. They're called balance.

If you need some authoritative permission, here are the releasing words of Abraham, the collective Consciousness that has come through Esther Hicks for the last 25 years:

> If we were standing in your physical shoes, that would be our dominant quest: Entertaining Yourself, pleasing Yourself, connecting with Yourself, being Yourself, enjoying Yourself, loving Yourself. Some say, "Well, Abraham, you teach selfishness." And we say, yes we do, yes we do, yes we do, because unless you are selfish enough to reach for that connection, you don't have anything to give anyone, anyway. And when you are selfish enough to make that connection—you have an enormous gift that you give everywhere you are.[6]

Now that you've got permission, maybe you need a little prompting in some really *selfish* things to do. Here's a short list of things that clients have confessed they've wanted to do, longed to do, and admitted their Inner Voice persistently prodded them to do. Finally, when they felt strong enough, deserving enough, or exhausted enough, they listened and acted.

Some Ideas for Nurturing Yourself

- An open-ended Sunday afternoon wallowing in magazines.
- Delving into the mysteries of your new Kindle, iPhone, iPad.
- Taking yourself to lunch at the restaurant you've always felt was too expensive.
- Watching the playoffs all day (choose your sport).
- Exploring the wildlife preserve 10 minutes from your home.
- Working on your long-lost collection of poems.
- Poking around in the new crafts shop or hardware store in your neighborhood.

- Sitting quietly and thinking of how you'll express your affection to your partner, like you did when you first discovered each other.
- Attacking the overstuffed, chaotic closet shelves that have been bothering you for years (some of us *do* think this is fun).
- Writing a letter to a treasured friend you haven't had contact with for way too long.
- Writing in your journal; starting your journal.
- Playing your trumpet.
- Playing with your pet for more than 30 seconds between work and bill-paying.
- Going to the zoo.
- Getting the massage you've always craved.
- Buying 17 sacks of candy you loved as a kid and eating as much as you want.
- Shopping (or browsing) for yourself alone.

By now, your own mental list has probably started knocking, or you think of the one you once scribbled out and tucked way back in your desk drawer. Go ahead. Schedule your self-nurturing date.

Self-nurturing, as many spiritual mentors teach us (see Cheryl Richardson[7]), is first a demonstration of our self-esteem, our self-respect, and our sense of deserving. Wendy Kaufman in *Miracle Journeys* points out that all the carefully planned private sessions of scented baths and candles (or center-ice seats at the hockey game) will do nothing if we don't bring our sense of deserving to the activity.[8] If we're drawing the water and lowering the lights only because we think we should, we might as well go empty the dishwasher instead.

To get your feet wet, even if it seems forced or rote at first, take the steps, do it, and act as if you do deserve it. Often the act itself will draw you into it. Ignore your three-page list of Unconditional To-Dos that's knocking heads with the single item on your self-nurturing list. Give yourself a little push. Draw the bubble-bath water anyway. Pull on your team t-shirt and get your buddy out of his garage. Your mind will gradually follow your body.

A wonderful exercise, very similar to the self-nurturing date, is what Julia Cameron calls "The Artist Date."[9] This is a specifically scheduled time—with yourself only—to do anything you've wanted to do for so long (she recommends once a week). It's your private time, with no restrictions, demands or provisos from anyone else. The Artist Date is meant to help unloosen creativity, however we choose to channel it. Like the self-nurturing date, it's also meant to free us from our lifelong constraints and self-denials.

I'd better warn you, though. As much as you may have wished for "the time" to really let yourself have this date, you may find countless inspired and ingenious reasons to avoid it. You suddenly remember it's your turn to chauffeur your daughter's class to the science museum. Your eye lights on the crammed briefcase you brought home from work. You decide to get ahead on the laundry this week, so you jump up to gather the dirty piles from every room. You feel an inexplicable drive to go and get the old radio fixed, even though it's been sitting in the garage for months and no one in the house cares about it anyway.

Realize that these debates, detours and supposed necessities are only your Inner Judge in disguise. The more we succeed in listening inside and acting, the more the Judge tries to sabotage our growing self-respect. These counterfeit absolute musts, which you know you could forget, postpone or get someone else to do, are only the Judge pounding again, and maybe last-gasping, that old message that you really don't deserve to nourish yourself.

Cameron recognizes that the date with ourselves is one of the hardest things for most of us to keep. In her work as creative coach, lecturer and seminar leader, she recounts the confessions of many people who have ignored The Date, tried to avoid it, or caved to yet another excuse masked as imperative.

"There are as many ways," she says, "to evade this commitment as there are days of your life …. Watch how this sacred time gets easily encroached upon." She wisely cautions us: "Recognize this resistance as a fear of intimacy—self-intimacy."[10]

What have we to fear from being alone with ourselves and hearing what we have to say? When will we learn that we're really our own best friend? Extraordinary, exuberant life coach and spiritual teacher Tama Kieves advises us to trust our "own way. No one can give you this way. No one can take it away either."[11] A Unity booklet on spiritual preparation for Easter advises us:

> Be true to yourself…. When you question your actions
> or the path you should follow … listen…. Listen to your
> heart, and know it will lead you in the way that is true
> to yourself—your spiritual self—for I am in you and
> you are in Me. When you listen to your heart, you are
> listening to Me.[12]

If you succumb to that advance load of laundry, forgive yourself. All you need to do is reschedule your self-nurturing date. Your kid or partner or dog will forgive you. Forgive yourself.

As you listen for the right actions, you'll get more comfortable with your Inner Voice. You'll turn to it more often, ask more precisely, and follow it more easily more of the time. To help and accelerate your practice, here are some reminders of its basic, blessed characteristics.

Five Truths About Your Inner Voice

1. It is here, always available, wherever you are, however you feel, whatever you've done.
2. It is solely on your side.
3. It knows what's absolutely right for you.
4. It is your friend, your ally, your guide, your ultimate supporter.
5. It is always with you and for you.

Whenever you're feeling perplexed, uneasy, anxious, mad, frustrated, sick or any other way you don't want to feel, ask your Inner Voice. Listen.

Answers Delayed?

Sometimes, though, despite all our sincerity and stillness, the answer doesn't come right away. This is not our Voice's fault. It continues to shine like a beacon, although our fogs of fear, confusion and anxiety may obscure it for a time.

In these cases, frustrating as they are, my best advice is to do nothing.

To reassure you of God's total presence, even though it doesn't seem to be showing up in your life at the moment, any of the above truths may help. Or not. Go about your daily business. After a while, as your mind processes your fears, gets tired of them, or deals with whatever is blocking the Voice's message, you'll calm down a little.

Don't lose heart. Ask again, forget it, and resume your activities. To do so is itself an act of faith. By acting normally, you're really telling yourself that you don't have to yield to the tyranny of the apparently pressing issue. You're declaring that you, not it, are in control. You're loosening the paralysis and mental hold the issue has had on you.

The answer will often come when you're not even thinking about the problem. In the grand tradition of Newton and Einstein, who puzzled over why their best answers always came to them in the shower, much of the time our answer appears in like ways. When I'm doing something unconnected and by rote— folding the laundry, feeding the fax—the answer pops up. You've probably had this experience too but haven't thought much of it.

Connection with our Voice and God, like Vitamin C, needs daily doses. In your practice sessions (What! Not regular yet!), repeat the thoughts that most comfort you. In odd moments, driving, waiting, walking, repeat them. In times of turmoil, when all you can think of is how vile you/he/she/they are, repeat them. In times of happiness, contentment, satisfaction, joy, repeat them. They will all help you find your Voice.

Finding My Voice

When I first learned about the Voice through *A Course in Miracles*, I had many doubts, probably like you, and questioned incessantly. As I tried to sort it all out, writing helped, and the following piece evolved.[13] It's here to encourage your own self-discovery.

The Voice

In the *Course* study group, Mark kept talking about some mysterious inner voice. When you quieted your mind enough, he said, it would speak to you.

Sure, sure, I thought. I've always had a voice, maybe five or six. They figure things out, make lists, tell me how stupid I am, and once in a while congratulate me on a good phrase or chicken dish.

I suspected that this wasn't what he meant. "Hey, Mark," I asked, "what's the big difference between this voice of yours and all the regular stuff that's always going on in our heads?"

Mark didn't answer right away. For a moment, he seemed to be listening. Then he said slowly, "It gives you peace."

I shrugged. My voices gave me peace. Sometimes. For a minute or two, when I weighed all the unpleasant alternatives, sorted out the infuriating contradictions, reached some kind of uneasy conclusion, or finally told any or all of them to just shut up.

I glanced around at the other people in the group. Two of the men were chuckling, and one woman kept her eyes on the floor. No one jumped in to contribute or explain.

Did they know something I didn't? How could you hear something you didn't hear?

A few mornings later, doing the daily *Course* lesson, I was trying hard to pay full attention and take it all in. Eyes squeezed shut, I craved some psychic spectacular, or at least a figure in light.

My mind went blank.

Something said: You want results. You must learn it's not the results that matter, but the process.

"Huh? Who's that?" I said. This couldn't be one of my voices. They were never so sure and authoritative. *Something* was speaking in my head, and I couldn't deny its odd sense of truth.

I turned back to the lesson, but my mind wandered to the next 12 hours. As usual, I was soon whirling with plans, obligations and tasks—anticipating, worrying, bargaining, shifting this to accommodate that, battling each passing hour. My forehead ached with the day's impossible pieces, and it had hardly begun.

Then, cutting right through, It spoke: *Give up. There's nothing you have to do.*

I waited. As if obeying, I opened the *Course Workbook* to a lesson way beyond the one I was on. My eyes teared as I read the passage:

> Instead of words, we need but feel His Love.
> Instead of prayers, we need but call His Name.
> Instead of judging, we need but be still and let all things
> be healed.[14]

My frenzy stopped. And, incredulously, disappeared.

I can no longer deny it. There is a Voice, different from any I've known. Those others occasionally give answers, but mostly they find fault and heckle like monkeys. Maybe they fade out for a while from exhaustion or disgust, but you can bet they'll return, in full-blast confusion.

This Voice, though, is certain. It's calm and strong. It commands without censure and doesn't waste words. Past all my nonsense, it centers right in.

My head may be reeling with all the pros and cons, what ifs, thens and maybes. Once I find the courage to ask, the Voice always responds.

Still doubting at times, I test it. A petulant child, I know this time I'll catch it and bombard it with questions. As I flirt with questioning at all, my words barely shaping or starting to surface, the answers emerge.

The Voice is not stern or forbidding, a harsh father or unapproachable judge. When I need explanation, it comes. When I crave reassurance, it's there. When I cry out inside on the edge of despair, the Voice soothes and softens my pain.

I'm learning to trust it, in any condition—at midnight or morning, alert or bone weary, in my room, on the road, in front of my friends, expansive and loving, or depressed and self-judging.

Even though I feel unworthy of asking, my mistakes go unnoticed. My regrets of "too late" don't estrange. My red shame at too many petty reactions is gently dismissed.

I can ask anytime, use any words, and repeat, if my fear is that great, every hour. The Voice never fails. No ego-bound guilt can stem its appearing. The Voice knows no limits in love.

All I need is to give up my words and their fighting, let go of directing how the world should behave. All I ever need do is be still and just listen.

Then the Voice, always present, I hear. The Voice, Self-assuring, is here.

With such assurances and your new discoveries, you're much closer to giving up the old habitual trashings of your life. You're more ready to take in the Voice's messages and act on them.

Next I'll introduce you to one of the most helpful ways I've found, as have many clients, for looking at your life differently. This is the idea of reframing.

Reframing will help you loosen that great stone of guilt and paralysis that has blocked you from yourself and weighed down your heart and life. Reframing will let you dissolve that boulder into pebbles and then sand, which trickles out, harming no one. Free of this weight, with your Voice, you'll see what the events, choices and people in your life were teaching you. You'll find out how you can now use reframing for quicker and greater growth toward your Dream.

CHAPTER 5
Draw a New Picture of Your Life: Reframe It

How do you reframe your life? I'll tell you again about Tom, whom you met in the Introduction. With a long and accomplished career, he'd been the director of a leading Eastern art museum, acquired the best works, and discovered, developed and exhibited promising new painters. He'd always had a secret Dream of painting himself, but he abandoned his art in his early 20s, feeling, he admitted, "not good enough."

On Tom's retirement to South Florida, he craved to resume his painting but felt he was "way behind," sure he had lost the talent his early art teachers had praised. He condemned himself daily for not going back to painting. He was also secretly panicked about beginning. Instead, Tom spent his time in superficial social activities with other retirees, telling himself without conviction that he was enjoying life and battling guilt and multiple fears.

After we met at a local art exhibit and I told Tom about my coaching work, he asked to work together. In our meetings, Tom told me more about his desire to teach and admitted, red-faced, that he knew teaching was an excuse to avoid painting. He felt it was too late to begin again, and his eyes misted as he talked about his love of painting.

I thought of Julia Cameron's description in *The Artist's Way* about people who take on jobs and careers on the edges of the work they really want to do. Like composers who become arrangers, painters who become illustrators, writers who become agents, dancers who become costumers, she calls them "shadow artists" and observes generally they were encouraged by their families to pursue more economically viable careers.[1] Economics is certainly a consideration, and many creative people maintain "day jobs," combining them with creative endeavors. True shadow artists, though, are motivated by insidious underlying reasons. They are "[t]oo intimidated to become artists themselves, very often too low in self-worth to even recognize that they have an artistic dream."[2]

I didn't mention any of this to Tom. He was just beginning to open up, and I didn't want to shut him down. I knew that his self-condemnation kept him from painting now, when he had the time and resources, and that he'd become increasingly frustrated and guilt-ridden.

I asked Tom to think about his past experiences, pointing out how rich his experiences had been and how they could be applied in his painting. I explained a major principle of this book: There are no mistakes; every one of our experiences has a purpose.

When I pronounced to Tom that he'd made no mistakes, that his talent was God-given, and that he deserved to pursue it, he shouted, "Wow! That's the best news I've heard since my retirement package came through."

As we worked together and I encouraged Tom to meditate about answers, he came to five realizations:

1. His lifelong desire to paint could not and should not be denied.
2. It was implanted by God.
3. His career hadn't dulled his artistic sense but in fact had enhanced it.

4. His life was in divine order: What his museum directorship had taught him was exactly what he needed for painting now.
5. He was now ready to relabel his "interminable detour," as he had called it, as his "thorough preparatory period."

A willing and consistent student, Tom now understood that his detour had allowed him to learn a vast amount about art and to refine his critical skills, judgment and discerning eye. He realized that his shadow-artist plans for teaching art wouldn't satisfy him now.

Tom also accepted that his longing to paint wouldn't go away. It had to be honored. With the guidance of his Inner Voice and my encouragement, Tom "stepped off" (in Wilbur's phrase) and gathered the courage to take the first step. He converted his poolside cabana—a contemporary translation of enlarging his tent—into a studio and planned a modest painting schedule, a half hour a day.

At our most recent visit, Tom jubilantly reported that, after his daily meditation, most days he paints for three hours. He still goes out with his friends, but now he limits the visits. Soon he'll have enough work for a gallery show, and we've started working up his publicity plan and the creation of his artist's statement.

What Is Reframing?

A major turning point for Tom was reframing his past—using new words to think differently about old events. Reframing has been with us since people realized they could think. Simply put, it's seeing and labeling things in another way. Politicians do it all the time (not "go to war" but "deploy"), as do preachers (not "lazy bums" but "our less fortunate brethren"), detectives (not a "socially disenfranchised individual" but "the perp"), and parents (not "my son is creating great neo-fusion-rock-n-rumble music" in the garage but "a racket and waste of time").

In counseling and psychology, reframing is often seen in terms of clients' personal "stories," that is, their outlooks and perspectives about their lives. The founders of Project Resilience, an organization dedicated to helping people overcome troubled pasts, make a great observation: "The organizing themes of some people's stories are constructive ... other stories are destructive."[3]

You probably know many people with destructive organizing themes about their lives—they're the ones who keep you on the phone with a litany of horrible events/circumstances/people-whodone'emwrong. Occasionally, though, people surprise us with positive themes. A friend who had recently gotten divorced told me he was quite bitter about the split, in which he lost his business. He said he was swearing off women, at least for a while. Then, perking up, he said, "I can always make money. Tomorrow I'll look into some new business opportunities."

I was rather astounded, because not many people have such confidence, especially about their financial abilities. My friend certainly needed to work on his relationship skills, but he had an unusually affirming perspective or story about himself and earning money. When I next heard from him, he'd already landed three contracts.

Most of us, unlike my friend, probably hug our destructive stories. Tom's "interminable detour" was part of his "I'll never paint" story. I recently heard one from a 42-year-old man:

> I came from a poor family. My parents couldn't afford to send me to college, so I never got anywhere. I'm not dumb, but I'll never be anything more than a laborer because the world doesn't recognize someone without a college degree.

Of course, we could list many successful people who had some or no college and followed their dreams nevertheless: Bill

Gates, Michael Dell, Rachel Ray, Halle Berry, Henry Ford, Ted Turner, Pablo Picasso, Eleanor Roosevelt, William Faulkner, Thomas Edison, Walt Disney, Doris Lessing, Frank Lloyd Wright.[4]

How would reframing help the man whose story I heard? The Project Resilience founders Wolin and Wolin tell us, "Reframing capitalizes on the subjective nature of personal stories to uncover underlying, underemphasized themes in people's stories that are potentially helpful."[5] By recalling and recounting our strengths, triumphs and overcomings, we give ourselves credit for them and see ourselves in a new light.

I like the advice of Abraham: "If you want your fortunes to shift, you have to begin telling a different story."[6] A reframe of the laborer's story might go like this:

> My parents could never send me to college. But I've made the most of what I've got. People respect me in my job, and I'm very good at it, even if it isn't in a big office. Why couldn't I take a few classes at night? I know more about building construction than all those supervisors and engineers I work for. Who knows, I might get a college degree yet.

When we tell our stories to a helping professional, a friend or ourselves, we begin to recognize and verbalize our assets and victories rather than our casualties and faults. Wayne Dyer in *10 Secrets for Success and Inner Peace* recommends accepting our past, honoring and finally transforming it with "a new job description."[7] Tom did this and reframed his many years of other pursuits not as failure but preparation. He was no longer stopped by his former sentence of himself.

Reframing has been repackaged—reframed—lately by social and futurist gurus as "paradigm shifts." "Paradigm" is from the Greek, meaning an example, a pattern, or map to understand and explain aspects of reality. The inspirational business leader Stephen Covey puts it this way:

> In scientific circles, dramatic transformations, revolutions of thought, great leaps of understanding and sudden liberations from old limits are called "paradigm shifts." These offer distinctively new ways of thinking about old problems.[8]

What's a paradigm shift? A fancy way of saying, "Hey, we're going to look at things differently. We're going to throw out the old ways of thinking and doing and bring in new ones."

In many fields people are reframing former precepts. Our views of the universe have changed radically based on new discoveries (dark matter, string theory). Our views of the human body have expanded tremendously with alternative and holistic practices and knowledge (yoga for stress, mind-body connection). Personal growth and fitness magazines regularly feature articles to help readers re-view their attitudes (get off the couch, get off the chips). One article advises readers blatantly to reframe themselves by turning their "so-called faults into assets" from "procrastinator" to "contemplative," from "impulsive" to "spontaneous," from "scatterbrain" to "multitasker," and from "pessimistic" to "realistic."[9]

Businesses are constantly reframing to meet market demands, and many company heads recognize the importance of reframing for survival. In an insightful article about business leadership in times of recession, two business writers observe, "'Reframing' can move a company from adverse times back toward good times. That's what Lou Gerstner did in fine-tuning, improving and realigning IBM."[10] Do we really need to mention Apple?

Seeing Differently

IBM's Gerstner saw things differently—and more positively—than the facts before him. As scientist-metaphysician Joan Borysenko says, "The same set of facts can look very different when viewed through someone else's eyes."[11]

You may know that classic Japanese story in which three blind men are asked to describe an elephant. The first states, grasping its tail, "Oh, it's a tiny, short, curly thing." The second runs his hand over its ear and exclaims, "It's a fantastic flapping bird that creates huge gusts of wind." The third, feeling its trunk, pronounces, "It's a snakelike beast with a great, winding body."

Why these three vastly different descriptions? Obviously, each man was feeling a different part of the elephant. None felt or saw it in whole.

On more daily terms, we all know about the famous glass of water. The facts are incontrovertible: One glass, one amount of water.

Each of us sees the glass as either sufficient or not. Why?

It's certainly not the properties of the glass or the water. It's what we bring to the material facts before us. Our mental programming, assumptions and conditions dictate our thinking, and therefore our description, about the glass and the water:

"Oh boy, there's half a glass left!"

"Oh no, there's half a glass left!"

Our words are determined by our outlook, mindset, beliefs—our frame. As we reframe our perspective, we will express ourselves differently.

Many Words for Reframing

This long discussion is meant to help you get the full essence of the term *reframe* and apply it to yourself. Here's a list of synonyms so you can see the many shades of meaning. As you think about your own life and labels, see which definitions strike the perfect chord.

Reframing means to:

- Relabel, restate, reinterpret, recast, reslant, refocus, reformulate, rethink.
- Reconstruct, recreate, reconstitute, remake, redesign.
- Remold, reshape, refashion, rebuild, redirect, reposition.
- Change, shift, convert, transform, alter attitude and perspective.

Use these definitions to erase and replace your old damning labels so you can:

- Restore, reinstate and reconnect with your best self and highest dreams.

Believing Is Seeing

The opposite words we use to describe the glass and water show that our words express our perceptions and beliefs and govern our experiences. Our words are powerful determiners. As we saw in Chapter 3, Jesus said it this way: "For everyone who has will be given more, and he will have an abundance. Whoever does not have, even what he has will be taken from him" (Mt. 25:29).

People usually quote these words in reference to material things and they get angry. As I mentioned earlier, they condemn this declaration as grossly unfair, sure it predicts that "the rich get richer." This is a fairly accurate interpretation, but not because of some Unjust Cosmic Wealth Dispenser.

Rather, Jesus was referring to a *mindset*. If you have a rich consciousness, that is, if you've told yourself and have reframed your idea of yourself as prosperous, successful, accomplished and enthusiastic, you'll attract experiences that demonstrate these qualities and what you believe about yourself. Please excuse me for editing the Bible: "For everyone who has an outlook of abundance, prosperity will be given."

If you feel depressed, hopeless, weak, feeble and frustrated, and you believe that the other guy always gets the breaks, your experiences will reflect these feelings. Whatever you assert and believe, life will prove you right. As real as the outward events seem, they don't make the difference. Our expectations and consciousness do. Once again, "out there" is "in here." Listen to others much wiser than I am:

Einstein says, "Reality is merely an illusion, albeit a very persistent one."[12]

The metaphysician James Allen explains:

> Every man is where he is by the law of his being; the thoughts which he has built into his character have brought him there.... Every thought-seed sown or allowed to fall into the mind, and to take root there, produces its own blossoming sooner or later into act, and bearing its own fruitage of opportunity and circumstance.... Good thoughts bear good fruit, bad thoughts bad fruit. The outer world of circumstance shapes itself to the inner world of thought.[13]

It's simple: Our positive thoughts attract positive experiences; our negative thoughts attract negative experiences. As we think and verbalize, we create our worlds. The ancient, newly rediscovered and phenomenally popular Law of Attraction attests this, with Rhonda Byrne's *The Secret*, and more offspring than you thought it was possible to attract, including the ultimate laurel of cultural acceptance, *The Idiot's Guide to the Law of Attraction*.[14]

If we believe the world is evil, people can't be trusted, we never have any "luck," and we keep lamenting to everyone who will listen—you guessed it—we'll have unfortunate, sad and tragic experiences that support our beliefs and words. If we believe our life is hard, aimless and haphazard, and that nothing good ever happens—right again—nothing will. If we believe in our ability to attract wealth, like my divorced friend who declared he could always make money (and he did quickly), we'll always be solvent. In *The Power of Intention*, Wayne Dyer enlightens us to the rattling truth that even our difficult relatives exist only in our minds![15]

Whether we know it or not, we all act from how we think and express ourselves. For example, some people always respond the same way when you ask them how they are or what's new. They shake their heads and sigh, "Oh, same old, same old." Why do they give this answer? Because this is the reality they've created and choose to believe. A proverbial infinite loop: they believe it, they verbalize it, they experience it, they believe it. Spiritual teacher, scientist and visionary Gregg Braden puts it concisely: "We are in fact architects of our reality."[16]

An Example: Greer's Prophetic Words

A friend and colleague during my typing period kept proving this "same old" thing, although I'm sure she wasn't aware of how she dug her own rut. Greer always wore jeans and a black turtleneck sweater, even in summer. She smoked incessantly and spoke in a deep voice, punctuated by the predictable cough. She had no patience with irrelevancies or things she couldn't see and always got to the bottom line. In fact, one of her favorite words was "literally."

At first Greer seemed gruff and forbidding, but when you talked with her, her eyes softened and a smile lit up her face. I liked her for her individuality, sense of humor and good heart. We'd met in the local stationery store comparing the merits of paper finishes. I was a novice at the business of typing papers and dissertations for students near the university neighborhood we lived in, and she'd been typing for several years. As we recognized common interests and became friends, she generously showed me, a potential competitor, the ropes of the business.

Greer was also a rather talented craftswoman. Between typing assignments, she created original, fanciful necklaces made of ceramic beads in the shape of flowers and small animals. Creative, charming, delicate, and, given her appearance and manner, definitely unexpected. The necklaces looked like primitive art, and I loved the one she gave me for my birthday.

She started selling the necklaces at crafts fairs and even got a commission from a major department store. She kept talking about her Dream—retiring to New Hampshire to work full-time on her crafts.

Every time I saw Greer and asked how the necklaces were going, whatever her latest sale, order or prestigious placement in a New York boutique, she'd say the same thing: "Nothing ever changes."

I couldn't fathom why she repeated this, with her two businesses going so well. Once I asked her. She shrugged and took a drag on her cigarette. "That's the way it is. That's the way of the world."

Greer kept typing and making her necklaces. I moved away and heard that one thing did change: She had exchanged her typewriter for a computer. Greer kept typing and only dreaming of New Hampshire.

Recently, more than 18 years after I'd left the area, I phoned her and we visited. She was still living in the same walk-up apartment. Another thing had changed: she'd redecorated her three rooms, exchanging the severe black and white theme for brown and moss. She'd bought and sold the New Hampshire house, was typing some, and continued making a few necklaces. After almost two decades, Greer had gone a little more high-tech and softened from black to brown, but she kept fulfilling her main mantra: Nothing much had changed.

A Lesson in "Reality"

Greer had talent and drive. She was unable to deny her creative urges and Dream in spite of her resolute belief in "literal" reality. She stopped herself at a certain point; what seemed like cynical philosophy or admirable realism was really self-defeatism. The result was that she cut herself off from what she really wanted to do. Maybe she really didn't want things to change. Maybe she had reached her "Upper Limit," as Gay Hendricks says, the maximum we allow ourselves of success or any other good thing.[17] Greer's "same old" song was her way of not allowing herself more success, so she clung to the secure and safe status quo.

Greer's words have always stuck with me. I fully believe that they, and the attitude behind them, kept her from reaching her Dream. She pronounced, therefore she believed. What she believed she produced in her life.

What's your story? A version of Greer's? A family myth you've bought? Identify some of your own limiting beliefs so you can then reframe them. Here are a few examples to get you started.

"Same Old" Limiting Beliefs
- Jody's the talented one in the family. I'm the efficient one.
- I'll never make more money than my father did.
- I'm just like my sister—can't stay away from those desserts.
- No one in my family ever goes to college.
- I'm no good at relationships.
- I always get three colds every winter.

- I can't save money.
- My ideas excite me at first, but when I start a project I can never finish it.

Who says? Who or what is binding you? In your mind's eye, is your father standing over you, threatening bodily harm? Is your mother taking away your allowance, or your car? Are you making such sweeping verdicts based on past actions?

Think about the people you know—partners, relatives, friends, mailbox acquaintances. I hadn't realized Greer was so rooted in her belief until long after I left the neighborhood. I wondered how much her litany had affected my outlook. How long had I subconsciously accepted her view, and how much had it stopped me from moving out and away sooner, physically and mentally?

The following questions will help you uncover the mental atmosphere that surrounds you and may affect you more than you realize.

"Same Old" Questions and Answers

- Do you know people who say things like Greer?
- Are they dissatisfied, unhappy, sarcastic?
- Do they regularly catch the illnesses of the season?
- Do their lives show evidence of their chorus?
- Do you hear yourself often agreeing with their chorus?
- Do you find yourself repeating it to other people?
- What are such words keeping you glued to?
- What are they keeping you from breaking out into?

You can certainly ask and answer these questions in solitude or meditation. Another good way is with a friend who doesn't have the "same old" perspective. Your friend should be someone who doesn't have an automatic advice reflex and someone you trust with your confidences and innermost feelings.

Sit together quietly, with open-ended time and no distractions. Have your friend read you each of the questions and wait patiently for your reply.

As freely as you can, answer each question aloud.

Practicing this exercise in the networking group I belonged to, one member said it helped to shut his eyes while he spoke. That way he didn't see his friends' reactions and wasn't tempted to play to them or start a conversation. Another said she tape-recorded the session. When she played it back, she was astonished to hear the extent of her negative perceptions.

See It Differently

As this exercise shows, the first step in reframing is to notice and admit that you're stuck. Your habitual outlook is what's keeping you bound.

When you reframe, you see yourself and your circumstances with new eyes, new definitions, and new assumptions, even if they're not in front of you yet. The hoped-for circumstances, your Dream, cannot help but appear as you keep concentrating on your new thoughts. Abraham talks about it in terms of alignment with Source, Dyer in terms of intention: "Change the way you look at things, and the things you look at change."[18] *A Course in Miracles* puts it this way: "From new perception of the world there comes a future very different from the past."[19]

The outer reflects the inner. The inner governs, shapes, creates, controls the outer.

Try a little test. The next time you're in a high-rise building, look out the window from the ground floor. What do you see? Probably a few buildings, cars, people walking.

Go up to the top floor and look out. What do you see? Of course, much more. What changed in the area you saw from the ground floor? It's a lot smaller, blending into other parts of the scene.

What's happened? You've refocused your sight. Not on the single patch called buildings, cars and people but on the larger whole. In other words, since you see a different landscape, you've changed your mind about what reality is. Despite the eternal protests of cynics, reality is what we think it is and therefore experience.

Rex's Reframing

A client applied this principle to his own life. When Rex began his doctoral studies, he gave up a rather prestigious position in a stockbrokerage firm, in which he had managed several dozen people. To get the class schedule he needed, he agreed to a job much lower on the employee ladder. His duties were largely rote, and he used little of his creativity and management skills. Harder to swallow, his new superiors were people he'd previously managed. As he needed, though, the hours were flexible, and he could take the necessary courses.

At one of our visits, Rex lamented that he was working extra hard and felt like a "peon." To his humiliation, he said his new superiors were giving him "a hard time," and he didn't know how he'd stand it.

I asked him whether he recalled why he had made the change.

"Yes," Rex said, "so I could take the classes I need."

"How long will this continue?" I asked.

Rex hesitated, figuring. "Until my coursework is finished—maybe another two years."

"So," I said, "not the rest of your life?"

Rex looked aghast. "Oh no! Maybe even only 18 months."

"Then?"

He smiled, getting the point. "Then I can go back to my leadership job, or one a lot like it."

As Rex spoke, I drew a diagram:

Leadership ▶ Humble Job ▶ Doctorate ▶ Leadership
   ▶ Using Your Full Potential ▶ Rest of Your Life

Studying the drawing, Rex saw he had misjudged himself from a very narrow perspective, the ground floor of the earlier example. My diagram helped him survey his present job and his life from the penthouse.

How does Rex's reframing apply in your life? Toward your Dream, what interim sacrifices do you need to make, always reminding yourself they're only interim? What larger perspective can you direct your mind to apply now?

Our minds are our most powerful allies—or enemies. We must guide them like workhorses and lead them away from the ditches of depression. One of the definitions of reframing is to relabel, and when we begin to use relabeling words, we redirect our minds onto the right and glorious roads.

CHAPTER 6
Reframe Your Words

Our words reveal to everyone what we're feeling and thinking. Like Greer's, our favorite expressions reveal what we believe, and they shape our experiences.

The principle that words have great force is an ancient and powerful one. Chants, prayers, mantras, commands and names attest to the power of words, as shamans, priests and political leaders have known for centuries.

The Old Testament writers knew the power of the word. "Thou shalt also decree a thing, and it shall be established unto thee" (Job 22:28). The act of creation was first a spoken one: "In the beginning was the Word, and the Word was with God, and the Word was God" (Jn.1:1).

The Greek term used here for Word, *Logos*, signifies more than mere words. Make it a part of your vocabulary and thought: *Logos* embodies the supreme Word that we can trust, count on, and evoke with rightful power in every circumstance.

Jesus consistently demonstrated the power of the Word and its effects. Study his imperative words:

The Power of the Word

- As His fame grew, "many who were demon-possessed were brought to him, and he drove out the spirits with a word and healed all the sick." (Mt. 8:16)

- When a leper asked for healing, he touched the man and said, "'Be clean!' And immediately the leprosy left him." (Lk. 5:13)

- To a man with a withered hand, he said, "'Stretch out your hand.' He stretched it out, and his hand was completely restored." (Mk. 3:5)

- To a child who had seizures, he verbally "rebuked the demon, and it came out of the boy, and he was healed from that moment." (Mt.17:18)

- To a woman who had been crippled and bent over for 18 years, he declared, "Woman, you are set free from your infirmity." He then put his hands on her, and she instantly straightened up. (Lk.13:12-13)

- To a man who lay sick for 38 years by the healing pool of Bethesda, he directed, "'Get up! Pick up your mat and walk.' At once the man was cured; he picked up his mat and walked." (Jn. 5:8-9)

- To His own devilish temptations of materialism and worldly power, he proclaimed, "Worship the Lord your God and serve him only." (Lk. 4:8)

- For his friend Lazarus, who had been dead for four days, Jesus performed the supreme feat. In a loud voice, he commanded, "Lazarus, come out!" Lazarus walked out of the tomb. (Jn. 11:43-44)

We have this same power to speak our words, drive out our negative and fatalistic "spirits," and resurrect our lives. We have the power to recharge our faith and become whole, to command our personal devils to get behind us. They've been blocking our way much too long.

Speak the words that are right for you, and they'll become true in your life.

- As you think, so you speak.
- As you speak, so you think.
- So you live.

Speaking Our Words

We don't have to enlist our new words only in severe situations with dramatic declarations. Everyday instances may be more important than critical episodes. Tama Kieves quotes a Tibetan proverb, and I'm sure every other culture has its own version: "If you want to know your future, look at what you're doing in this moment."[1] We build our lives by our choices, day by day, moment by moment. We build our lives thought by thought, phrase by phrase, word by word.

Compare the following sets of sentences.

▸ I'll never finish this.
▸ I'll take this in small steps to completion.

———

▸ I've avoided this.
▸ I've needed more time to warm up to it.

———

▸ I'm terrible at this.
▸ I'll get better with practice.

What do the first sentences of each set have in common? You instantly see their negativity, driven by self-condemning words: never ... avoided ... terrible.

The second sentences? At the least, they're less disparaging. Contrary to what you may be thinking, they don't ignore reality. Look where Greer's "reality" got her, or didn't get her.

Like most of us, you're probably pretty good at using the first sentence in each pair. How do these words make you feel?

Read the second sentence of each pair. How do you feel?

When I asked a friend these questions, she exclaimed, "Wow! The first sentence fastens an albatross around both my ankles. The second is a divine cooling breeze sweeping into the endless sweltering summer of my guilt!" (Excuse her literary allusion and hyperbole; she's a writer too.)

My friend was right. The second sentence in each set gives us compassion, charitableness, hope, forgiveness, perseverance. Each describes the same event as the first sentence but in words that don't make you want to go run and hide under the bed.

Reframe your words. Recast them so they don't blame and attack you. Talk to yourself with words you'd use with a dear friend or your own beloved child or pet. Reframe with generous glue.

Use the Right Glue

The words we use with ourselves stick. They set up patterns in our minds and bodies and draw our blueprints for the future. By our words and labels, and our beliefs in those of others, we glue ourselves to the past and forecast bad patterns for the future.

Our self-pronouncements are first cousins to this chapter's earlier "same old" limiting beliefs, cementing them to us like extra pounds. Your self-pronouncements are the reasons you're restless, depressed, hard to live with, frustrated, guilty, too fat, too gaunt, feeling caught in a dead-end job, and mad at the world. Our treasured judgments help us rationalize why we can't reach our Dreams. Here are a few most of us have verbalized or heard (ad infinitum) from others:

Our Disparaging Words to Ourselves

- I'm no good at numbers, so I couldn't succeed in business.

- I'm not a morning person. How can I become a personal trainer and meet clients who need to be at the gym at 7 a.m.?
- I don't have the discipline to succeed.
- I can't ever get anywhere on time. How could I run a courier service?
- Following through has never been one of my strengths. I'll never finish this painting/poem/song/scrapbook/exercise program/diet/course/project.
- The spare room has too much junk in it. How could I ever set up my workspace?
- I just can't write this book any faster. (Oops!)

Come on. I know you've already thought of your own self-derogatory statements. Write them down now.

Reframing Our Self-Disparagements

When we reframe with new glue, we jettison old predictions, expectations, stereotypes, entrenched personal habits, family patterns, societal pronouncements, collective assumed inevitabilities. Choose a few of your self-condemnations and reframe them. Here's a start from the list above.

- I can get all the accounting help I need to succeed in business.
- I can make a new habit and enjoy the freshness of the early morning.
- I can take the spare room inch by inch and clear it out.
- I write this book, as long as it takes, with consummate thoughtfulness, care and love.

We have a choice in our thoughts and beliefs. Abraham says that beliefs are only thoughts we continue to think.[2] Unclump that knot of thoughts; pull the knot apart and replace the strands with better thoughts—and you will have better beliefs.

In *10 Secrets for Success and Inner Peace,* Wayne Dyer says this kind of relabeling transforms the beliefs that we've stamped as our limitations.[3] We're not the horrible and unalterable masses of hopeless confusion our negative pronouncements would have us believe. We can fashion immediate and perfect self-perceptions, and we're flowing, unfolding, glorious beings with the unlimited capacity to change for the better.

As we gently unglue our old labels and strip them away, our reframing words (and worlds) become easier to create. Then our words prompt us naturally to the leads, ideas, actions and life we desire.

A Reframing Story: Greg and Jim

With this background, I want to tell you about two friends, Greg and Jim, who had contrasting outlooks and longstanding assumptions about each other. These, and the judgments of Greg's mother, affected their views of themselves, their success, and ultimately their friendship—until they both reframed.

Greg, an international business consultant, asked for my help with an article for a professional journal on consulting, and after that a book. At an early meeting, we talked about reframing in the context of business expectations and employees' different lifestyles in international firms. The discussion prompted him to tell me about an unexpected and surprising call from his old friend Jim.

Greg and Jim had been best friends since childhood, growing up in the same neighborhood in a New York City suburb. They went through elementary and high school together, entered the state college, and joined the same fraternity.

Greg's mother always liked Jim. As the boys were growing up, he visited frequently for supper, and she would extol Jim's virtues to Greg. Jim was "such a nice boy, so well-behaved." He always got good grades and helped his mother with the groceries.

Greg often burst out with enthusiasm, indignation or anger, no matter who was in hearing distance. He devoted his energies, at the sacrifice of good grades, to rallying schoolmates to different causes, often with international bases. Greg's mother encouraged him to remain friends with Jim, hoping some of his exemplary traits would rub off on Greg.

After college, both young men returned to their hometown. Jim quickly got a job in a local insurance company, with excellent prospects for quick promotion to regional manager. Several months later, he married Sharon, the girl he'd dated throughout high school and college.

Jim and Sharon bought a modest but comfortable house and rescued a golden retriever from the pound. A year later they had a baby boy, and two years after that a girl. Sharon became active on the local school board, and Jim was elected captain of the community park beautification committee.

Meanwhile, Greg rented the small converted garage of an old house not far from Jim's. Greg had no trouble getting jobs but couldn't seem to keep them. He went from one to another and began taking night courses at the local university in international business, which had been his passion since college.

Greg dated a succession of girls, occasionally bringing one home to his mother's for Sunday dinner. The relationships never lasted more than six months. His mother longed for a daughter-in-law she could give her best recipes to, grandchildren she could spoil, and a full family table on Sunday.

She kept telling Greg to settle down into a steady job and come to church with her, where he'd surely meet a nice girl. Greg's mother repeated the refrain he'd grown up with: Jim was so successful. Why couldn't Greg be more like him?

After three years, Greg gave up his apartment and local girlfriends and moved to an even smaller apartment in the city. He got another job and managed to save enough for a monthlong trip to Europe, where he visited several major firms. On his return, he established his own consulting company. Now he travels regularly to major European cities, has two associates, and teaches a course in international business at a prestigious university.

Whenever Greg visits his mother, she tells him the latest news about Jim: his big new home, beautiful lawn, lovely children, wife's promotion to president of the school board, and Jim's latest award for top insurance sales and position as regional manager. Then, even though she smiles thinly when Greg tells her about his current accomplishments, she always shakes her head slightly. Greg knows this is her unconscious expression of the regret she still feels that he couldn't be more like Jim.

Recently Jim had a heart attack. He recovered physically but was kept in the hospital for six months with major depression and suicidal tendencies. Having had no contact for years, he called Greg.

To Greg's astonishment, Jim poured out a confession. "I always admired you," he said. "Even in college you were a maverick. You never settled for what everyone else did. You weren't satisfied, you pushed beyond. I wish I'd had the courage to do what you did, go out on my own. I did what was expected and safe. You took off and followed your dreams."

Surprised and moved, Greg thanked Jim and related how his mother had always held up Jim as the model son. Greg admitted that he'd envied Jim his family and wished he could find the right girl, as Jim had.

Then Greg reminded Jim of his accomplishments as a superb manager, salesman, husband and father. What Greg really did was to reframe Jim's self-judgments. As the conversation ended, Jim said he felt better for the first time in months, and they promised to stay in touch.

The Lessons of Greg and Jim's Story

In this story, I don't mean to criticize anyone's mother or imply that one lifestyle is intrinsically better than another. A Dream and achievement of quiet stability is just as valuable as one of sophisticated international business and travel. Rather, the story illustrates three significant points:

1. Our best choices are those truest to ourselves.
2. Our choices can be interpreted in dramatically opposite ways, even by people who think they know us well.
3. When we reframe, we see things in a larger, fuller, higher perspective.

To Greg's mother, Greg was a failure; to Jim he was a hero. To Greg's mother, Jim was successful in terms of traditional expectations and social stereotypes. To Jim, Greg was successful in terms of individuality, courage and entrepreneurship. To Greg, Jim was enviably successful in his stable and satisfying marriage.

I'm sure Greg didn't set out deliberately to frustrate his mother or willfully go against her cherished values and standards. There was nothing wrong with her desires for him except for one thing—they weren't his.

Greg found it hard to hear his mother's regular disapproval but recognized he couldn't meet her expectations. He knew he had to develop himself, find his true occupation, and go after what he loved. Greg's Inner Guide, consciously labeled or not, told him his mother's wishes weren't for him. He risked her displeasure, followed his Voice, and finally reached his Dream.

Apply Greg and Jim's Story to Yours

1. Do you recognize yourself in any part of this story?

2. Does it apply to someone you know?

3. Are you more like Jim or Greg?

4. What can you learn from their different paths and the consequences?

5. Who in your life has done the following?
   - Labeled
   - Expected
   - Predicted
   - Circumscribed
   - Judged you

6. If you're doing all these things to yourself, whose voice(s) are you hearing?

7. Can you see that these voices no longer have power over you?

8. What could you tell yourself to really know this?

9. How do you need to reframe your history, actions and choices to stop judging yourself?

10. Especially, now, do you want to:
    - Label
    - Expect
    - Predict for yourself?

Think about these questions and your most heartfelt responses. They're the key to clearing the way to your Dream. Write down your answers and come back to them in a few hours or tomorrow.

When you return, study what you wrote. Can you improve on anything? See how the words you use reflect your outlook? With this awareness, you'll find it easier to rephrase and reframe more regularly.

How I Reframed Writing This Book

To show you I'm not immune to my own advice, I've applied the questions from Greg and Jim's story, and many more, to writing this book. It was born, one bright morning, in gray ruminations about the "wrong" choices I'd made and what I was labeling as the grand canyon between where I was and my lifelong Dream. From these thoughts came an essay called "Trust Your Life," parts of which I shared earlier.[4]

As this essay developed into the outline for the book, I finally figured out, as I've nagged you to do, that my life has indeed been in divine order. All my choices and paths had led me precisely to this perfect point. Then that sneaky god of self-condemnation threw another rock in the road.

"How dare you think you're a book writer!" it shrieked. "You're a short-thing writer! Essays and stories. You could never last through a whole book!"

These decrees paralyzed me, and I wrestled with them for weeks, writing nothing and spiraling down into worse and worse feelings. Finally, I turned to my Inner Guide. As always, It came through loud and clear.

"Hey," It said, "you need to see this differently or you'll never write anything. What's a long book, really?"

Dunno.

The Voice answered. "It's only a series of short things. How long is a chapter in a book? Short, like an essay, right? You've written a lot of essays, haven't you?

I guess.

"And published a few?"

Yeah.

"So ...."

Oh!

That did it. What was I writing? Not an overwhelming, insurmountable, impossible, interminable book. I was writing a long series of short essays! With this thunderbolt, I tore into this volume's first "essay" with gusto and gratitude.[5]

Wayne Dyer in *10 Secrets* encapsulates the experience, like mine, of anyone who's facing, and freezing at, a huge project:

Transcending labels, particularly those that have been placed on you by others in your past, opens you to the opportunity of soaring in the now in any way that you desire. You can be all things at any present moment in your life.[6]

The lesson was strengthened as I browsed through a Unity booklet on Easter. The perfect words suddenly sprang from the page, and I've translated them into affirmations. Apply them in whatever ways you need.[7]

Reframing Affirmations

- I believe in my Inner Guide.
- I listen to my Inner Guide.
- Others' negative opinions cannot hurt me.
- I give up thinking thoughts different from what I truly wish to achieve.
- I see all elements of my life as part of the perfect Whole.
- I am willing to change my mind.
- I know how to change my mind, my words and my labels.
- I replace my negative labels with health, wholeness and perfection.
- I replace my negative labels with right guidance, success and prosperity.
- I am willing and able to become all that I desire to be.
- My right labels and expectations carry me surely into my Dream.
- I see and think of myself as a successful _____.

- I see myself with eyes of love.

These affirmations and this chapter show you that there is certainly "another way of looking at the world."[8] When negative labels pop up, you'll reframe them, and as you keep practicing, you'll get better. The following diagram should help.

Steps to Reframing

First, Thank Yourself in Advance for the Answers.

Then:

Reflect

Rethink

Replace

Restate

Rename

Relabel

Relieve

Re-feel

Re-see

Reclaim

Refresh

Re-act

Rejoice!

Granted, reframing isn't easy, especially because we've all been so negative for so long. Many people have taken the necessary bold steps. Like Tom, they may have started by branding their past as hopeless or wasted, but now they know it's an integral part of the inevitable, divine order of their lives and the future they want to create.

They've successfully burst out of long-held boundaries. They've acted on fresh, audacious, deliciously freeing perceptions of themselves, even after they, or all their relatives, or the world, thought it was too late, unattainable, stupid, ridiculous or wrong.

You can reach this new way of seeing yourself by reframing in the ways outlined here, and others your own Guide may reveal. Muster your courage and look at your life beyond the assumptions, hereditary sentences, and supposed literal facts. With this perspective, you won't be pulled down or tread water, like Greer, or make choices you regret, like Jim. Instead you'll gain a freedom of outlook and expanded horizons. You'll start to express and act on what you've always suspected or known is in you.

Inherent in reframing, as you may have noticed in the exercises, is an equally important element. This is forgiveness, not only of your past and everyone in it, but of everyone in your present, including yourself. A big order, of course, and in the next chapter, we'll look at the many ways forgiveness benefits you, how I can prod you to practice more forgiveness, and how it helps you reach your Dream.

CHAPTER 7
Forgive a Little:
People You Know, People You Don't

Why do you need forgiveness to reach your Dream? When you're not forgiving, you're angry and tight. You're holding onto old hurts and hugging your rightness around you like a parka against the stinging winds of change. Your arms are crossed and your mind is crossing out possibilities.

If you think about it, what we can't forgive is really *who* we can't forgive: nonrelatives, our parents, our partners, and ourselves. We're going to look at each of these in turn—and do something about them.

Why? Because they're impeding your progress toward your Dream.

Why again? Because you're expending your energy keeping your resentments warm, lamenting, bemoaning, crying, cursing, kvetching. You have little left over for actively pursuing what you want to do.

Here we'll look at forgiving strangers, acquaintances, friends and parents, and everything applies as well to parental surrogates and other important relatives.

As you get better at forgiving these people, you'll also, maybe automatically and seemingly miraculously, start to forgive your boss, co-workers and colleagues.

A caution—the words in this chapter demand nothing less than giving up all your cherished reasons, rationales, righteousness, excuses, yes-buts, indignation, desires for revenge, and anything else you're keeping safe and secretly relishing about everyone you feel has done you wrong. The psychiatrist and superb *Course in Miracles* teacher Jerry Jampolsky calls forgiveness "the ultimate challenge."[1]

Are you up to it?

Too often we hold on—to hurts, slights, insults, betrayals, wrongs, angers, resentments, annoyances—and on and on, through months, years, decades, and, before we blink, a lifetime. You know the stories—maybe you have one—of brothers estranged for 25 years over an argument they can't even remember, of mother and daughter who exchange only frosty greeting cards at Christmas, of childhood buddies who parted over a single remark, of career-long quietly seething resentment at the boss.

This is only one type of nonforgiveness. I'm also talking about all the mountains of gripes you—and all of us—have built, even nurtured, over the years. They're a huge trunkload, ranging from very big—the person who cheated you out of a large sum or walked out of what you thought was a great marriage with no warning—to very pesky—the proverbial uncapped toothpaste tube, the empty dish left in the refrigerator, the tool not back where it should be.

These resentments, whatever their size and import, poison our outlook and color our perspective black, black, black. Despite passing years and fleeting time, most of us are stuck. We're stuck in a mindset that may have originated in our fifth or 25th year. We change outwardly, but inside we stay in that mental timeset.

Charles Dickens' Miss Havisham in *Great Expectations* is a perfect symbol of a stuck mindset. The main character, Pip, discovers a very old woman who lives surrounded only by wedding decorations and trappings. She wears an ancient wedding dress and a full veil, her face by now very old.

Pip learns she's been living this way for years. From the moment the letter arrived from her fiancé telling her he would not appear, she preserved everything, even to wearing only one white shoe, which she had strapped on at the moment she received the letter. All the wedding accoutrements remained frozen in time, like her mind, covered in cobwebs and encrusted with dust.

Like Miss Havisham, many of us remain intensely wounded, nurse the wound, and refuse to move forward. We hope against all evidence of the mounting years that the longed-for and long-gone groom, parent, happy event, feeling or approval, will finally surface. We rob ourselves, like Miss Havisham, of every other aspect of life.

Our resentments usually go back to childhood. Louise Hay sums it up: "We all have family patterns, and it is very easy for us to blame our parents, or our childhood, or our environment, but that keeps us stuck.... We remain victims, and we perpetuate the same problems over and over again."[2]

One of Wayne Dyer's *10 Secrets* for lasting success and inner peace is to give up our personal histories. We "hang on to past pains, abuses and shortcomings as calling cards to announce a 'poor me' status to everyone [we] meet.... 'I was abandoned as a child,' 'I'm an incest survivor' ... 'My parents were divorced and I've never gotten over it.'"[3] As he says, the list could go on for hundreds of pages, and maybe yours does.

If you don't want to stay a victim, and I assume you don't because you're still reading, there's a lot you can do. First, consider a few principles that apply to everyone and everything we should forgive. Of all the writings in forgiveness in many disciplines, I've chosen these because they mean the most to me. I've applied them many times, and continue to rely on them (more or less successfully—I too have my personal story, with hundreds of pages).

Six Universal Principles of Forgiveness

1. It's okay to get angry.

You *are* entitled to feel anger at the other person's wrongdoing. You are entitled to burst out with disappointment, shock, rage. Those emotions are cathartic and healthy.

But here's the big BUT. Too often we hang onto these emotions. We never seem to express them enough. Any slight reminder starts us off again. They become our chronic reaction, hardening in us like coal.

This is the unhealthy part that translates so often into physical symptoms and full-blown illnesses. As many publications now attest, individuals who hold longstanding resentments are at greater risk of cancer than others who let out their pent-up feelings and let them go. Louise Hay suggests enlightening correspondences between emotional causes and physical illnesses; for example, abscesses develop from fermenting thoughts over hurts, arthritis results from criticism and resentment, bursitis is associated with repressed anger, glaucoma with resolute unforgiveness, and malignant growths of all kinds with rehearsing old hurts and building resentment.[4]

Go ahead. Express your anger.

2. It's not okay to cling to your anger.

Express—Yes. Ruminate, obsess, linger, cultivate, replay, grind away—No. This is the stuff of disease, depression and decrepitude.

Maybe you're thinking this sounds too much like an indiscriminate, unfounded generalization, but not only mainstream medicine finally recognizes the destructiveness of anger. Look around. Generally the most sour, frail people are those harboring the most held-to resentments and blame, sometimes for generations.

Look at your own anger. You've probably stayed stuck in it for too long, hardly noticing it because it's gone underground, buried beneath your daily goings-on. You can be sure that anger is siphoning off your energy, enthusiasm and hope. It's plugging up your joy in living now and tainting your outlook for tomorrow. It's obstructing your ability to marshal positive energy and emotions toward your life Dream.

If you want to continue to live with this malevolent outcome, fine. Stop right here. If you want to free yourself, continue.

3. They needed to do that.

This statement about whoever you're so mad at is the first real step in forgiving others. The declaration may go against all apparent logic and the rage in your stomach. You may have been in the fury habit for so long that it feels natural. We need discipline, self-control and determination to start changing that habit of mind.

How? Reframe your accusations and condemnations in the perspective of the statement above, impossible as it may seem at first. You'll get used to the idea that the culprit's misdeeds or terrible actions weren't entirely personal, aimed specifically and maliciously at you.

On the other hand, maybe they were. You've remained convinced that the object(s) of your fury acted completely, willfully toward you and you alone. That's certainly possible.

Go deeper. *Something* was precipitating that person's nefarious action, something outside your particular presence, and something probably very deep inside.

Okay, maybe you say their action was in reaction to your own. That's quite possible.

Something was operating in them even beneath this. We're not out to psychoanalyze this person for his or her actions; we simply want to see that what you've always seen as the dreadful act stemmed from a very old, deeply intimate need of theirs and not primarily something precipitated by you or the circumstances.

That need, I'll bet, was something many of us carry around (Dyer's "'poor me' status") and keep ourselves suffering with— lack of childhood love and support, rage at an absent parent, frustration at a stalled career, jealousy of everyone, feelings of unworthiness, and so on.

In other words, they needed to do that.

4. It was the best that they could do at that moment.

This is a hard one, especially because their action resulted in hurt to you. When you realize that they needed to do it, for their own convoluted, unforgiving, transferential reasons, you can also take in this principle.

To do so doesn't mean we're condoning or excusing them. Rather, we realize that at the moment of the unforgivable action their level of maturity allowed them to act in the best way they knew how. This is another way of saying that they weren't aiming their entire quiver of poison arrows only at you.

In fact, they could have acted no differently. As horrible as the action may have seemed to you, given where they were in their development and how they handled the circumstances, they were doing the very best they could. Even with good intentions, like, for example, most parents have, they may not be equipped to respond, advise or support our Dreams, much less our daily highs and lows.

5. What was done simply "missed the mark."

The sin you feel was perpetrated upon you can be seen another way, reframed. In Jesus' original language, Aramaic, the word for "sin" also meant an error or mistake. From this standpoint, a sin is not irrevocable, to be pushed in our faces at the Last Judgment. It is simply a mistake and requires correction.

Author and Unity minister Eric Butterworth writes that sin is only "missing the mark."[5] As we forgive others their mistakes, we also forgive ourselves. How? Jesus said, "Do not condemn, and you will not be condemned. Forgive, and you will be forgiven" (Lk. 6:37). Jampolsky comments on these commands with great wisdom:

> Whenever I see someone else as guilty, I am reinforcing my own sense of guilt and unworthiness. I cannot forgive myself unless I am willing to forgive others. It does not matter what I think anyone has done to me in the past or what I think I may have done. Only through forgiveness can my release from guilt and fear be complete.[6]

Can you stretch your mind to take this in? Yes, it is a stretch. We rush to condemn, blame and harden our heart at the other. This reflex produces only more of the same suffering for us and does nothing to loosen our own baggage of anger, resentment and hatred.

Instead, see the wrongdoing as simply missing the mark. This view helps you get some distance, put some space between you and the action. The detachment helps you stop the blame and take the next constructive action for yourself.

6. Continued resentment and blame, especially if not faced, hurt only yourself.

Hugging the other person's wrong to you only glues it closer. Dr. Fred Luskin, co-founder and director of the Stanford University Forgiveness Project, paints a graphic picture: "By carrying around these hurts, you are letting the person who harmed you continue to inflict new bruises. You are renting space to him in your head."[7]

Luskin's first book is called *Forgive for Good.* This title not only refers to time but our own health and well-being. The subtitle is *A Proven Prescription for Health and Happiness.*[8] Since we create our own realities, what we concentrate on grows, or, as in the Law of Attraction, what we focus on is what we get.

Forgive Strangers, Acquaintances, Friends

Are you ready to tackle a few impossible people? When we think of them (you know the ones), Jampolsky's label of forgiveness as "the ultimate challenge" hits even harder.[9] If you've ever tried to forgive, really forgive, anyone—from that person closest to you to the driver in the other lane—you'll likely agree with him.

How to start? Butterworth's wise answer sounds strangely like reframing: "Any time you feel a sense of guilt, a sense of unforgiveness ... if you take a good look at yourself, the chances are that you will find there is much you can do today by getting a new attitude toward the people around you."[10]

Strangers

Start with people who may be a little easier: strangers you don't have much history with. Maybe the guy who unthinkingly bumps against you on the street, the woman who pushes in front of you in the grocery checkout line, the rude customer service rep.

Your first responses, naturally, will be anger, annoyance, irritation, indignation. You'll probably take one of two roads: Curse them out for all to hear, or swallow your ire, glare and curse inwardly. As you know by now, neither reaction helps very much.

I'm not suggesting you simply ignore the event (nor would Dr. Luskin); your reflexes should be acknowledged. I am suggesting that you change your habit of response.

Of course this takes practice, and if you practice in advance, you'll be that much more prepared. First, see the offending person surrounded in light. You may have to force yourself, but draw on your meditative practices and give it a try.

Then, follow Jampolsky's excellent suggestion:

> If you feel tempted today—regardless of the seeming justification—to blame anyone, remind yourself that in the loving eyes of God we are all sinless and innocent.[11]

The more you repeat and hold to such thoughts, the calmer you'll feel. When I've been able to catch my habitual damning reaction, I've experienced several blessed results, and they've dissipated my wrath like a sudden rain shower purging August humidity.

1. Despite the seeming affront, you'll feel calm, unaffected, even benevolent. Where did your rage go?

2. With hardly an effort, you'll come up with the appropriate response. To the street bumper, it may be "Excuse me, I didn't see you." To the line pusher, "If you'd like to get in front of me, just ask." To the rude rep, "It sounds like something may be bothering you. I know the phone company is proud of its record of courtesy."

3. When you respond in these ways, some people may give you only a dull, impenetrable grunt, but most of the time,

out of the blue, they'll apologize. They'll often spill the "reason" for their offensive behavior.

People have told me, "Sorry, I'm worried about my son. He left for college across the state yesterday in his new car and I haven't heard from him yet." "Sorry, I'm in a big hurry because my dog is panting in the hot car." "Sorry, I didn't get much sleep last night because the basement got flooded and I heard water rushing all night and the plumber still hasn't shown up."

Their responses have often led to sympathetic, supportive conversations, even in the space of a few minutes. Both of us left feeling better.

Acquaintances and Friends

Like strangers, and every person in our path, we encounter acquaintances and friends for a reason. More accurately, we attract them (Abraham, again). Sometimes the reasons appear obvious, as when a stranger gives us directions in an unfamiliar neighborhood or a friend springs to our aid in a crisis. Other times the reasons are not obvious at all and may take months or years to dawn, as when a stranger crossing the street smiles at us for apparently no reason, or a friend gets insulted over something miniscule and hangs up on us.

Whatever the immediate or deep-seated reasons, we can be sure of one thing: we attract relationships with acquaintances and friends, like those with everyone else, to learn. If we don't learn from one person, another with similar traits, quirks and even hair color will materialize until we do. They'll make us grow, nurture our sense of good, stretch our love—and teach us to forgive.

We should know, too, that only a few people are real friends. This is how I know: time passing between contacts makes not a speck of difference. Neither of you ever needs to make excuses. No matter how much time has passed, both of you can hardly talk fast enough for everything you want to share. A friend I hadn't heard from in six months summarized it perfectly. She wrote, "No apologies. Time between emails doesn't matter. Friends are friends. Time between anything doesn't matter."

A lot of people are acquaintances. We have pleasantries, even closeness, but nowhere near the intimacy and rushing joy of being with a friend. Acquaintances don't last as long as friends— there's nothing solid that joins and sustains.

One day, neither one of you calls back. When the "use" of a certain person is complete, in our learning, receiving and giving, then that person fades from our lives.

We must be true to ourselves about whether they continue to nurture us or not.

As we grow in understanding and consciousness, some people drop off. If we try to resurrect a friendship like this, it's usually stilted and uncomfortable. At the holidays, nostalgic, have you ever spontaneously phoned your high school best-friend-in-the-world you haven't talked to in 30 years? What happens? Small talk, exchange of children head count, too many repetitions of "How the hell are you?" and "How great to hear your voice!" Sadly, you've got to admit the magic vanished, probably not long after the lockers got aired out.

A friend reminded me of the wisdom of that anonymous quotation: "Don't worry about people from your past. There's a reason why they didn't make it to your future."

We need not feel guilty about how people weave in and out of our experience. As Werber says in *The Journey With the Master*, "They are in your cycle of experience and have crossed your path for a purpose."[12]

Forgive that former friend for no longer being your buddy. Forgive yourself for the lingering feeling of betrayed loyalty and your inability to recapture the old closeness and easy fun. You've both changed and grown in different ways, have traveled different roads, made different choices. Overlook the faults and memorized wrongs, be grateful for the former camaraderie and joy, and bless that friend for the help and affection you gave each other all during those old times.

Real friends, on the other hand, can feel more like family and are family to many of us. Although without blood ties, we often feel more connected to friends on more levels than to family. In fact, we often attract friends with qualities we wish our family members had.

Friends, of course, are the people we feel a soul connection with—we're comfortable, relaxed, talkative and unashamed of admitting our most secret thoughts. In addition to mightily enjoying their company, we unhesitatingly help them, and they do the same—like encouraging us in our ridiculous Dream. When we are angry at them, we're not only disappointed, and sometimes dismayed, at their behavior, but also really mad at them. In retaliation we may do or say things we regret. There's a better way to respond.

Forgiving Friends

No, you don't have to become a doormat. Rather, remind yourself of the five principles above and then practice the steps below. They really apply to any relationship and are especially effective with friends, because we generally bring a little less baggage than to our relationships with parents or partners.

The first step is enormously important. It sets the tone for the others and assures you will complete them in the right spirit.

1. Meditate on love, pure love, pure Love. Forget your hurt, your rage, your disillusionment. Forget your friend. Just bathe in Love.

2. Ask your Inner Voice (yes, it's still there waiting for you) what you did to cause or contribute to the situation. Maybe it was something you didn't do or say or failed to make clear. Maybe you sent a mixed message. As you become open to some candid introspection, answers will come. Jot them down to remember them.

3. Ask your Voice what you should do next, what to say, what steps to take. Listen and obey.

4. You may entertain dismissing the situation or behavior, not making a big deal of it. Only you know if you can do this without it nagging at you, or if it's a ploy to avoid facing it with your friend. If you can honestly find in yourself no vestige of anger, even a little irritation, and if you really do feel at peace with this thought, then let the incident roll off you with generosity and kindness.

5. If you can't reach that point (and most of us can't), then it's time to talk it out. I recommend you make notes beforehand on what you want to say. Preparation helps you from blabbering, blathering or blasting out.

Choose a quiet spot, preferably not over the phone—too much opportunity for evasion and miffed slam-downs—and preface what you're going to say with assurance of continued love and your sole intention of air-clearing and strengthening the relationship.

By now, if you've followed the steps above, you should have dissolved your anger. Couch your grievance in terms of your feelings only; don't indulge in accusations or demands for explanations. Then allow your friend to respond.

Next, listen. Your friend's intention may have been completely opposite to the assumption you made and got enraged at. Your friend may also voice some gripes about you. Breathe deeply and listen without springing to your own defense or yielding to self-protective rationales.

End by committing to new actions. For example, you can both promise not to react with hurt when the other wants to go out only with a third friend; to behave better in the situations that have caused misunderstanding ("Okay, I'll call if I'm going to be late." "I won't discipline your daughter anymore."); to air feelings right away so your grievances don't fester and build up. Finally, eat something sweet together and, if you're moved to, hug.

A Lesson in Love: Forgiving My Friend Jen

Sometimes the story doesn't end so happily. As I said earlier, friends' interests or growth may not keep pace with ours. Despite the friendship's duration, rich history or satisfaction, you have to face the reality that the friendship no longer works, and either you or your friend does something to jettison it altogether.

I learned a painful lesson about friendship and honesty with a friend I'd met through a writing critique group a few years ago. Jen was bubbly, extremely intelligent, wickedly funny, and, at a moment's notice, always ready for new adventures. On many Saturdays we'd take a bus downtown, get off as our whims dictated, buy ice cream and ethnic foods, and eat as we walked. We'd admire the buildings, exchange sly remarks about the people passing, and issue witty pontifications about life, art, our writing, and the other, obviously inferior writers in our group. We laughed so much we often had to stop walking to lean against a lamppost and catch our breath.

One night, the phone rang. I groped for it and squinted at the clock: 2 a.m. It was Jen. I thought, My God, what's the matter? She said cheerily, "Hi! I wanted to say hello. Can you talk?" I was shocked but pretended I didn't mind her calling at that hour, which she never had before. After she'd recounted her day's activities and her cat's antics, we said goodnight. I was so angry I hardly slept.

Three days later we had lunch together in a local restaurant. As we finished our coffee, I brought up the call and asked her not to phone at that time any more. I expected her to nod, shrug and say, "Sure, I understand." Instead, I was bowled over by what happened.

She launched into a screaming surge of words in a high-pitched voice I'd never heard, like a child stuck with a knife. People stared and I tried to calm her, but as we left the restaurant and walked to our neighborhood, she kept up the torrent, hardly taking a breath and apparently not caring who heard or what they thought. I couldn't get a word in as she continued that screaming flood of recriminations of me and curses and accusations of the rest of the world for not understanding her.

After this, Jen never answered my phone messages or called me again. Eventually I stopped leaving messages.

For a long time, I asked myself what I could have done differently. After finding out that her late-night call wasn't an emergency, I could have immediately asked her not to do so again after 10 p.m. I could have acknowledged to myself that she'd been insensitive and inconsiderate. I could have called her the next morning and told her how I felt. Her reaction might have been similar, but it was probably worse because I brought it up three days later, a measure of my own lack of courage.

Of course, it was also Jen's choice to react the way she did. She seemed to take my single request (not unreasonable) as a negation of everything good about our friendship, a total obliteration of my affection for her, and an annihilation of her very worth as a person.

I later realized I'd never known Jen as well as I thought. Obviously, she was deeply disturbed about something that brewed under the surface very close to her vivacity. Looking back, I see now that she had major emotional problems, and my criticism must have triggered some traumatic early childhood scenario of rejection.

Although I never had the chance to speak with Jen directly again, I've forgiven her for her psychological problems and myself for assuming she was more mature than she demonstrated and for not being more forthright and acting immediately. I've been helped by using the steps I gave you earlier, especially seeing Jen surrounded by an accepting, vibrant light, all emotional scars healed, all insecurities assuaged. I picture myself in this same light, which lovingly expands to encompass us both, and I see us holding hands and smiling at each other.

Love, finally, is what forgiveness is about. Love works when we envision anyone bathed in it and project it to them. It works even for those whom we rightfully expect should love us, we assume love us, and of whom we can list 5,328 reasons showing how they haven't.

Forgive Your Parents

These words apply, most of all, to our parents. Are you rebelling already, saying, "No way! Not in a million light-years!"?

Parents may be the hardest for us to forgive. Our society encourages us to blame them. Shrinks push us to cough up all the wrongs they did to us. Child psychologists warn of all the harm they can do at every developmental stage. Books tumble out regularly commanding parents, sometimes with astoundingly opposite advice, how not to irreversibly damage their children.

Louise Hay describes the black straws we keep grasping at when we think of our parents. For example, "What they did was unforgivable. They ruined my life. They did it on purpose. I was so little, and they hurt me so much. I'm right and they are wrong. It's all my parents' fault."[13]

We trusted them, loved them, and had every right to expect the best from them. Like so many of you, my parents, too, betrayed my trust, undercut my aspirations, and too often simply weren't there.

Now what?

As adults and maybe parents ourselves, we have a choice:

- Never forgive them. Continue to wallow in the blame and make them responsible for all the excuses we've made for not reaching our Dreams.
- Forgive them now. Even if it takes a lot of practice and back-sliding. Even if it takes teeth-gritting will power and extraordinary determination. Even if it takes many tears.

Whatever the extent of your disappointment, disillusion and disgust with your parents, they've served an important, noble purpose in your life. Radical as it may seem, I believe, with Hay, that we choose our parents before birth to learn valuable life lessons. Our higher Self knows the experiences we need to grow spiritually, and these start with our nuclear family. We chose our particular parents, Hay says, "because they were perfect for what we wanted to work on overcoming.... The lessons we learn seem perfectly matched to the 'weaknesses' of the parents we have."[14]

She admonishes, "So whatever you came to work out with your parents, get on with it. No matter what they say or do, or said or did, you are here ultimately to love yourself."[15]

This is great advice. Here are a few reminders to nudge you along the way:

Four Reasons to Forgive Your Parents

1. They were really doing the best they could at the time. (Sound familiar?)
2. They were acting out of their own low self-worth, deprivation and guilt (and probably the ways their parents acted toward them).
3. Inside their adult shells, they're little children, crying for love.[16]
4. They love you in spite of everything they said and did and you said and did. If you give them a chance, they will finally tell you. *They love you.*

With these boosts, ask yourself a few wriggling questions:

Four Questions to Ask Yourself

1. Do I want to continue to be miserable?
2. Do I want to stay negatively tied to my parents, mentally and emotionally, even if they're no longer physically here?
3. Do I really want to let go?
4. Do I really want to grow up?

If your answers to the first two questions are "No" and to the second two "Yes," keep reading. Otherwise, throw this book down. I don't want to butt into your misery.

If you're still holding the book, know this: Even if everyone around you can't seem to get along with, much less forgive, their parents, that's no reason for you not to do so. You don't have to be swayed, influenced, limited or dissuaded by anyone else's patterns. "My sister can't get along with my parents either." "None of my cousins has a good relationship with their parents." The job, and choice, are yours alone.

Re-Establishing Communication

How wonderful it could be, after you've forgiven your parents, to establish communication on new ground, autonomous ground, where the affection and love remain but the destructive aspects disappear. This is attainable, but only if both sides not only want it but are willing to relinquish long-held beliefs.

Maybe you're saying at this point, "Oh, sure, my parents will change. When the Red Sox win the World Series." Well, *that* happened, after over 50 years. There's hope for your parents.

There's more than hope. You may find, as so many have, that as you change and relate to them differently, something magical happens: contrary to everything rational, they change too. A truism of family therapy says that the actions, thoughts, feelings, and words of one member cannot help but affect those of the others.[17] It doesn't matter whether they live in close proximity or thousands of miles away. Once you think and act differently, so does the other person (kind of like family quantum mechanics). The catch, of course, is that *you* have to start to think and act differently.

Whether your parents are living or not, try it. You've got to do your forgiveness work *first* and resolve not to react in the same old ways to the destructive and negative family dances. These suggestions will help break the dams of decades of resentment, guilt and regret.

Five Ways to Communicate With Your Parents

1. Meditate

Picture them, separately or together, and see them with light surrounding them. Hold this image as long as you can, with no thoughts, judgments or dialogue. See them in light as they are. Infuse the picture with love. Feel only love. This technique is an absolute prerequisite to any of the others.

2. Visualize

As if you're looking from across a room, see them sitting with you in a pleasant setting, maybe a lovely living room or favorite childhood spot. Feel only peace in this setting. Hear all of you speaking in pleasant conversational tones. You don't have to know the words or subjects. Only see this scene taking place.

3. Write them a letter

Tell them what you really want to say. Let yourself write what you've wanted to say all this interminable time. You never have to mail this letter, and no one else has to see it. You can still use it—it can become the basis for a real conversation with them.

4. Visit with them

Choose a pleasant, convenient private place. Using your letter as a guide, outline what you want to say. For example, tell them you want above everything to improve your relationship and enjoy each other. Ask for their total attention, without interruption, and pledge the same when you've finished.

Talk to them as if they no longer suffer incurably from all the faults, hang-ups, and closed minds you've always known them to have. Talk to them as if they're really listening. Talk to them as an adult. Talk to them as a friend.

5. Listen to them

How much have you really listened? Whether in person or your mind, they will respond. Use your inner listening and guidance. You may find yourself having a dialogue with them, on a much different, deeper level than ever before. You may discover facets about them they never revealed and that they're people you never really knew. It's time to see them as beyond parents and as individuals in their own rights.

When you reach out in these ways, your parents, possibly to your amazement, may respond very differently from their habitual patterns. Change may not take place immediately, and several visits may be devoted to clearing the air. All of you may get enraged, let off steam, cry, or clam up for a while. This is all part of the process. Just keep seeing them in light and giving them love.

If, after several attempts, communication on new ground still isn't possible, accept this too. Love them and see them in the best way you can—maybe for holidays only, maybe for unsolicited advice that they need to give, maybe for children or grandchildren. *Your* relationship to them will have changed. You will have forgiven them.

An Illustration: Letter to My Father

Once in a personal growth workshop, I wrote a letter to my father, who had died 10 years earlier. He was a very closed and distraught man who had much talent in music, had studied at Juilliard, and played the violin like a concert artist. He never realized his potential—now I would say he never followed his Dream—and this ate at him all his life. With a growing family, he settled for a second-rate administrative job that used a sixteenth of his intelligence, and he barely tolerated the small-mindedness of his boss and everyone else around him.

To his family, my father was emotionally absent most of the time. His primary method of showing affection was the sarcastic putdown or blanketing silence that permeated the whole household, punctuated by unpredictable thunder bursts of temper. Yet, when my mother complained to me about him, or more accurately, complained under her breath in my hearing, I always defended him.

In the workshop, at the leader's instruction, I wrote him a letter. The first few lines were stiff and awkward, but soon, despite the fact that I was sitting on a metal bridge chair in an overheated roomful of people, I was alone with him and he was there.

I could hardly write fast enough, pouring out everything I'd kept bottled up during the years he was alive and all this time since his death. I hope this letter helps you acknowledge, cleanse and heal some of your own issues with your parents.

Dear Daddy,

Please, see me, Daddy. Notice me. Talk to me. You've always been so preoccupied with work. Or too tired after work to do anything but sit in front of the television and fall asleep.

How often have I seen you smile? Maybe three times in my life. Once on vacation when two fawns pranced across a field. Once when a neighbor's kid crawled into our bushes. And once, the time I cherish most, when you smiled at me.

One Sunday, when I was about 10, we'd had a houseful of relatives visiting, and you and Mom took them from our neighborhood to the highway. The kitchen and living room were piled with dirty pots, dishes and glasses on every surface. While you were out, I did sinkful after sinkful of dishes, put everything away, and wiped every surface.

As I was rinsing out the sink, you came home. You looked at me in the kitchen and smiled. You said, "You're a good kid."

I've carried these four words with me throughout my life. They were the only compliment you ever gave me.

Everything else was storms and crises, fuming and cursing, or worse, ignoring my presence. Look at me. See what a good kid I turned out to be. See what I've done. Could you say those words again now and be at least a little proud of me?

Daddy, I'm not only thinking of me now but you too. As you kept away from me, you kept me away from knowing you too. I want to.

Do you know my second most cherished memory?

We went to a concert together, just us, during my college freshman year. I don't recall any other time we went out alone. I felt very grown-up in my skirt and blazer and little earrings, coming right from school on the subway to meet you outside Carnegie Hall. We had hamburgers and French fries in a place across the street and almost really talked for the first time.

I vaguely recall telling you about my classes and friends. Across the table, for the first time I had your attention. You even told me a little about your music studies.

The concert was sublime, although I've forgotten the program. Mostly I remember sitting next to you, looking at you from the side of my eyes. Then we took the train home.

You began having pains on the train, and there was nothing I could do. You kept groaning, trying to stifle them, and I hear those groans today. When we got home, you took some potion that helped momentarily.

There was nothing I could do.

It was only weeks afterwards, at midnight in your and Mom's bathroom, that you crashed into the glass shower door and collapsed on the floor.

I know you were struggling, for years and years. Your last illness was a gathering, a collection of everything that bothered you, stuffed down for so long the lid had to burst.

I understand and forgive you. Forgive me, too, for intruding on your life and making you have to earn money at something you hated instead of following what you loved.

I'll learn from your strength and grit, your intensity and passion for music. I'll learn from your insistence on doing a thorough job and seeing it through, and your outraged disdain for slackers. I'll learn from your love of quality and genuineness, whether of violins or cars or people.

Daddy, you were the best you could be for me.

I love you and forgive you.

Your Parents Are Role Models—One Way or Another

As I wrote this letter, I finally stopped concentrating on my father's temper and shell-like withdrawals and saw him with positive qualities. I recognized him as someone I'd never thought of—a positive role model.

Think about it. Maybe you had great role models: a mother who is, or was, a successful businesswoman combining her career with gracious and joyous nurturing of her family. A father who is, or was, a courageous entrepreneur who built a flourishing company, with branches in the United States and abroad. Maybe they weren't afraid of money, success or radiant health, or supporting their children in what they truly wanted to do and watching them bloom. Wonderful!

Maybe not. My mother was a talented but frustrated artist, my father a talented but frustrated violinist. Both were angry at life and felt victimized by it. By my choosing them, what, in Hay's words, were the life lessons I needed to learn?

This question was an underlying impetus for this book. To use my own talent, in writing, I needed to learn not to see life as against me or myself as a victim of it. I needed to love myself enough to nurture my talent, allow it, not deny it as they had, and learn that I could indeed trust my life and reach my Dreams.

My parents were additional models for Cameron's "shadow artists."[18]

My mother, with her artist Dream, became a textile designer. My father, with his violinist Dream, became a weekend player (with me accompanying him on the piano), and mostly a listener and concert subscriber. I must face the fact that I, too, chose a shadow career in writing, despite all the help it brings others, that of coach and editor to other writers. Here was another impetus for this book—to learn from my parents as role models in shadow careers and make the transition from my own.

An Illustration: Michael's Parents as Role Models

One of my clients, Michael, told me about his parents when we talked about fear of success. He had what might be called hybrid (and I don't mean today's "green") role models. His father was forthright, hearty, a lover of life, relentlessly positive, and said what he thought without hesitation. An Italian immigrant, he came to the United States at age 30 with $40. He also possessed a guarded family recipe for sublime tomato sauce.

Michael's father went to the first restaurant he saw and worked at anything they gave him—trash collector, dishwasher, potato peeler. Gradually, as he learned English and the restaurant ropes, he was made second cook, then first cook, and finally manager.

When the boss wanted to retire, Michael's father bought the restaurant from him and immediately introduced his tomato sauce into several dishes. Word spread, and the restaurant became known for that delicious sauce. With his father's outgoing personality, acceptance of everyone, hearty sense of humor, and refreshing candor, the restaurant became a meeting place not only for neighborhood regulars but also for politicians, real estate developers, the mayor and visiting senators. After a few years, Michael's father opened a second restaurant, as successful as the first.

Michael's mother was different. Concerned mightily with what others thought, she took great care in how she responded and rarely said what was on her mind. Instead she hinted, insinuated, tiptoed around the issue, and, yes, controlled others through these actions. Michael grew wary of answering any question she asked, recognizing his response might be used against him in some way.

Michael was most like his father—direct, forthright, tolerating "no BS," daring, and highly energetic. The first in his family to go to college, much less get an advanced degree, he loved to defy precedent. As I helped him with his graduate studies, I often had to advise him (I was more prudent and politic) to wait until his degree was in his fist to inform the college advisors and administrators what he thought of the system. When Michael told me about his parents, he commented that as much as he loved and admired his father, Michael also was very grateful for his mother.

"Why!" I asked, incredulous.

"She showed me what not to do, how not to be," he explained. "She was so subtle and devious that I knew I had to go the opposite way, almost for survival. I saw the time and energy she spent on all the machinations and involvements, and I said to myself,

'Oh no, I'm not going to get hooked into using my time like that.'"

Michael also commented that his chosen career, as a small business consultant, probably stemmed as much from his mother's model as his father's.

"With his courage, creativity and drive, he taught me to be direct, innovative and audacious. But she taught me persistence in what you want and how to uncover all the subtleties. She insisted on information, understood people's motivations, and pursued her goals. In business, as powerful as direct leadership are the unspoken motives and forces that operate beneath the surface pleasantries. If you don't find these out, they can torpedo a business."

Michael's reflections prompted me to think more about my own parents. For all their "shadow" careers, they nevertheless taught me much. By opposites, they showed me the importance of straightforward communication and the destructiveness of anything else. They showed me, by their own unhappy examples, the supreme importance of developing your self-worth and self-love, and by doing so, acknowledging your talents and following your Dream.

They also gave me dance, piano and flute lessons, took me to the ballet, opera, concerts, museums and plays. They subscribed to sophisticated, well-written magazines and acquired a rich library of literature. They gave me the love of drama, art, music, knowledge, and, most important, reading and writers. Despite their shortcomings, they gave me these lifelong gifts, which not only continue to nurture me but serve in developing my own talents.

Your Parents, Your Role Models

Are you prompted to think about your own parents? Think a little more:

- Which one are you emulating most?
- Which one would you like to emulate more, or not at all?
- How can you reframe your perceptions of their negatives into positives?
- How can you learn from them now?
- Most of all, are you ready to use their best and forgive them?

However you answer these questions, forgiveness is the key. Here are six powerful methods to encourage your practice.

Six Prayers for Forgiving Your Parents

1. Close your eyes. Mentally list all the negatives you can think of about your parents. Keep at it until you feel you've finally run out. Visualize them with those negatives flying around their heads. See the dark negatives shooting off into space.

   Creep up on a positive or two. Admit to a few more and write them down. Command the positives to surface and surround your parents. Surround the whole picture with light and let it blaze.

   You may experience peace, warmth and relaxation. Stay in this feeling as long as you can. Know that it is being transmitted to your parents. Open your eyes gently.

2. If you're stuck in the mantra, "It's all my parents' fault," repeat the following five times a day: "My parents treated me the way they had been treated. I forgive them and their parents too."[19]

3. Reverse your roles. For a moment, see *yourself* as the parent, doing what your parents did to you. See them as the child. If

you're a parent now, you may have found yourself, probably in horror, echoing your parent. Perfect.

Now say, "Mom/Dad, I forgive you. I really forgive you. You were acting out of your own best understanding. You didn't kill me. I am still here. I forgive you."

4. Go back mentally to when you were a small child. Even if you don't remember exactly, imagine that you do. How did you see your parents? You trusted, loved, admired and wanted to be with them. Become that child. This is the truth, beneath all the adult overlay. Bask in the feelings.

5. Refuse to keep playing the "game of guilt," as Jampolsky calls this, the ping-pong of our continual abrasive interactions and resultant bundle of negative feelings towards others.[20] Among the many wonderful exercises in his *Goodbye to Guilt*, he suggests a prayer for stopping the malevolent ping pong game:

This is my instant of releasing you, _____, and myself from a guilty and unforgiving world. Together we can join in seeing a healed world free from guilt.[21]

6. Louise Hay gives us affirmations to neutralize our carefully guarded collection of negatives. Like catching a spark that flips out of the fire, catch your negatives and extinguish them with any of these:

   • I am willing to go beyond my own limitations and judgments.

   • I forgive them, whether they deserve it or not.

   • I release myself from prison. I am safe and free.

   • I give myself permission to let go.[22]

You can let go. Allow yourself the redemption and freedom from your own prison of condemnations. Your parents deserve it. You do too.

The more you forgive your parents, the freer you'll be to see them, and everything, differently. This includes what they did to you, how you've suffered since, and how you think they stopped you from achieving your life's Dream. They didn't.

You did. This, in the end, is why it is so important to forgive your parents. They're not hampering you now, whatever your impressive edifices of rationales and evidence. Practice forgiveness of them in the ways suggested here. They will help you, as we'll see next, to forgive the other two most important people in your life—your partner and yourself.

CHAPTER 8

Forgive a Lot:
Your Partner, Yourself

Our lack of forgiveness is all too often at the core of what's blocking us from realizing or even acknowledging our life Dream. As we've already seen, holding back forgiveness builds emotional walls and physical blocks in us that won't allow love to be fully expressed. These blocks are why we can't seem to muster the energy to commit to and pursue our Dreams.

When we do forgive, the energy that "protected" us with the armor of righteous anger is released. The energy of forgiveness is then "transformed into productive, constructive, loving energy" we can channel into whatever we choose, including health, abundance and accomplishment of our cherished Dream.[1]

You've now learned of many techniques for forgiving strangers, acquaintances, friends and parents. You can use these methods for two more important people, your partner and yourself.

Forgive Your Partner

If you don't have a partner, read this section anyway. You'll gain more insight into yourself and how you function. If and when you do desire a partner, you'll be forewarned and forearmed.

All the principles that apply to forgiving your parents apply to forgiving your partner. In fact, it's a truism in psychology that our partners reflect aspects of our parents. Incidentally, our troubles and frictions with bosses, co-workers and colleagues often uncomfortably replicate our relationships with parents.

There's more to make you groan. What irritates us in our partner is an aspect of what we don't like, haven't changed, and haven't forgiven in ourselves.[2] How many times have you blasted your partner, outwardly or silently, for something? Then you notice, a few minutes, days or weeks later that you've done the same thing.

When you do it yourself, some little voice in your head assures you, "Oh, it's okay. I can leave the wet towel on the floor ... drink from the dirty cup ... not fill the gas tank ..."

What have you done? Forgiven yourself. When? *Instantly.* You don't parade around all day in a huff, answering yourself in monosyllables, never cracking a smile, and doing what you have to do grudgingly, if at all.

I once heard a lecture by the wonderful family therapist Virginia Satir. She noticed, to the audience's embarrassed laughter, that there are over 200 ways of washing dishes. She knew from the trenches, or the sinks, what's *really* important in a partner relationship. I recalled a passionate argument with my then-husband about how much detergent to squeeze into the basin. With my present precious man, I still get irked when I see how lavishly he shakes the scouring powder onto an encrusted pan. One remedy for our reactions—and toward forgiveness—is to face ourselves and recognize that what annoys us in our partner is something we actually do or secretly would like to do—I'd love to lavish the cleanser but my (overly) thrifty side says no. Another remedy is to talk.

I wish our language had a better word for "communication." The word doesn't do justice to the flow and glowing exchange, the lifting of anger and resentment, the greater closeness and satisfaction, when two people open up to each other with what's in their minds and hearts.

Communication with your partner is one of the roads, although not always a smooth one, to forgiveness. As many professionals have written about, gender, socialization, culture, personality types, even occupations govern the differences in how we think and communicate. The more you know your partner, and the differences, the more you can understand, communicate well, and forgive.

Read up on different communication styles—between men and women, the intellectual and the artist, the Italian and the Japanese, the younger and the older (a great eye-opener is Morrison and Conoway's *Kiss, Bow, or Shake Hands*[3]). Some of the generalizations seem to be stereotypical or downright untrue for your partner, but you'll come away with some insightful nuggets. You'll recognize your own communication style better and how it can be tempered.

With your enlarged view, the first thing to forgive your partner for is being born into a family or culture with mores different from your own. Our upbringing is often at the root of conflict— you hold the fork a certain way, your partner holds it another way that looks really stupid to you. You make little of birthdays, your partner wants a party of 300 closest friends.

Recognize that no matter how proudly we think we've separated from our nuclear family, we bring its customs and traditions into our primary relationship. We were probably attracted to our partner in many ways because of the differences in our upbringing.

A friend who was senior vice president in a large company and had to prepare a major presentation for a new account lamented to me privately that his wife wouldn't leave him alone. Brad was working feverishly on this presentation in all spare moments, and Elise kept making plans that involved him: take the kids shopping for school supplies, visit the summer camp in advance, have dinner with the in-laws, help the neighbors move.

Brad thought of his father, an attorney always with a briefcase full of work at home. His mother always kept the house quiet and the children away while his father worked in his study. Why couldn't Elise be like that?

He went into a huffy silence and buried himself more in his work. His wife responded with her own icy silence and served his meals in the kitchen while she ate with the children in the dining room.

Brad didn't want things to continue like this. The atmosphere at home was unbearable, and the children had started to act scared and were beginning to clam up themselves. Brad couldn't concentrate on his presentation.

When he asked for my help, I suggested that he and Elise carve out an hour when they wouldn't be interrupted and listen to each other's sides. I asked Brad to list what he thought was at the heart of the issue and to suggest solutions. Together we created 10 points:

Brad's Partner Talk

1. Tell Elise about his schedule for the presentation, with specific details about the many facets, the synchronization with other people involved, and his schedule for completion. Remind her this is all in addition to his regular professional obligations.

2. Tell her his mother always protected his father from household "intrusions"; that's how she was brought up and that was the role she accepted.

3. Tell Elise what this presentation and getting the account means for her and the family: He'd be almost assured of an important promotion. This would mean a much larger salary and more ability to buy things for the family that he and Elise have wanted for many years.

4. Tell her that her plans for him feel like unreasonable demands on his time. Because of his schedule, he feels every spare moment counts.

5. Tell her that he understands that she and the children have needs.

6. Tell her that he doesn't intentionally mean to ignore or shut out her and the family or put them second.

7. Tell her that for this short period of time he needs her cooperation and support.

8. Tell her that once he delivers this presentation, they can plan when to do the necessary things and make dates for some fun things with the children.

9. Suggest that together they make a list of these dates they both can look forward to and share them with the children.

10. Suggest how they can enlist relatives, neighbors and friends to help in things that need to be done now without him.

When Brad next saw me, his face was glowing. He told me all about his "real talk" with Elise. They agreed beforehand neither would interrupt the other, and, to his astonishment, she listened quietly while he told her, list in hand, what was on his mind. Then, as promised, he listened to her and was shocked at what she had to say.

She interpreted his "holing up" (her words) as ignoring his family. Tearfully, she told Brad she was always afraid that her marriage would be like her mother's—her father, for business and other reasons, went his own way and was rarely home. Elise thought that family didn't mean anything to Brad anymore. She was sure he was hatching a plan to leave once he gave that presentation.

When Brad assured her he had no such thoughts, she admitted trying to pile on the duties and dates to try to force him back into the fold. Then she cried in earnest. Her father, she confessed, had buried himself in outside activities until, as she ruefully said, "they buried him." Underneath all her anger at Brad, she was afraid he was headed for the same fate.

Hearing these words, Brad's heart melted. He reassured his wife that he wanted nothing more than to deliver the presentation successfully and regain balance with the family. He offered to devote Saturday afternoons to her and the children. Elise offered to keep the children away from his study and bring Brad most of his meals so he could keep working. She even helped collate his handouts. Hugging, they forgave each other for their icy silences and earlier assumptions based on their childhood experiences. Together they started counting the days until the presentation date.

Maybe Brad's exact issues aren't yours, but I'll bet there is more than a little similarity. The content may change, but the core issues are almost universal. As Brad's story shows, partners often don't really know how you feel, what you're thinking, or what's motivating your behavior.

That little word *communication* is the key. It's your responsibility to initiate it, the sooner the better. Your partner can't be expected to know the intricacies of the demands on you, the pressures you feel, or your feelings about what you need to do. You must enlighten your partner. Of course, if the situation is reversed, your partner must enlighten you. This holds for large issues, like getting through a presentation, and smaller ones, like getting the groceries.

Talk with your partner. The more you communicate now, the less there will be to clear out and forgive later. As you talk, focus on listening and understanding, not on being right or proving your partner wrong (a sore temptation for all of us). You've probably heard the axiomatic question, "Would you rather be right or happy?" Insisting on being right and going to all kinds of lengths to prove it rarely solves anything between two people. The satisfaction of the one who is right is short-lived, and the brilliant list of reasons for rightness and demonstration of logic arguments usually alienates them further.

Instead, concentrate on hearing your partner's side and perspective. Like Brad, you may be surprised at the mistaken assumptions and erroneous conclusions you hear. Recognize, too, how many of us come from different backgrounds and parental role models.

A Larger View of Forgiveness

As I said earlier, it's a truism and metaphysical truth that what irks us in another reflects something in ourselves. A friend reminded me of his Talmudic scholar grandfather's favorite maxim: "What you hate, you become."

Hay extends this ancient wisdom: "Relationships are mirrors of ourselves. What we attract always mirrors either qualities we have or beliefs we have about relationships."[4] This is true of parents, partners, children, bosses, co-workers and friends. It follows that what irritates us in anyone else is a quality we possess.

Is he always late? Is she messy? Are they critical of almost everything?

Are you?

Or are you the polar, righteous opposite—obsessively punctual, ridiculously neat? Indiscriminately praising everything under and over the sun?

Brad finally saw, as he criticized Elise for being inconsiderate, that he was as much at fault in trying to shut out her and the children. He saw, too, that, like his father, he felt it was his right to have his family completely subservient to his needs and will. He realized that Elise wasn't against him, throwing activities in his way for spite, but acting out of her own fears. Once he admitted his traits and beliefs to himself, it became easier to admit them to his wife, and to forgive both himself and her.

As you forgive, a surprising thing will happen: You are also forgiven. Like Brad's wife, your partner may surprise you by becoming not only receptive but relieved to finally talk about the issue. Elise showed she wasn't against Brad but supported him by offering to accommodate his needs.

What if your partner isn't as willing or receptive to talking as Brad and Elise? If your partner rebuffs your attempts to communicate and continues the wall of silence or unrelenting TV watching, then ...

Reframe Your Image of Your Partner

Whatever unflattering image you've held of your partner—uncooperative, against you, torpedoing your project or Dream, uncommunicative, paying too little attention to you—reframe your image. It's a powerful word and works in every sphere, from changing your belief about the inevitability of flu season to your sour perception of your future to brightness to your labels about your partner.

1. Admit to yourself that your partner has developed in ways you find hard to take. Maybe he or she has become a "different person" from the one you knew before.
2. Replace this image—which will inevitably lead you to more anger and recriminations—with one in which you see your partner as the person you were originally drawn to.

3. Refeel your feelings from that time. Picture where you were, what you did and said, and how joyful you were together.
4. Hold this image in mind every time you're tempted to replay the old angers and hurts.
5. See your partner as open to your invitation to talk, eager to share and help heal the rift or unspoken, blocked areas between you.
6. Picture your partner participating, willingly and joyfully.
7. Above all, every time you see, talk to, or think about your partner, look with soft eyes and think to yourself, "I see only the divine in you." (This is a translation of the traditional Sanskrit greeting "*Namasté.*")
8. Expect your partner to respond to the positive image you're holding.
9. Remind yourself that underneath all the "stuff," your partner really does want closeness, acceptance and love, wants to help and support you. That's why you became partners in the first place.
10. Don't push, press or try to will your partner's change. Practice allowing, letting go. Affirm, in Catherine Ponder's words, "I fully and freely release you. I let go and let God have His way in your life."[5]

As you change by seeing your partner differently, your partner will change. Abraham puts it clearly: Focus on and saturate your mind with what you *want* in the relationship.[6]

Outer reflects inner …

How will you know you've successfully reframed your image of your partner? There are several touchstones:

1. Your anger vanishes. You no longer respond automatically with teeth-gritted seething, nasty little retaliations, incessant eye-rollings, grunts in answer to everything.
2. You aren't incensed by the things your partner does that previously crazed you. Instead, you respond in neutral, reasonable tones, probably to your partner's shock.
3. You feel lighter, even buoyant. You've jettisoned a few tons of useless baggage.
4. You feel quiet, almost confident. On some level, you know your partner won't be able to resist the power of love.

As you practice, you may be shocked—your partner is responding to the image you've held. Maybe not overnight, or in big chunks, but a little at a time. A lot of the things you used to fight about, or that enraged you, have disappeared. Who changed?

Keep practicing. You both deserve a richer, more satisfying, and fun relationship.

Forgive Yourself

I've often heard people say, "I'm harder on myself than anyone else." Somehow, we're not as gracious, bighearted or generous with ourselves as with others, even those we feel have greatly wronged us. This protestation has always sounded slightly self-righteous to me, but it's true for a lot of us. We may gain a little ego-pride from this stance but rarely any joy.

Maybe we don't think much consciously about our lack of self-forgiveness. Our regrets and self-recriminations may only rise up at birthdays, quiet times or tragic times, and, like the ultimate wave faced by a surfer, threaten to engulf us and knock us permanently to the bottom.

Many people make the mistake of equating forgetting with forgiving. They believe that ignoring, covering over, distracting themselves from, and not thinking of their perceived offense or sin is the equivalent of forgiving themselves.

Not so. Your nonforgiveness of yourself, like your denial of your Dream, continues to keep you bogged down, obsessed with negatives. Your preoccupations with your "sin," obvious or just under your conscious surface, build a shield of negativity around you. This shield keeps the good away from you that you want, hope for, and even take steps toward. (Repeat after me: The outer reflects the inner.)

An Illustration: Sandra Couldn't Forgive Herself

Lack of self-forgiveness usually leads to self-punishment. A client of mine unfortunately illustrated this to perfection. Sandra was dedicated, intelligent and eager to better herself. Her graduate program was tough: She had to complete one paper about every 10 days.

We met weekly to work on the papers, and after every meeting she diligently went home, typed out a draft, and emailed it to me. I critiqued her draft and quickly returned it to her. We continued these steps, shooting drafts back and forth, until the paper was as good as we could make it.

However, every paper the professor returned had a big red "C" marked on it. I couldn't understand it—the more we worked, the lower her grades. After the fourth "C," Sandra was in jeopardy of suspension, because her graduate program, like many, required maintaining a B average.

At our next meeting I sat her down. "Sandra," I said, "I'm puzzled. We work very hard, and you go home and produce good drafts. I critique them and you follow my instructions. Then I tell you to go to final print and hand in what I know are well-done papers. You shouldn't be getting Cs."

Sandra's face contorted and she looked down. "I was hoping you wouldn't notice." Then she sobbed out the story. "After you say go ahead and print the final draft, something takes over, and I can't hand in the final paper. So I go back to an earlier draft, usually the second or third, and send that in as the final."

I was astonished, and even a little angry. All our work!

I controlled myself. "Why are you impelled to do such a thing?"

She was silent for a long time. Then, lips trembling, she blurted out, "I never told anyone this. No one ever found out. When I took the entrance exam for this program, no matter how much I studied, I didn't feel prepared. I knew someone—on the inside. They got me the answers to most of the questions. I—I cheated to get in."

The light dawned. "Sandra," I said, "you've been punishing yourself ever since. Because you cheated you felt you didn't deserve to stay in the program?"

"That's right." She looked at me almost gratefully for understanding and not reprimanding her. "That's why I couldn't bear to submit the final drafts."

I then talked to Sandra about forgiving herself. What she'd done to gain entrance was wrong, certainly. Since then her grades on quizzes and exams had been fine, and in our visits she certainly showed understanding of the material and even demonstrated creative thinking. I asked her to recognize a wise observation from Abraham about our wrongful thoughts: "No matter how awful you think they might be, all were of value in the evolution forward."[7] Sandra acknowledged this and realized how she was hurting herself by hanging onto her guilt.

I helped her see that she was now a different person from that cheating one, more mature and dedicated. With sniffles and

167

thanks, Sandra saw she could now let that guilt go, and she promised not to torpedo herself any longer. She recognized that she had been punishing herself and resolved to keep alert to instances in other areas of her life. A good point—for all of us.

Sandra chose to defeat herself in schoolwork, but many people elect other ways to punish themselves. In *The Secret of Instantaneous Healing,* minister and author Harry Douglas Smith asks, "Is illness your way of punishing yourself for some sense of personal guilt?"[8] To illustrate, Smith recounts the story of a young man who was always considered the exemplary good boy. At age 17 he committed a minor crime. He kept the secret to himself. As he grew older, all those involved either moved away or died, and no one else knew about it.

This was enough. He developed severe pains in his stomach and back and went to a succession of physicians, who prescribed many kinds of treatment, but he was never relieved. Still a young man, he walked bent over and with great effort, unable to engage in any normal activities.

It was only when he went to Smith for consultation and confessed his guilt and self-denunciations that the young man saw what was really causing his illness. In the book, Smith recounts what he told the young man:

> You made a mistake. But is that any reason to bind your life to that mistake? You are just as much in error right now, reliving that awful night, as you were in living it then.... Remember the words of Jesus: "Go, and sin no more."[9]

What we don't and won't forgive ourselves for happened in the past, maybe recently, and more likely a long time ago. More than likely, we, too, like Smith's young man, have changed and grown, more than we probably give ourselves credit for. Why are we still punishing ourselves?

We Only Missed the Mark

Eric Butterworth in *Discover the Power Within You* reminds us that what we so quickly label sin is only missing the mark (the original meaning is related to archery); we made a mistake. Playing with the word *mistake*, I saw it more deeply:

Mistake = miss take = missed the take = my take on this was missed.

What do you do when you miss the mark? What does the archer do? Takes up another arrow. What does the sculptor do? Takes up another lump of clay. What does the writer do? Takes up a fresh piece of paper. What does the chef do? Takes out another bag of flour. Can you picture any of them collapsing on the floor and sobbing that they feel so guilty for their mistake they can't go on? I can't.

If you feel your mistakes are irretrievable or completely uncorrectable, think of the athletes on national television—football, baseball, tennis, soccer stars. When they make a mistake, it's exposed before millions of people and can cost them and their employers millions of dollars. They don't have the luxury of running off the field into the locker room sobbing and lamenting. Maybe they frown, curse under their breath, or bite their lip, but they get right back into the game and try again.

Reflecting on *A Course in Miracles*, Jampolsky puts it succinctly. Every time we cut ourselves off from self-love by self-condemnation, we can simply choose "another way."[10] This is to climb back on the horse, no matter how badly we think we've bruised our derrière.

Not Forgiving Yourself

In fact, not to forgive yourself is the ultimate arrogance. *Huh?* Arrogance, as Robert Schuller tells us, refuses to change its mind, rejects advice because someone else said it, or doesn't want to give anyone else the credit.[11]

By incessantly berating yourself, you're telling God you know better: "Ha, I foiled You! You thought You were all-powerful? I'll show you. I've done such horrendous things that I'm beyond forgiveness."

Of course, this stance is monumentally self-defeating. Cleverly, it also keeps you separate, special. You're the poor, martyred center of attention, the irredeemable reprobate that everyone feels sorry for or gets mad at, or in some other way is always forced to pay attention to. At what price? What do you possibly gain but more misery?

The Prodigal You

Whatever you've done, however horrible you're convinced it was, you can be sure that someone else somewhere at some time has done it too. If you knew them personally, and they were sincerely and truly repentant, wouldn't you forgive them?

Don't priests, ministers, rabbis, therapists, counselors and parents forgive?

This is the essence of Jesus' story of the prodigal son (Lk. 15:11-24). We're all prodigal sons, straying from our Father for various times and reasons, all flawlessly rational and defensible, but all, in the end, hollow.

Look how the father in the story received the son—no recriminations, no punishment, not even a reference to forgiveness. When this son, the younger one of two, condemned himself, the father instead commanded a celebration: "For this son of mine was dead and is alive again; he was lost and is found" (Lk. 15:24).

For us now, as long as we wander lost in the land of self-hatred, we hang onto the deadness of a heart hardened against ourselves. We stay lost to enjoying life, to receiving the love of others, to giving ourselves acceptance, and to releasing the energy to go after our Dream.

Maybe you identify instead with the older son: "Hey, what about me, the responsible one who shouldered all the duties, the one who didn't run away but sacrificed his youth, got no rewards, and stayed home and obeyed his father?"

Maybe you've been unable to forgive those who "put" you into the situation and yourself for taking it on. Like the older son, you're mad: "Don't I get any credit?"

You bet. Do you know what the father said to him? "My son ... you are always with me, and everything I have is yours" (Lk. 15:31).

In other words, the Father was as generous to the older son and saw him with the same love as the younger one. The younger one was wrong, saw his wrong ways, expressed remorse, and was rewarded. The older one was right, wanted acknowledgment of his right ways, and was also rewarded.

Who's your Father? God, your beautiful Inner Self. Who's the Son? You again, in your human, stumbling guise, but ever growing and reaching toward the light. The Father forgives, no matter over whom, for what, or for how long.

Here we're talking about the idea of grace. What's grace? Simply put, it's unearned and, we may think, undeserved love, acceptance and forgiveness. *Daily Word* enlightens:

> God's grace reveals itself to me in many forms.... I can never—and need never—earn, repay or deserve it.... Grace is infinite—love without limit and without end.[12]

Jesus again instructs us. Peter asked him how many times we're expected to forgive our "brother" who does us wrong and suggested seven times as an appropriate number. Jesus' reply must have shocked him: "I tell you, not seven times, but seventy-seven times" (Mt.18:22).

This purposeful exaggeration, says Butterworth, rather than to be taken literally, connotes "infinity": "Forgiveness must be perpetual, a state of consciousness and not just an occasional gesture."[13] If this dictum applies to your forgiveness of everyone else, how much should it apply to forgiveness of yourself?

Divine Order Strikes Again

Remember sneaky old divine order? We've made all our "mistakes" so we can grow. Wayne Dyer refuses to flinch at the divine order in our lives:

> As tough as it is to acknowledge, you had to go through what you went through in order to get to where you are today.... Those dark times, accidents, tough episodes, periods of impoverishment, illnesses, abuses and broken Dreams were all in order.... Embrace them from that perspective ... and then understand them, accept them, honor them, and finally retire and/or transform them in your own way.[14]

This advice also counters our whining question, "Why me, Lord?" Asking why is a perfect method of procrastinating, as Hugh Prather (quoted earlier) unflinchingly tells us, and keeps us from acting to get out of our tight spot. The real answer to "Why?" is this: We experienced all the painful events and feelings because we needed them. Our soul—our wise Inner Self—arranged them for our growth.

Making Amends

Sometimes, in addition to bleating "Why?" we hang onto self-condemnation for things we can easily rectify. It may take gulping down some pride, mustering some courage, and taking an action we're too embarrassed or uncomfortable to take, and these feelings are exactly why we should act. We'll not only have less to forgive ourselves for, but we'll gain more compassion and growth from the dread action.

Return the book to the library. Call and apologize. Write the letter. Send the thank-you gift. Make the date you've been avoiding. Explain why you did/said/didn't do/didn't say it. Repay the debt. Arrange a payment plan.

If you think you absolutely can't do it—whatever it is—prepare. Talk to a neutral person about it. Start writing down what you want to do or say. Rehearse.

For example, you can start by saying, "This call is long overdue. I've wanted to tell you this for a long time but haven't had the courage. I've always felt sad about _____."

A family friend taught me this lesson. He visited my husband and me to explore avenues to raise the necessary funds for a new business he wanted to start. After my nice dinner (only semi-homemade), as we discussed his financial circumstances, Gardner became so anxious and agitated that he shouted and left abruptly. Fifteen minutes later, he called from his car in a rage. He said he couldn't find his good pen and accused the valet of stealing it.

I spoke to the valet manager, who assured me his people did not steal from the residents' or guests' cars.

Later that night, Gardner phoned again and said simply, "I apologize for my inappropriate behavior. I found my pen wedged between my car seat and the door."

I admired Gardner's dignity and courage, and his language. He didn't berate himself but labeled his actions as simply "inappropriate." I thanked him, complimented his action, and suggested several other avenues he might investigate for funding.

When you face up and make amends, what's the worst that can happen? The other person could say, "It's about time, you so-and-so!" Or, "I told you you were wrong, but you never listened." Or, "I hear you, but it's been too long and the hurt is too deep. I never want to speak to you again."

Any of these responses is possible but hardly probable. Even if the response is the last one, you will have taken the risk for yourself. You're not in charge of how and if the other has changed or softened. You can then say, "I wanted you to know and I wish you only the best." If the person hangs up on you, you've done what you needed to.

Most of the time, none of these things will happen. A friend told of a family situation that you may relate to. For many years, she'd been estranged from her sister, who now lived across the country. Growing up, they'd been very close, and my friend could hardly recall why they'd stopped talking. Year followed year, and my friend could never bring herself to call.

We talked about this notion of forgiving yourself and making amends, and her voice became husky. "I really want to heal this rift. It's been so long. When my sister hears my voice, she'll probably slam down the phone." Together, we arrived at what my friend would say, and she promised she'd make the call the next Sunday.

Sunday night, she called me, ecstatic. Hearing her voice, her sister had started crying with joy. Her sister confessed she'd wanted to call my friend many times but had stopped herself, thinking my friend would slam down the phone.

They had an hour conversation and straightened out what they needed to. Now they call, write, email, exchange photos of expanding families and new pets, and have the kind of wonderful relationship they had growing up.

Yes, to make amends takes courage and the willingness to make the leap. Whenever I've jumped, often holding my breath but daring to expose the egg on my face, the other person, like my friend's sister, has had one or more of these reactions:

1. Surprise
2. Delight
3. Gracious acceptance of what I had to say
4. Appreciation

With some people, a relationship has been resumed or started, with others it hasn't. Each time I've "cleaned up," I've immediately felt better, even joyful, lighter and freer daily. I've also become able to apologize and say what has to be said more quickly and succinctly, without waiting days, months or years.

If you cannot make amends in actuality, do so in your mind with the techniques we talked about in forgiving your parents and those in a wonderful audiotape by Michael Moran, *Heal the Past, Release the Pain*.[15] Set yourself a quiet time alone. Then visualize the ideal setting and sit down with each person involved. Say your words clearly in your mind or out loud. Listen for the other's response. You will hear. Allow the dialogue to flow, until you feel complete. Then consider the matter done, resolved, closed.

Use the Golden Key

If you've sincerely used these ideas, and you're still having trouble getting off the treadmill of morbid ruminations about yourself or anyone or anything else, here's another suggestion.

Every time your mind is drawn to, repeats or fixates on any past transgression, use the "Golden Key."

What's that? Not a hand-hammered shimmering pass to Vegas (perish the thought!), but a single commandment. Formulated by the brilliant metaphysician Emmet Fox, the Golden Key appears simple but is extremely profound: "Whatever it is, stop thinking about it, and think of God instead."[16] That's it? Sounds easy, but to act on this apparently undemanding principle takes persistence and self-discipline. It takes consistent self-forgiveness of those pesky, recurring self-recriminating thoughts that bob up uncontrollably. It's not how many times the thoughts come up that's important, but how often you let them take over.

When they do, immediately invoke the Golden Key. What do you replace them with? How do you think about God? Any way you wish. Fox recommends a psalm, a childhood prayer, even a simple sentence such as "God is all" or "I am at peace." Maybe you'll choose a favorite meditative word or phrase.

As we chronic dieters well know, retraining ourselves takes perseverance, vigilance, determination and sheer repetition. After a while, as you keep Golden Keying and replacing those tentacled negative thoughts with positive ones, the self-blames will surface less often, eventually fading out. Keep at it.

You can also use sentences more specifically directed to current issues. Hay offers some wonderful affirmations for forgiving that apply to others and ourselves:

Forgiving Affirmations

- I forgive whether I/they deserve it or not.
- I am willing to go beyond my own limitations.
- I take responsibility for my own life. I am free.
- I am grown up now and I take loving care of my inner child.
- I release myself from prison. I am safe and free.

- It is strong to forgive and let go.
- I refuse to limit myself. I am always willing to take the next step.
- I give myself permission to let go.[17]

A Universal Affirmation

This affirmation can help you accept forgiveness of your partner, yourself and everyone else in an instant. At a time when I felt in a downward spiral of lament over myriad sins, as if I were falling into an irreversible deep depression, a dear friend gave me this affirmation. It cuts through all that self-condemnation litter: "I forgive myself and I forgive all others, from the beginning of time to the end of time."

Say this over a few times to yourself. Again, a few more times, out loud.

Bellow it, sing it, shout it with different tones and accents. Do you feel a fantastic sense of power and freedom? Practice this often.

All our words here lead to one conclusion and command, given in *A Course in Miracles:* "Forgive, and you will see this differently."[18]

As you start forgiving, you'll see things differently and think differently. As you think differently, you'll let go of past guilt and turn away from it and all its hangers-on. You'll start entertaining new possibilities, new inevitabilities, about others and especially yourself.

With forgiveness, you'll lighten your outlook and release the energy you used in holding onto those condemnations. Instead of crying about what's behind, you can shout about what's ahead.

Give yourself this gift. Forgiveness makes you feel so much lighter, makes you inexplicably bubbly and excited about life like an unsullied child. Forgiveness gives you a vibrant energy that you haven't felt since you fell in love for the first time. It uncovers what you've secretly yearned for all this time. Give yourself this marvelous gift.

It will give you the courage and sense of deservingness to think about your Dream again with gusto and strength.

PART III
ACTIVATING:
GETTING TO YOUR DREAM

CHAPTER 9

Discover Your Dream: Envision and Name It

Maybe you already know what your Dream is. Some people recognize it early—a scientist I know told me that at 18 months he was trying to heat his jar of baby food on the stove to see if it changed color. At age 3 Mozart was picking out chords on the piano.[1] More recently, Arnold Schwarzenegger, world champion body-builder with multiple top titles, and later governor of California, announced at age 13 to his parents, "I want to be the best-built man in the world!"[2] I knew from very early that writing was my path and Dream. Do you have a parallel story that your great-aunt loves to repeat?

Even without a prophetic family tale, I'll bet you've got Dreams. What Dreams have been jabbing at you, pricking like a splinter, itching like a gnat bite?

What Happens When We Deny Our Dream?

Maybe you've already discovered your Dreams won't go away. Dyer knows this:

> That silent inner knowing will never leave you alone. You may try to ignore it and pretend it doesn't exist, but in honest, alone moments of contemplative communion with yourself, you sense the emptiness waiting for you to fill it with your music.[3]

I believe this constellation of denial contributes to many illnesses. When we deny our Dreams, they go underground and underskin. They fester in our subconscious and precipitate changes in our immune system and body chemistry. I've already talked about mind/body cause and effect, a connection increasingly acknowledged by medical, psychological and spiritual experts.

Even if you don't get sick, many things happen when you deny your Dream, or, in other words, don't express your potential and creativity. You get:

- Resentful
- Bored
- Stymied
- Angry
- Convinced the world is out to get you
- Frustrated
- Negative
- Stuck
- Addicted
- Self-hating.[4]

We all know people like this. You can see it in their chronic furrowed brows, downturned lips even when they smile, and sagging shoulders. Sadly, I've watched several family members who have denied their Dream. They go through the activities of living, sport pasted smiles when they have to, and most of the time act like curmudgeons with those around them. Worse, they develop serious illnesses.

Fear of illness or unpleasant temperament shouldn't be the main reason to get in touch with your Dream. The most important reasons are so you'll feel better about yourself and your life, you'll enjoy more things more often and—do we dare even say it?—you'll feel more joy.

As you march toward your Dream and achieve it, everything may not go smoothly. When you experience bad times, you'll see them in a larger perspective (reframe them), learn from them, realize you needed the lesson, feel more grounded, and won't blame the world or the garage mechanic for your "bad luck."

What Negative Others Will Say

Maybe you think you don't deserve your Dream. Maybe you've bought into the reactions of others when you finally confessed you want to become a stand-up comic, opera singer, or psychiatrist, or learn conversational Urdu so you can be a U.N. translator. You've probably heard it all:

- You shouldn't.
- It's ridiculous.
- You can't.
- It costs too much.
- You'll never make any money at it.
- It's too hard.
- It's such a long shot.
- It will take too much time.
- You are/will be too old.
- You'll never make it.
- No one in our family ever did that.
- You'll make me ashamed.
- There's too much competition.
- Your children/parents/job/dog/front lawn will suffer.
- Why do you want to do that?

If you need a quick antidote, one of the best I know is the often-quoted directive attributed to that supreme philosopher-poet Dr. Seuss: "Be who you are and say what you feel because those who mind don't matter and those who matter don't mind."[5]

Maybe Abraham knew Dr. Seuss:

> When a child has a dream and a parent says, "It's not financially feasible; you can't make a living at that; don't do it," we say to the child, run away from home…. You must follow your dream.[6]

This radical advice applies to us all, if not literally, at least figuratively. I would add, Don't run away mad.

In addition to these two remedies, I ask you to remember what we've discussed about forgiving. Here's where they apply, big time. Hard as it may seem, the first thing to do is forgive these people, these voices, for what they're blaring.

Maybe it will help to know where these strident, immediate hit men come from: their own unfulfilled Dreams, lifelong sense of inadequacy, deep feelings of being nondeserving, and yes, envy that you're even daring to voice your own Dream, much less do anything about it. Start clearing your mind.

A Prayer for Forgiving Others Their Negativity

- ♥ I thank you for your interest, (*name*), and your caring.
- ♥ I thank you for reacting and responding.
- ♥ I thank you for showing me, by your reaction, that I'm on the right track.
- ♥ I thank you for strengthening my resolve to pursue my Dream.
- ♥ I forgive you for your anger and rancor. I have had these too.
- ♥ I forgive you for your apparent lack of understanding and support.
- ♥ I know these come from your own fears.
- ♥ I know they have nothing to do with me.

♥ I wish you strength and self-nurturing.

♥ I wish you the courage of your own Dreams.

♥ I free you from my anger.

♥ I forgive you and bless you on your path.

You may have to repeat this prayer, or another of your own, many times before you really believe it. As you've undoubtedly already seen, most of us have become so accustomed to negative mental reflexes and mindsets that it takes consistent, deliberate repetition to change our psychic habits.

As you forgive others for their negative messages that get in the way of your Dream, so you may have to forgive yourself again—for all the years you denied, buried and minimized it. For all the times you felt you could do even one small thing, take the smallest step, and instead you chose primetime TV.

You have the chance to turn yourself around, turn it all around. Instead of seeing your life as a long, pathetic series of excuses and avoidances, see its perfection. Here's some help:

A Prayer for Forgiving Yourself for Denying Your Dream

♥ I thank my life for its divine order.

♥ I thank my life for showing me what I need.

♥ I thank my life for giving me the path, however twisted it seemed, to now fulfill my Dream.

♥ I thank my Self for guiding me where I've needed to go to learn, grow and develop up to today.

♥ I am ready now to forgive myself for what seemed wasted.

♥ I am free now to gather the harvest of my life and bloom where I've been planted.

♥ I am free now to go forward with love and gentleness to fulfill my Dream.

Enthusiasm for Your Dream

Have you ever noticed how a small change affects everything around you?

Think of a time when you were so tired all you could think of was flopping into bed. Then, because you're an avid James Bond fan, you noticed the newest Bond movie on TV before it even hit the theaters (admittedly a rarity). What happened? Where did your fatigue go?

One of the major books of Norman Vincent Peale, the great minister and prolific advocate of positive thinking, is called *Enthusiasm Makes the Difference.*[7] This declaration remains astutely true. I've proved it often enough. Some days, after lunch, I live only for a nap (guilty secret) after putting in a bare amount of work. Then I check my email. Two article acceptances and an invitation to send my latest children's book! The nap jumps out the window, and I jump up and tear into the work at hand.

It's the same when you finally uncover your Dream. You may be dragging to work every day, wondering how you'll get through all the nonsense. Then, one morning, you decide to register for that course you've been putting off that you need to get your real estate license. What happens? You walk faster, your mind gets clearer, you even look forward to seeing your co-workers. You can't wait to get home and fill out the form.

Your energy gets released and your enthusiasm propels you forward. Why? You've finally begun to do what your Inner Self has been urging you to do all this time.

Your Job

Whatever your employment in the so-called real world, this is your real job: to find out what you really want to do—and start doing it. Most of us ask, generally late at night or after a particularly grueling stint of work, why we are here. The answers, when we Wiki or otherwise search, range from assertions that life is a gigantic gaffe of the Universe to the highest calling to develop ourselves into spiritual beings.

It's no secret that I tend to the latter. With good reason. Many wiser than me have declared it. American philosopher Eric Hoffer declares, "Man's only legitimate end in life is to finish God's work—to bring to full growth the capacities and talents implanted in us."[8] Spiritual teacher Catherine Ponder (whom you may have noticed is one of my favorites) informs us, "Your deepest desires are God's for you."[9] That aggregate of enlightened Consciousnesses, Abraham, says, "It's not your work to make anything happen. It's your work to dream it and let it happen. Law of Attraction will make it happen."[10]

Muster Your Courage

Are you nervous? Do you doubt you can achieve your Dream? If you're itchy and dissatisfied, great! That's a sure indication that you know what you should be doing and have been denying it. Unity minister and teacher J Douglas Bottorff says this:

> Dissatisfaction is always a signal that we are not living life to its fullest available potential, that we are somehow thwarting the expression of a quality of experience we know instinctively we can and should have.[11]

Spiritual teacher and author Bruce Wilkinson reminds us that denying our Dream produces our chronic sadness, anger, frustrations and illness. Our Dream is always outside of where we're comfortable, and usually scary.[12] At the Unity services in New York City's Lincoln Center, which I attended regularly when I lived in the city about 20 years ago, deeply insightful minister Olga Butterworth used to call this feeling "divine discontent." We're denying our high calling.

Our high calling may seem monumental, horribly distant, impossible, overwhelming, full of hubris and arrogant assumption. Know that the longing for your Dream is placed in you by God. When you acknowledge the desire, the "how" will be revealed, the steps will start surfacing. Hear the often-quoted words of a man who certainly proved its truth: "If you can dream it, you can do it" (Walt Disney).[13]

Focus on your Dream and not the fears, as Wilkinson reminds us. Even Moses, Joshua and Jesus had fears about their missions, and probably even Oprah. Repeat affirmations like Disney's. You need to feed your mind with these bolstering truths. If other people don't chip away at your self-esteem, your own doubtful voices will try to do so. Position your armament and defend yourself.

You'll be doing more than reacting; you'll be nurturing your courageous, confident, bold Self. Depression will lessen; anticipation will increase.

A Radical Treatment

Still not convinced? Still avoiding? Still too painful to think about—the fear of failure, success or surpassing your parents? Still tuning out your Dream with all the incredible distractions our age has provided: TV, CDs, DVDs, radio, movies, magazines, newspapers, Net surfing, blogging about your latest lunch, and endless computer chats with others who are also avoiding themselves?

Okay. I'm calling in the EMT: Extended Metaphysical Treatment. It's what Cameron calls "Reading Deprivation": you must starve yourself for a day or a week of all mental stimulants.[14] Turn 'em off, close 'em up, hide the movie schedule, kick the mouse out the back door.

This may sound ridiculous, radical, impossible. Much as you may not want to face it, all such adjectives are resistance. Are you that much afraid of silence, of being alone with yourself?

Give it a try. Start with an afternoon or evening. Then stretch it to a day.

You're asking, What will I do instead? The answer is of key importance and leads to another question: What would you really like to do?

Let your imagination fly.

As you do what you've decided to, observe your thoughts. First they'll be full of the day's trivia and then harangues about how ridiculous this is, how bored you are, and how you should be doing, doing, doing. As your complaints and criticisms wind down, you'll find yourself daydreaming about a perfect life or set of activities, possibly very close to what you're doing, or visualize yourself in these. You're now resisting the resistance and getting closer to identifying your Dream.

As it creeps up, give it more attention. Daydream consciously. Rivet your attention on it and fill in the details. Don't stint, limit or censor yourself. See it so clearly you can touch and taste it and you're convinced you're really living it. As many spiritual teachers (and brain researchers) have pointed out, the mind doesn't know the difference between an imagined scenario and a real one—you imagine your child is in an accident and your heart races, you imagine you've gotten that fantastic promotion and your heart races. Maybe that's why Einstein said that imagination is more important than knowledge.[15] Imagine your Dream life with gusto!

Details and variations you may never have thought of before may blossom. Listen for them, see them, welcome them. They're emerging after eons underground and finally airing themselves;

they're your soul talking to you. Let those rushes of relief or elation wash over you.

You *can* stand it.

Questions to Hone in on Your Dream

What Dreams, secret, guarded, or otherwise, have been jabbing at you, nagging, pricking, despite your best efforts to ignore them? What Dreams do you find yourself dreaming when you allow a moment to look out at the sky or the field? What do you dream your life really could be like, if only ...?

Still having trouble? A friend's brother taught me the importance of asking ourselves questions about our Dreams. He became discontented and restless, even though he was very good at his job in an ad agency. He wanted to explore other things that would give him greater satisfaction. But he'd been at his profession for so long he didn't know what else he could do. I devised the following questions (with appreciation to minister and spiritual teacher Terry Cole-Whittaker) to shake him up a little and expand his thoughts.[16] Try them yourself.

1. What do I *really* want to do?

   No shoulds, ifs, approvals.

2. What are my most deeply felt goals about my life?

   No excuses, regrets, yes-buts.

3. What could my best Dream do for my career or job position?

   If it's nothing, so be it. Have the courage to admit this.

4. What am I afraid of losing or seeing happen if I trust my needs and wants?

   Cough up your fears. Do they involve others? How?

5. What would I be afraid of if I were happy right now?

   Maybe a strange question, but think about it. Who would you hurt, deprive, disappoint?

6. How willing am I to face others to defend and fight for my Dream?

Could take a lot of listening to hysterics, accusations, recriminations. Are you willing to stay centered, simple and strong?

7. How important is my Dream to me?

The world, a lot, sort of, so what? Be honest.

8. What will it do for me:
   — Economically?
   — Emotionally?
   — On a soul level?

9. What is the ideal life I envision for myself, if I could have it any way at all?

No censoring or gap-finding. Suspend all trumpets of impossibility and self-ridicule. Go back to those pictures from your electronic deprivation.

10. What satisfactions, fulfillments, joys would this ideal life give me?

Fully imagine how you would act and feel. These should go beyond the standard comforts, such as financial security, possessions or a lot of leisure time. As many retired people have found, comforts as an ultimate goal can get very stale very quickly. The brilliant children's author Maurice Sendak was right: "There must be more to life than having everything!"[17]

If you take the time to thoroughly think about and write down your responses to these questions, you'll arrive at answers. They may be what you've long suspected or real revelations. Think about them, use them, get used to them.

More on Recognizing Your Dream

The eloquent, compassionate and gentle philosopher and mythologist Joseph Campbell instructed us with a statement that has become a byword in self-improvement and life coaching circles: "Follow your bliss."[18] What is it you *love* to do and can do well? Listen to yourself; listen to your heart.

Again, courage! A beautiful passage from the Unity booklet I recommended earlier, *Spiritual Preparation for Easter 2000*, tenderly prompts us:

> Be true to yourself.... When you question your actions or the path you should follow ... listen.... Listen to your heart, and know it will lead you in the way that is true to yourself—your spiritual self—for I am in you and you are in Me.... When you listen to your heart, you are listening to Me.
>
> Whatever comes your way, whatever choices you have to make, follow the course that feels right to you. No one else knows what your path is or should be.
>
> You are here now, to live wholeheartedly, with zeal and enthusiasm. Listen to your heart.[19]

Courage again—when you receive your heart's answers, know you've been given the ability to carry them out. With your fierce desire to follow your Dream come the capabilities, possibly buried to you at the moment, to fulfill it. In my work, both for clients and my own writing, I repeat Paul's admonishment to Timothy: "For God did not give us a spirit of timidity, but a spirit of power, of love, and of self-discipline" (1 Tim. 1:7).[20]

Get Specific

It's time. Write down your Dream. Be very specific. Your mind and the Universe take your direction and act on it. Activate your own law of attraction.

If you put down "To be happy," this isn't specific enough and will depend on the specifics you choose. Write your end-goal Dream here. Many steps and subdreams will take place toward achieving it, and we'll work on those in the next chapter. If you have more than one Dream, put it down too (and kick out that voice that says, again, "Yeah, when the Red Sox win the Series!" You know what happened.). Here are some examples from clients and friends:

Dreams

- Become a college professor.
- Be a social worker.
- Paint full-time.
- Open a dessert catering business.
- Own my own real estate firm.
- Run an adoption agency.
- Have a business consulting practice.
- Stay home with my children.
- Write novels. (Sound familiar?)
- Become an opera singer.
- Become a film producer.
- Teach piano from my home.
- Teach history.
- Carve exquisite duck decoys.

Stare at your list. Take it in. Make it yours. Then take some index cards and on each one write or type your Dream, with your name, in the present tense:

"I, Marcia, am now a full-time painter."
"I, Gary, own my own real estate firm."
"I, Lynn, now stay home with my children."

Make six or eight of these cards, and place them around where you'll see them: on the refrigerator door, in the sock drawer, next to your phone, on the bathroom mirror. I've got one near my never-ending grocery list and one next to my computer. Even if, after a while, you no longer look at them consciously, you'll automatically see them peripherally, and they'll become part of your consciousness.

This new message will begin to replace all those old can'ts, shouldn'ts, and should haves.

What If You Can't Identify Your Dream?

Maybe, unlike some people who always knew they wanted to be an actor, singer, scientist, philanthropist, you never really had a strong feeling about your Dream. You couldn't quite pinpoint it, but know only that you itch with dissatisfaction, the daily gratifications aren't enough, and somewhere, somehow, there's got to be more.

If this is the case, it's time to make another list.

20 Things I Really Like to Do

These can range from the frivolous to the somber. They can be things you've done or would love to do every day, things you want to do, have done a few times, or things you've never done but wish you'd let yourself do. As silly, stupid, pig-headed, selfish or unattainable as they may seem, don't judge, censor or dismiss any of them. Here are some examples from other people's lists:

1. Watch cooking shows on TV.
2. Visit fabric shops and sort through lace trimmings.
3. Listen to music.
4. Paint with watercolors.
5. Watch construction sites.

6. Play with model trains.
7. Work out at the gym.
8. Read Bible stories.
9. Work with numbers.
10. Play with my kids.
11. Practice the clarinet.
12. Dance.
13. Paint watercolor scenes.
14. Bake.
15. Work in the garden.
16. Organize the CDs.
17. Rewire a lamp.
18. Read world history.
19. Learn Spanish, for real.
20. Listen to other people's troubles.

Look at your list, study it. Picture doing all these things. What are the top five? The top two ... one? Maybe two or more are related and are really parts of the same deeply felt desire, like painting with watercolors and browsing through art supply stores. What makes you cheer inside? What makes you say, when you imagine doing it, "Yeah—this is it!"?

If you're having trouble coming up with your list or want to confirm your answers, try one or both of the following meditative techniques. They follow from listening to your heart.

Two Dream-Catching Meditative Techniques

Each of these requires outer and inner quiet. By now you must have certain favorite ways to calm yourself, so now is the time to use them.

The first technique is adapted from several Unity *Daily Word* passages and lessons.[21]

Listen for Your Dream

1. Tune out whatever is happening around you.
2. With eyes closed, tune into yourself. Focus your attention on your body, your mind, the images flashing across your eyes, the sounds around you, or anything else in your universe.
3. Say to yourself, "I am awake and aware spiritually."
4. "I have moved beyond my senses."
5. "I am guided by divine understanding alone."
6. "I am no longer limited by facts and reasoning."
7. "I am consciously connected to the wisdom of God."
8. "I am consciously connected to God's purpose for me."
9. "I hear and feel this purpose now."
10. Just listen.

Repeat these sentences as you need to. Listen.

Look especially at number 6. It's one thing to repeat affirmations, but "denial" is equally important. It's very important to consciously recognize that you don't have to hook in to what seem to be facts, reasons, circumstances. The torpedoing skeptics and hard-headed pragmatists are always so proud: "Face reality," they proclaim. Well, you don't have to face reality. It will only hamper you and delay your Dream. Reality is what we choose it to be and what we concentrate on. Reality, we should always remind ourselves, is malleable.

The other technique is a slightly more graphic variation. It's from *A Course in Miracles*: "My only function is the one God gave me."[22]

Listen for Your True Function

1. Again, quiet your mind.
2. Tell yourself you now listen for the answers.
3. Tell yourself you know the answers.
4. Repeat several times, "My only function is the one God gave me."

5. Many thoughts will surface. Notice them as interference and let them pass by. Repeat the previous statement.
6. After a while, the interfering thoughts will lessen. As they do, and you relax, say the following:
7. "On this clean slate, let my true function be written for me."
8. Listen.

How will you know and feel the truth of the answer? You'll feel a calm, a sense of relief, as if something suddenly fell into place, an *Ahhhh*. You'll feel a sense of rightness and peace.

Frank McCourt, teacher in tough New York City schools for 30 years and author of the Pulitzer Prize-winning best-seller *Angela's Ashes*, put it another way: "It's a great thing to know why you were put on this earth. I was a teacher ... but all the time I was a writer not writing." This quotation appeared in a mailing I once received to subscribe to a writers' magazine. I didn't subscribe but kept the mailing, because his words are so true.

Trust Your Answers

Before he died, McCourt found his calling and followed it passionately, with great success. By now, hopefully you have too. Whatever has been revealed, trust it. Trust your peaceful feelings, in body and emotions. Trust the vision of your perfect, ideal life. The strength of this message *is* God's will for you.

Stop worrying—about the how, the who, the where, the when. You've hit on the What. Trust, and swig another dose of Abraham:

> All the resources you will ever want or need are at your fingertips. All you have to do is identify what you want to do with it, and then practice the feeling-place of what it will feel like when that happens. There is nothing you cannot be or do or have. You are blessed Beings; you have come forth into this physical environment to create. There is nothing holding you back, other than

your own contradictory thought…. You are powerful Creators and right on schedule…. Just practice that and watch what happens.[23]

Be assured that you can achieve what you Dream because it is implanted in you. What's been revealed, your preference and greatest joy, indicates your gifts. You wouldn't yearn to follow your Dream if you didn't have the tools and talents to fulfill it.

If you need more support, remember this: God has given us the best telephone service we could ever subscribe to. The contract is infinitely renewable, with no fine print. It's one verse in the Old Testament: "Before they call, I will answer; while they are still speaking I will hear" (Isa. 65:24).

The Dream you've just identified is the answer. It was ready *before* you called; your itchiness told you that. You are assured of being heard, even while you're speaking (tell that to your impatient relatives). You can speed-dial back any time; the contract includes unlimited, infinite-distance minutes.

With this assurance of Ultimate Phone Support, you're ready for more.

The next chapter will guide you from trusting to believing in your Dream. It will take you from believing to knowing you deserve it. Then you'll have the foundation for acting to bring your Dream into your life in all the radiance and wonder you formerly thought was impossible.

CHAPTER 10

Take the Leap:
Believe in Your Dream and Deserve It

The two verbs *believe* and *deserve* are twins. Each is a necessary part of the other and nurtures it. They are also essential preludes to acting, the subject of the next chapter. Believing comes before acting, impels us to act, and can't really be separated from acting. We can hardly believe unless we feel we deserve. These are the engines that drive us to act and propel us to the success we crave.

Believe

Okay, you've identified your dream with confidence. The next step is to believe it. What about all those doomsayers? They keep creeping in, like ants, harder to get rid of than a cold. Those messages cling like dirt:

- You don't have the aptitude.
- You're afraid.
- You'll look ridiculous.
- You need more money, education, time, talent, help, friends, cooperation, quiet, supplies, room, etc.
- Our neighbors don't do these things.
- Our family doesn't do these things.
- Our people don't do these things.

This list is endless if you let it keep going. Well, don't. As metaphysical teacher Harry Douglas Smith says, "Life is choking on the sludge of negative normals."[1] That's what these negative, wet-blanketing statements are—what other people are convinced is normal. Shut them out and concentrate on the beautiful, clear, unequivocal, peace-producing messages from your Inner Guide.

Avoid a Trap

When we finally identify and acknowledge our Dream, our first reaction is elation. Our next is generally to look around—at our house, apartment, office, title, paycheck, life—and groan, shaking our heads: "It's impossible! I'll *never* get out of this!"

Who says? Others have, many many others.

One of the best antidotes for this attack, which I had often during my typing years, is the advice I got when I went to see a psychic—the only time I've ever gone to one. I'd barely sat down when I sobbed, "All I ever do is type. How can I ever get out of this and start writing in earnest?"

Her answer has stuck with me for decades: "Accept where you are now. However hard or even impossible it is, love it. Love it 100 percent and more. The more you love it, the sooner you'll shoot out from it."

At her words, the image burst into my mind of a large, strong bird fluttering its wings and emerging from a leaf-covered nest. It spread its wings and soared into the sky.

Can you love where you are? This is part of your lesson and discipline. Focus only on loving it, despite all the gripes, impossible duties, demands, people, schedules. The sooner you start loving where you are, the sooner you'll no longer need it and the faster you'll soar from it.

Some help:

Catherine Ponder counsels, "Stop talking about the problem [or your boss]. Place it lovingly in the hands of the Father."[2]

The wonderful Unity teacher and writer Mary Kupferle published many essays, and each title brings showers of buoyant hope: "Everything Is Working for Good," "God Is in This Experience," "God Will Turn It to Good," "Let the Divine Plan Unfold." These are only the titles of essays in two of her books.[3]

Learning these lessons, from my own and others' almost unbearable experiences, I wrote an essay called "Are You Blooming or Wilting Where You're Planted?"[4] As the lessons surfaced, I shared them and share them now: In this loving process, thank yourself for where you are. You've chosen this situation, given it to yourself as a life lesson for many reasons only you can fathom and tease out (at some time), a lesson to be learned as you dance toward your Dream.

If the negatives keep recurring, counter them with your own repetitions.

Repeat what your Inner Guide has told you, like a refrain, a chant. You know how sometimes we can't get a certain song out of our heads? Invoke this technique consciously. Your Guide's message is a song to keep in your head and drown out the unremitting voice that screeches, "You can't do it!"

The commitment to your Dream requires discipline, concentration and belief in yourself and what you can do. God told Neale Donald Walsch, "The people who make a living doing what they love are the people who insist on doing so. They don't give up. They never give in. They dare life *not* to let them do what they love."[5] Henry David Thoreau's imperative has often been read, on everything from t-shirts to mugs to mood rings: "Go confidently in the direction of your dreams! Live the life you've imagined."[6]

Words to Believe By

Jesus repeatedly taught the crucial importance of belief. Hear some of his words:

- What things soever ye desire, when ye pray, believe that ye receive *them*, and ye shall have *them*. (Mk. 11:24 KJV)

When a father brought his son to be healed of "madness," he said:

- If though canst believe, all things are possible to him that believeth. (Mk. 9:23)

When a woman's daughter seemed dead, he told her:

- Fear not: believe only, and she shall be made whole. (Lk. 8:50)
- Ask, and it will be given you; search, and you will find; knock, and the door will be opened for you. (Mt. 7:7)

Only when we believe, at least a little, will we be answered in what we ask; only when we believe that we'll find will we search; only when we believe the door will open will we knock. That is, Jesus is asking us to take the first step by acting *as if*, by believing enough to act. He promises that our action will be rewarded by what we desire.

This instruction is very close to another of my favorite directions from Psalms. The Lord says: "Open wide your mouth, and I will fill it" (Ps. 81:10). Again, we're required to take a specific action. To take it, we must believe it will bring us what we want: ask ... search ... knock ... open your mouth. That is, believe, believe, believe in your Dream.

To do so, we're also required to use our self-discipline to turn away from our fears and ambivalences, and especially the material evidence in front of us. Look below the crust of perceived reality to the substance of faith.

Have Faith

Faith is the essential ingredient for any accomplishment, from baking a cake to building a city. Most of us, in our eyeball-focused materialistic culture, haven't been schooled in faith. We've been taught to believe only what our senses confirm, to our detriment, depression and aborted development. Many things we do require faith in ourselves to successfully complete the activity, but we take them for granted, like driving, preparing a meal, swimming, buying a gift, balancing a checkbook (for some of us).

Napoleon Hill advocated a major principle of faith: Whatever we can conceive, and then believe, we can achieve.[7] People who've accomplished great things—Columbus, Da Vinci, Edison, Marie Curie—reveal the visions they conceived, the kind of extreme faith they had in themselves, and what they had to see beyond their senses. Their successes came, finally, often after years of disappointments and failures. We're often prone to say, "Yeah, yeah." They were geniuses, they were famous, they were in other eras. They didn't have my kids, mortgages, bosses, broken-down cars.

We can always find excuses. We can also always find people who overcame their excuses: the rock and rap stars who started as poor near-delinquents; the many actors, athletes, politicians, publishers, business leaders and medical professionals who started with almost nothing materially but had the courage to see and act beyond their physical surroundings to their Dream.

All of them once felt exactly like you do.

You don't believe it. You're saying, "They had talent, they had charisma, they were good-looking, they didn't have my short-comings."

Marilyn Monroe couldn't act very well. Oprah Winfrey struggles with a weight problem. General Douglas MacArthur was a clotheshorse. General Colin Powell has a little-known speech impediment. A baseball player for the St. Louis Browns, Pete Gray, lost an arm in childhood (and a movie was made of his life). Carl Joseph, who was born without a left leg, is in the Florida

Sports Hall of Fame, earned 13 letters in high school sports and played college football. He never wore a prosthesis.[8]

Maybe you're saying, "They haven't failed so often as I have, not by a long shot." Oh, really?

Inspiring Failures

- R. H. Macy failed seven times before his store in New York became a success.
- English novelist John Creasey got 753 rejection slips before he published his 564 books.
- Babe Ruth struck out 1,330 times, but he also hit 714 home runs.
- Before he isolated what made the light bulb stay on, Edison failed 10,000 times!
- Margaret Mitchell received rejection letters from 38 publishers before publication of *Gone With the Wind*, which won the Pulitzer Prize, became a now-classic movie (1939) and made Clark Gable as Rhett Butler the heartthrob of generations of women.
- The original *Chicken Soup for the Soul* was rejected by 140 publishers. Since its publication in 1993, sequels and spin-offs have been going strong for 15 years.[9]

Failure at one attempt—or 10,000—doesn't mean *you* are a failure. It simply means you have failed at that attempt. "Failure," said Henry Ford, "is the opportunity to begin again, more intelligently." He should know. In 1945, his company lost $20 million in a Brazilian rubber plantation venture for tires—the equivalent of $200 million in 2010.[10]

As Ford's words and the people in the list above show, they didn't attach themselves, or their Selves, to their failures. What set them apart? Faith in themselves, in seeing beyond their momentary failures, appearances and self-judgments. Faith in listening closely to and following their Inner Voice. Maybe they didn't hear a voice, but called it drive, passion, desire. What was normal for others wasn't for them. They had faith in their own normals.

Their normals didn't come from doing what they'd always done, what others had always done, or from ignoring their true desires and Dreams. They weren't content to be, in psychologist James Hillman's graphic description, "huddled in the mean of the bell curve."[11] Their normals, as Tama Kieves says, didn't "come from choosing comfort in the moment—over comfort in [their] lifetime."[12] They weren't afraid to break out, rise above family, friends, limited expectations, squashing labels, to follow their normals.

Your true normal, whatever particular expression it takes, is what's vibrating inside you and it comes from the Divine: *"The true normal for each one of us is exactly that which is normal to God—* beauty (whatever the apparent physical appearance may be), love, abundance, health, success, peace, harmony, joy. These are the normals we must accept and in which we must believe for ourselves."[13]

The Friend Within You

A great way of seeing our true, maybe maverick, odd, noncon-forming, iconoclastic normal is as a friend. This keeps your Dream intact and your Voice in the forefront. Your Friend is at once a comforter, bolsterer, guide and leader. This is Earnest Holmes' description:

> The Friend within you is continuously looking after your well-being.... Possibly it will be difficult for you to believe that there is such a Friend, but He is there at the very center of your being, directing your thought and

causing you to triumph over every defeat, for He is an unconquerable hero.[14]

A wonderful promise from Psalms corroborates Holmes' declarations. It promises the constancy of our Voice and its sure direction: "I will instruct you and teach you in the way you should go; I will counsel you and watch over you" (Ps. 32:8).

Use your Voice, your Guide, your passion, your drive, your certainty in the rightness of your Dream. Whatever you need to do to keep believing in it, do. This is the fuel that will power you to reach the destination of your Dream realized.

What's to stop you from believing you can reach your Dream? Absolutely nothing.

You Deserve It

To succeed at reaching your Dream, another ingredient is absolutely as important as believing. This is feeling you deserve it. If you feel you don't deserve it, for whatever reasons, you will torpedo yourself. "When we have strong beliefs that we don't deserve, we have problems doing what we want."[15] A while ago, I was struck by the truth of the title of a lecture by motivational speaker Nancy McFadden: "Stay With Yourself When No One Else Will: How Self-Esteem Affects Your Success and Impacts Your Creativity."[16]

You can remedy this feeling of nondeserving instantly, without even thinking about it, without making a journal entry or confessing to a shrink why you don't feel you deserve your Dream. A longtime friend, a rare person who doesn't avoid the truth about himself or his friends and isn't afraid to speak it, gave me a wonderful affirmation. If you're lamenting over not believing in yourself and wavering with deservingness, make these words your mantra: *I forgive myself for having believed for so long that I was never good enough to have, get or be what I want.*

If you're uncomfortable or anxious reading this, or so nervous you can't help laughing in a high-pitched voice, the message is definitely for you. Memorize the sentence. Plaster it around the house and repeat it so often you begin to believe it.

Practice deserving. Mothers are notorious for taking the raggedy heel of the bread, serving everyone else, and for themselves scraping the dregs of the pie plate. These choices become an unfortunate mindset and infect everything else. Wives are notorious for putting off their Dreams until their husbands are settled in careers, their children are grown, their elderly parents are cared for, their church has had its last supper, and so on.

Elizabeth Gilbert, in her irresistible spiritual chick lit odyssey, tells of the epiphany that she had never asked herself what she really wanted. When she dared herself and finally did, her answers ranged from a new linen shirt to living in Italy.[17] You don't even have to leave your house—but you can choose the better piece of toast (I love it dark), take the neater piece of cake, give yourself a daily 15 minutes alone with a cup of tea, buy that outrageous pair of jeans (not your grandmother's overalls). "Too much of a good thing," said sexy stage actress, playwright and movie star of the early 20th century Mae West, "is wonderful."[18]

With this permission, grow your deservingness and dreams. Know they have a purpose, your purpose, and they've been instilled in you. One of my favorite reminders is Julia Cameron's assertion: "Our creative dreams and yearnings come from a divine source."[19] Your desire and God's desire for you are one and the same.

When we catch ourselves thinking (again) that our desires and dreams are frivolous, bad, silly, ridiculous and exclaim, "Oh, I'll become an interior designer ... God willing," we should stop and reflect. God's will is not frivolous or capricious; it's not a reward or punishment. In a heady passage, Eric Butterworth explains:

> The will of God is the ceaseless longing of the Spirit in you to completely fulfill in the outer the potential within you. The will of God in you is the pent-up energy of your own divinity that is seeking releasement and fulfillment in your manifest life. It is God seeking to express Himself as you.[20]

Remind yourself often that if it were not God's good will for you to experience fulfillment of the deep desires of your heart, you would not desire them in the first place.

Unity minister J Douglas Bottorff puts it forcefully: "To be true to your Self is to be true to God. To pursue your dreams is to do God's will. Everything else follows these two things."[21]

What's more—especially when that fear of inadequacy rises from your stomach to your throat—know that your desires carry the seeds of your ability to accomplish your Dream. Sure, you may need training and practice and experience, but the desire is not random. Take heart from McWilliams: "a deep desire ... also comes with an inborn ability to achieve that desire."[22]

If you're questioning your deservingness, don't. Your desire tells you that you unequivocally deserve your Dream. Otherwise you wouldn't desire it at all.

Accept your deservingness. Feel at ease with it. Dare to deserve. Dare to believe that all things are working for good in your life, toward your Dream. Give your Dream the energy it deserves.

This may mean giving up certain things, certain very cherished things that we've hung onto often for years. Like what? Give up thinking about your face (wrinkled), your feet (bony), your stomach (too big), your house (unclean), your desk (piled high), your finances (lacking), your work (chronically behind), your mate (chronically annoying), your future (scarily unknown). Give up trying to preserve an often worse enemy than all these: your status quo. The old comfort zone is a comforter we pull around us, with soothing snacks, and sink into, sink away from all but the necessities. Your Dream won't let you sink and snooze but prods you with what should be welcome discomfort in that zone.

When you marshal the courage to dare to dream, you open yourself to accepting and receiving. What? God's love, abundance, care, comfort, security, order, healing, reassurance, all-good for you, the sureness of your future in His loving hands. When you are attuned to God, a *Daily Word* lesson promises, nothing can stand between you and your bliss: "I am a divine being, blessed with miraculous gifts that allow me to rise above any challenge and live my dreams."[23]

Keep affirming. Here are some direct and forceful affirmations.

Affirmations for Deservingness

- I deserve to do what I've always wanted.
- No one stands in my way.
- I don't stand in my way.
- I was born to deserve what I've always wanted.
- I have enough time, money, energy, interest, cooperation from everyone around me to do what I've always wanted.
- Doing what I've always wanted to do is my natural state.
- Doing what I've always wanted to do harms no one.
- Doing what I've always wanted to do makes me feel good and keeps me healthy.

- Doing what I've always wanted to do blesses me and everyone I meet.

Why are such statements so important? We do create our own reality. We can change our thoughts, and thus our emotions, and thus again our experience.[24] Our inner governs our outer.

Choose What You Concentrate On

Toward your better creating and combining the concepts of the power of our thoughts and "Believing Is Seeing," U. S. Andersen sets forth four "mental conditioning laws" on really believing in your Dream.[25] These laws, re-enunciated by many contemporary spiritual teachers, apply in every area of our lives, and especially as we move toward our Dream:

1. We are what we concentrate on.

If we concentrate on failure, we engender feelings of failure. If we concentrate on success, these feelings come. It takes practice and discipline, though, to concentrate on what you *don't* feel like. Sometimes we need to pretend, act, imagine, act *as if.*

2. What we concentrate on grows.

We've all had this experience. Think about it. You wake up grumpy. You snap at your spouse and slap down the dog's bowl. Then on your way to the second cup of coffee, you hit your head on the kitchen cabinet door, curse and step on the dog's tail. The dog yowls, waking the baby, and your spouse yells at you. You haven't even gotten dressed for work. Your concentration on grumpiness and anger have produced these matchless experiences the first thing in the morning.

3. What we concentrate on becomes real.

The marvelous human mind believes what we tell it. What we tell it we come to believe—beliefs are a clump or bouquet of thoughts. Look at people with delusions. They truly believe they see and hear others or experience events the rest of us don't. They act on their beliefs. When we tell ourselves we're failures, can never finish anything, or will never get what we want, we believe these messages. What we're concentrating on has become real to us. So the next principle becomes true.

4. We always find what we concentrate on.

A well-known axiom declares that things don't just happen to us; they happen justly. "Justly" means that things happen just as we believe them. Haven't our dire self-fulfilling prophecies—"I was afraid that ...," "I *knew* that ..."—come about, to our disappointment, dismay or heartbreak?

As Andersen also points out, these four mental laws always work, whether we consciously apply them or not. "The greatest danger in your life lies in dwelling on failure. The greatest reward lies in thinking success."[26]

Visualize

With these four principles under your belt and in your head, it's time to activate your mind's eye. This means visualizing what you want, *as if it's* already *here*. Many fine books have been written about visualizing, and you may want to look at some, such as the classic *Creative Visualization* by Shakti Gawain and Wayne Dyer's *You'll See It When You Believe It.*[27] Whatever technique(s) you use, the main point is to picture in your mind the life that fulfills your dream—like a movie, photo or painting.

On the bulletin board near my desk is a picture torn from a supermarket women's magazine, I don't know how many years ago, of a cozy living room, furnished in a Southwestern theme. The room has two wood bookcases, a coffee table, and a TV console. Two Indian rugs hang on the walls, with elk horns mounted nearby. The chairs are rattan, roomy and slightly worn-looking, with Indian triangular-patterned throw pillows in dark reds and purple. The coffee table, with a dark wooden top and black wrought-iron legs, stands between them.

I don't like western decor and would never choose it. Nevertheless, the picture grabbed me for many reasons. The feel is homey, comfortable, somewhat haphazard. More than this, other parts of the picture sang, or twanged, to me.

Near one of the bookcases, at the back of the picture, is a computer workstation, with a page visible on a wooden paper holder. In front of the workstation sits a contemporary office chair, one of those inexpensive ones from a chain office-supply store. The chair has a black seat and black arms on an adjustable pedestal leg and is positioned halfway out of the desk, as if in use. Next to the chair on a pull-out stand is a printer, with a stack of extra paper on the lower shelf of the stand.

In the forefront, the coffee table in front of the rattan chair holds an old manual, black typewriter, like the Royals of the 1940s. A new sheet of paper is rolled into it. Next to the typewriter rests a coffee mug near two notebooks, and beside the shift key is a wadded-up ball of paper. Several others are strewn around the coffee table.

Why does this picture mean so much to me? It's the room of an active writer in the midst of writing! Looks like the person took a little break, in the throes of struggling to create (all the balls of paper), maybe to answer the phone or get a snack. The working environment is warm, easy, not formal or pretentious. It contains a relaxed blend of the old ways of creating and the new—the vintage Royal and computer coexist comfortably in different parts of the room.

This picture, which is still in my peripheral line of vision, is my visualization of the writing life. I look around my office area. It's in a corner of the living room, which is casually eclectic, semimodern, comfortable, cozy, with light wood bookcases and TV console. The sofa is a delicious caramel color, and the coffee table matches the wood of the bookcases. Things are quite haphazard, with piles of magazines and DVDs (my husband's passion) on the floor and coffee table.

On my L-shaped desk, the computer is nestled into the corner. The printer is at one end within arm's reach, and an open ream of extra paper below. My chair, bought at one of those chain office-supply branches, is all black with an adjustable pedestal leg. My files, papers and notes for current projects cover the desk. The ubiquitous mug of coffee rests on a coaster at my elbow.

On a small table across the room sits a typewriter. It's not a Royal but my precious royal blue correcting Selectric II, companion through many phases of typing, editing, whining and writing. It's missing half a letter, like a broken tooth, but has had only two repairs in the last 10 years and works like new. I use it for the occasional form or envelope and exercise it every Sunday so the oil doesn't congeal. Mainly I like it near me.

Does this picture parallel the one on my bulletin board? You betcha. The biggest difference is that I don't have balled-up wads of paper strewn all over. I deposit them into a wicker wastebasket near the chair under my desk. As much as I've visualized my perfect life and repeated countless affirmations, in choosing my surroundings I never *consciously* tried to reproduce this picture.

Visualization Practice

I recommend, though, that you consciously practice visualization. Many books are out now on techniques, but I've always liked Gawain's simplicity. She outlines four basic steps to help you visualize effectively. Here they are, with some description and hints I've found valuable for greater power.[28]

1. *Set Your Goal.* Choose something at first that's fairly easy to believe that you can gain in the relatively near future.

2. *Create a Clear Idea or Picture.* Mentally create, *see* the thing, state of mind, or condition that you want. Make it exactly as you want it. Quiet all those *buts* and *I don't haves*. Be very specific and include all the details, like in the photo I described above.

3. *Focus on It Often.* Think of your mental picture frequently, during specific times, such as the early morning and before you go to bed. Think of your picture also at odd times, while you're doing other things. You don't have to will it into existence with furrowed brow. As Gawain says, "Focus on it clearly, yet in a light, gentle way" (17). Pressing is counterproductive.

4. *Give It Positive Energy.* This energy combats all the negatives that too easily rear up. For an additional jolt, say affirmations to accompany your picture: "I have this now; I experience this now. This is real for me. I accept and deserve it." Or you can simply hold your picture in mind surrounded by light.

Another excellent set of techniques is given by the psychologist Lee Pulos in his CD *The Power of Visualization.* He suggests "putting on someone else's head."[29] This may sound slightly macabre at first but makes great sense.

Pulos tells of an essay writer who was blocked and had to get out an essay for a client. In a kind of displacement and replacement, the writer "put on the head" of a prolific writer he admired. The blocked writer convinced himself that he was now the successful writer, saw himself as the other, and visualized himself thinking and acting like the other. Having imbued the feel and personality of the other, the stuck writer broke through, forgot his own block and perceived shortcomings, and wrote a great essay.

This anecdote tells us that when we get out of ourselves, put a halt to our constantly rehearsed inadequacies and feelings of undeservingness, and concentrate instead on a goal or part of one, wonderful things can happen. However, we must take that disciplined step of closing the door on our negatives, shutting them up, or simply turning away from them and substituting other thoughts and words.

The award-winning writer and professor Joyce Carol Oates directs her writing students at Princeton to write under a pseudonym for a week. "It allows them a lot of freedom they don't have ordinarily."[30] Same idea.

I love the unabashed statements (I call them hard-core metaphysics) of the minister and prolific New Thought author Joseph Murphy. These words perfectly capture the as-if principle: "I become that which I contemplate. I now feel that I am what I want to be; this feeling or awareness is the action of God in me; it is the creative Power."[31]

By now you're familiar with meditative techniques from earlier chapters. Let's look at some specifics and apply them to visualization of what you want to achieve, see happen, and live.

Stepping Into the Essence of the Person You Admire

1. As always, sit in a quiet spot, alone, with no disturbances. What are the five or six areas you want to change? Write them down. You certainly don't have to tackle them all at once, but this list gives you the grand picture. Writing them all down also gets them out of your head so you stop the worry and self-castigations. A newly divorced friend listed these areas: easy fearless social conversation, weight loss, daily exercise, resuming the fiction writing she'd abandoned in high school.

2. Next, for each of the areas you put down, think of someone who displays or embodies what you wish you had, someone you admire, envy, wish you were. The person may be a friend, relative, acquaintance, stranger or celebrity.

3. Choose one of your areas. Start imagining how you'd feel if you were this person. From what you know directly, have seen, read or imagine, feel their personality flow into you, let their body slip over yours, let their mind come in, filling yours.

4. Get up, eyes closed if you want, and visualize and act out steps or actions that are part of your desired area. Here are suggestions adapted from my friend's list:

   - For easy social conversation, see yourself at a cocktail party or dinner, being introduced as your model would be. Talk, gesture and decline the calorie-laden circulating appetizers with wit and grace.

   - For weight loss, see yourself politely refusing that second helping or clenching your fist at the nighttime TV corn chips. See yourself choose from your closet the backless, sleeveless, waist-cinched slinky black dress your model wore on the cover of *Cosmopolitan*. See yourself take from the hanger the trim tennis whites your other model wore in the last Wimbledon. Act out putting on these clothes.

   - For daily exercise, see yourself in a snappy, matching nylon tank top and shorts, or, depending on your neighborhood, a stretched t-shirt and baggy sweat pants. Imagine yourself springing out to the gym bright and early, cheerily greeting others on the way (my personal un-favorite). Feel yourself full of energy, like your admired model. Where you are, stretch a few times, jog in place, do a couple of yoga postures (the Warrior, any level, is great for feeling power).

   - To practice your version of fiction writing, see yourself in your studio, unused guest room, corner of the bedroom, or wherever you'd most like to work. Your supplies are on a side table, your computer or pad at the desk or on the bed. An old lucky t-shirt or cap is hanging invitingly on a hook. Put it on. Flip on the stereo to your favorite music or CD. Pick up your pen. Remember your model, feel your model. Start writing.

5. Decide on the date, day and time you will put your visualization into practice and act. Next Friday night, at the office cocktail reception? At your next meal, cutting your portions in half, eating more salad, or skipping dessert? Tomorrow morning, meeting your neighbor at the gym? Saturday afternoon, setting up that spare desk in the bedroom and dusting off the old laptop?

6. Keep this date with yourself. If you feel the need, tell your partner or a good friend about your plan and ask for help in keeping your promise to yourself. If you like or feel the need, involve the other person—practice witty repartee, make a dinner salad together, agree on the time you'll go out to walk a mile around the park, clear the junk out of the spare room.

7. Keep a journal of your successes. This will help you stick to your plan and repeat it. You'll be motivated to keep setting dates and targets for the next steps. Give yourself credit for each step, and reward yourself (but not with corn chips).

Like a kid playing soldier or queen or movie star, when you become the character you're playing, many things happen. Your doubts, fears and tentativeness vanish. You become commanding, sure and strong. You act in the role naturally, without hesitation or inhibitions.

You unravel that tangled bundle of thoughts that produced the knots of undeserving beliefs. You realize you do have what it takes to dare to believe that all is working for good in your life. You're no longer a victim of life, God, your heredity, the weather, or the chili sauce you ate last night. You're not afraid of something bad happening when you follow your Dream.

Instead of waiting for the other shoe to drop, let the other shoe dance—dance with both shoes. You'll see how in the next chapter, as we ACT.

CHAPTER 11
Act!
Ensure Your Dream's Arrival

><⊶-0-⊶<

Yes, it's time. With the tools you now have, and the mental and spiritual fortification, we can start easy. Take my hand and trust yourself.

Act as If

Your visualizations and Andersen's four principles have prepared the way for this step. Acting "as if" means playacting in the best sense, imagining as if you already have what you desire, behaving as if you've already succeeded, figuratively standing straighter and sucking in your gut. If you need to, give yourself a little more juice with any of these reminders from spiritual teachers that have made their way into popular wisdom:

- Act as if until you become.
- Change your mind and your body will follow.
- Move your body and your mind will follow.
- Think as if … and you will.
- Fake it until you make it.

I'll add a couple:

- What you believe you don't have, you don't have.
- What you believe you have, you have.

Recognize the foundation of reframing? When you *see* things differently, you *act* differently. Instead of thinking and seeing yourself as a failure, think and see yourself as successful and accomplishing.

Do you feel like a fraud, a fool, a fake? Okay, but so what? Do it anyway. You'll be surprised at how quickly you get into the role and the part. It will get you closer to what you want.

Acting as If: Ken's Story

One of my clients told me how he applied this principle. Ken, whom I was helping to get his doctorate in business, was a salesman of computer hardware and software to large corporations. An engaging, outgoing good-looking man, he had been quite successful, earning large commissions. He knew his product and was enthusiastic about it. The year before he enrolled in graduate school he couldn't seem to make a sale, no matter what he did. His usual accounts weren't interested in expanding and new leads yielded nothing.

Ken had a fairly affluent lifestyle and was beginning to get worried. Although his company advanced him funds, he didn't like seeing his savings dwindle for daily living. His wife, a teacher, took a second job. Ken in turn got more depressed and felt hopeless.

Finally, after a particularly depressing weekend, where both he and his wife spent long hours alternately fighting and comforting each other, he realized he'd have to pull himself out of this downward plunge if he didn't want to declare bankruptcy. He started recalling the times he'd made fabulous sales. How had he felt? What had he done? What had he worn? How had he carried himself? What had he said?

With his wife's encouragement, Ken began to describe these times. Aloud, he pictured himself bantering with clients and prospects, surprising them with their kids' names and birthdays, making sales, giving presentations, answering questions, shaking hands with the CEO, signing the agreement, smiling broadly as he left the building, and coming home to share the jubilant news with his wife.

One bright spring Monday, despite lingering feelings of depression and doubt, and with very little money in his pocket, Ken chose his best suit and whitest shirt. He shined his shoes and put on his boldest tie. His wife polished his briefcase. Ken told me his heart was fluttering and his stomach was turning in knots, but he made himself look in the mirror and declare, "I am a success!"

During his visits to clients, many times during the day, especially when Ken was repeatedly politely refused, his depressed feelings threatened to overtake him. He maintained his stance. "I am a success!" he chanted inside and made himself walk with a jaunty, confident step. Many times he felt "stupid," he said, like he was acting, and it felt hollow, but he kept at it.

With one more name on his list, Ken almost went home. He felt the chances of a sale were slim, but he made himself go. When he emerged, he had a hefty order and a contract for two years of onsite technical support.

This sale broke Ken's slump and bolstered him tremendously. He went home, as he had pictured, and announced it jubilantly to his wife.

That sale signified much more. It showed Ken that he could have control over his thoughts, feelings and his very mind. It showed him that this control could happen when he acted and put on the costume of success. Ken hastened to add that it wasn't only because he put on his good suit. He'd done that before and had just sunk lower. He was successfu because he took charge of his mind and used all the tools he had—affirmations, visualizations and stern self-talk—to reverse his downward direction.

Sneaking Up on Acting as If

Like Ken, many have found that getting our bodies to go on automatic is the easier course, even if our minds remain unconvinced. Ken applied affirmations, although he didn't feel very self-affirming at first. Quaking is normal. Feel the quake and do it anyway.

Act like you've been there before.

Act like you're there already.

Be ready for more action. Jesus advised, "Be dressed ready for service and keep your lamps burning" (Lk. 12:35). Whether it's a burlap cloak or Brooks Brothers, be dressed for action and have your mental lamps lit.

Let's say you yearn to finish college or get a master's degree. It's time to act.

Rather, it's time to partialize. This is just a fancy word for breaking down the project into steps. Notwithstanding the people you hear about who are multitasking whizzes, everyone—please remind yourself—does anything and everything one step at a time. There's a logic, a sequence, to any endeavor. Everyone does it one minute, one day, one lesson, one course, one inch, one word, one page, one note, one brush stroke, one backhand at a time. As Woody Allen may well have said, "The novel of a thousand pages begins with the first cheese Danish."

Action Actions

- Pore over the ads for what you're aiming at.
- Make a list of places to explore, websites to visit.
- Better yet, get dressed and get out.
- Go visit the avenue to your Dream: craft shop, small business institute, art gallery, gourmet bakery.
- Swallow hard and start a conversation with someone who looks knowing.

- Ask all the questions that occur to you, and get their contact information for more questions later.
- Corral another person in the restroom and ask about the place and projects.
- Decide how you'll begin to present your Dream—sample framed collages, spruced-up vita, portfolio of your water-colors, free minisamples of your delectable brownie-blondies.
- Talk to your family about adapting and supporting you in your new endeavor.
- Start working on your project (even if it means first shoveling out the spare room).
- Make a schedule for yourself of hours/days/grabbed moments that you'll devote to the project.
- You're on your way!

When You Start Acting, Be Alert

When you start to act in earnest, another set of subversive messages may rise up in protest and try to keep or bring you down: it's too late, it's too much, I'm too old/young/inexperienced/busy/dumb/untalented ...

Another pull surfaces too. The more we fiercely desire to do more, be more, and have more, maddeningly, the more a part of us desires to do nothing. We prod and condemn ourselves at once. Psychologist, cultural anthropologist and futurist Jean Houston calls this "the lure of becoming and the sense of galloping sloth."[1]

Aside from this beautiful rhetoric, this is only your old self trying to sabotage you; it can't stand seeing you get somewhere. After all, you're upsetting the status quo, the comforting familiarity, negative as it may have been. McWilliams wisely counsels, "Be willing to be uncomfortable. Be comfortable being uncomfortable. It may get tough, but it's a small price to pay for living your Dream."[2]

Recognize that this is what's going on. You can dismiss these thoughts, flick them off like flies on your collar. Detach yourself from them, declare control over them, and assert they have no hold over you. Soon you'll be able to shake them off and eventually barely nod at them as you keep acting toward your Dream. They'll shrink to the corner, limp ghosts of the monstrous threats they were, and disappear.

Louise Hay offers a great perspective: Greet these thoughts kindly, like former friends you no longer care to spend time with. "Oh, you again. Hello." Recognize them, thank them and know they can't harm you.[3] Another perspective transmutes them. Your fears are really positives in depressive dress. Consider these:

Your Fears Are Friends in Disguise

- Fear is excitement camouflaged.
- Guilt is the fuel for personal change.
- Hurt feelings are caring in drag.
- Anger is a mask for acting differently and often radically.
- Unworthiness is the angel that tells you there's got to be more than this.
- Undeservingness tells you that you know there's an infinity to deserve.
- Doubts are confidence turned inside out.
- Failure, as Edison learned, is yet another proof that you're closer to the answer.

If you get off the track, practice Hay's greeting. Or apply Fox's "Golden Key" and think of God instead. Or mentally step back and visualize those destructive emotions as posturing punks in your path and out to intimidate you. Talk back out loud: "Out of my way! You can't stop me! You're nothin'!"

Your Attitude Counts

Quash those fears, recognize them as closet blessings, and start acting. When you do, your mind and emotions will generally follow. You'll forget your negatives, at least for the moments you're acting, and really believe you are where you've longed to be.

I must caution you about developing a mindset beyond visualization and positive pretending. We discussed it before, and people have had trouble with it since it was uttered in the first century. If you grasp its real import, you'll make it work in your favor. It's the basis of the Law of Attraction, the recognition of our oneness with our Source, and our acknowledgment that God is All Good.

This is Jesus' pronouncement that many people think is patently unfair:

> For unto every one that hath shall be given, and he shall have abundance: but from him that hath not shall be taken away even that which he hath. (Mt. 25:29)

As my country friend used to say:

> Them what has gits.
> Them what has nits, gits nits.

You know—the generally held angry, victimized and envious interpretation of this declaration is "The rich get richer." What it really guides us to is a mindset of expectation and belief: The rich get richer because they *expect* they will continue to be successful at making money. This is not to minimize their savvy and wise decisions, but the governing factor is their confidence in their ability to accumulate wealth.

Either mindset is self-perpetuating, if you allow it to be. When you let your negatives overtake you, you activate a "poor" mentality. In the same way, when you're acting "as if," you gotta believe. You've got to allow yourself to feel the energy, drive, motivation and enthusiasm you'd naturally feel if you weren't pretending. You'll be activating the "having" mindset, and when you have in this way, you'll get and will continue to get what you want. As Abraham says, "That which is like unto itself, is drawn."[4]

An Example: Abundance Attitude

The idea of abundant thinking is rooted in the parable recorded in Matthew 25:14-28. The master gives "talents" (coins in Biblical terms) to each of his three servants. To the first, he gives five, to the second he gives two, and to the third he gives one. The servants who were given the five and two talents "traded with" them and gained another five and two. The servant who was given the single talent hid it in a hole in the ground.

When the master came back and asked what the servants had done, the first two proudly reported their gains and the master was pleased, commended them, and gave them more. The third servant said he was afraid, and that's why he had hidden his one talent. The master was very displeased, called him slothful, and told him to give it to the servant who had made 10 talents. Thus this third servant ended up with nothing.

All the servants may have been afraid; we're not told. We do know that the servant who acted on his fear and hid his talent lost it. I'm not the first to see the metaphorical significance of this story. The translated word "talents" has multiple meaning for us today; our current use of "talent" as a special natural aptitude or ability derives from this parable.[5]

Despite your fears, trade on your talents, use them, invest yourself in them, take action. You will be rewarded. You get out of your efforts—and life—what you put in, and don't hide your head in a hole (or widescreen TV) in the ground. Take the risk in yourself and you will gain from taking that risk and using your talents.

Motivate Yourself to Act

As we know, deciding to act may be scary and hard. What will putting it off get you? If you keep on saying "Later," you'll end up with "If only." The co-founder of *Ms.* magazine, Letty Cottin Pogrebin, faced this very choice:

> Standing at midlife in the riflescope of mortality, I found ... to die with a major goal unachieved—or, worse yet, unattempted—would be a bummer, and clearly the thing I would regret most on my deathbed was having not written a novel. I vowed to start one immediately and finish it before my next decade birthday.[6]

Her novel took four years to write, and she completed it within the decade. *Three Daughters* was published by a major house in 2002.

Pogrebin was wise to recognize that an early desire is a lifelong one. Maybe she knew and felt what French author Anaïs Nin said so well: "The dream was always running ahead of me. To catch up, to live for a moment in unison with it, that was the miracle."[7]

I'm reminded of a friend who always wanted to be a lawyer. Waylaid by family obligations and parental messages not to aspire to such a grand career, she worked for years as a secretary in a law firm. Finally, after her children were grown, when she was 48, she said, "I'd had it. When I told people I was applying to law school, everyone said, 'You'll be so old when you finish!'"

With a twinkle in her eye, she told them back, "I'll be that age anyway!'" My friend got her law degree at 52 and now runs her own successful firm, specializing in family law.

When you're tempted to procrastinate yet again, think of this retort. Imagine how you'll feel later, when you are "that age," or more dramatically, like Pogrebin imagined, on your deathbed. What will you regret? What will you wish you'd done?

What will it take to take the first step? We saw action steps earlier. Fifteen minutes to make a call for hours of the dance class? A half-hour discussion with your mate to arrange babysitting? An hour on the Internet?

Each moment you have a choice—as Deepak Chopra says, we are "infinite choice-makers."[8] The well-known AA motto "One day at a time" can be adapted: One moment at a time. You have the choice to do it now, to recognize that what you choose now automatically replaces other, surely more comfortable options. If you're really committed to your Dream, you'll use that hour at night for Internet research on sculpting workshops instead of yet another rerun of *Little House on the Prairie*.

Acting in Time

As you get fired up about acting and taking a succession of real steps toward your Dream, yet another negative may almost automatically crop up. You think of everything you absolutely must do every day, in addition to your Dream-steps, and you scream: *But I don't have time!*

An article in a writers' magazine offers an excellent remedy for this negative mantra. Robert Busha suggests we reframe the dailies that plague us, the things we must all do over and over, the things we've just completed (laundry, dishes, shopping, teeth-brushing) and here they are again.

First, Busha points out that if we put them off until the last minute, of course they don't go away. They nag and sap our energy while we're trying to do other things. You certainly don't want this kind of intrusion when you've broken through what may be a lifelong block and are finally taking the first step toward your Dream.

In an innovative battle plan, Busha suggests what he calls "weekly anchors." List all your must to-dos—grocery shopping, cleaning the house, getting gas, the ubiquitous laundry. "Deal with them up front and in a regular way…. Write them on a spot of their own on your calendar." Why is this such a good plan? "They can solidly *anchor* your work, with all the other activities of your week flowing around them."[9]

By listing, planning and sticking to your plan, you'll gain many benefits: you won't have the necessaries hanging over your head. You won't waste valuable mental or physical energy worrying about them, resisting them, or lamenting how you'll ever fit them in. You'll know they're scheduled in good places and times. With this anchor, you can plan when and how to start the actions that will take you toward your Dream, letting them, as Busha says, flow around your regular demands.

He also points out another major advantage to such a plan: You can use your routine chore time to think about your Dream. Stocking groceries is a great time to do affirmations. Cleaning your place is perfect for visualizing your perfect work space. Folding laundry is great for working out your next step of action.

Everything Cooperates

When you truly, unequivocally decide to act, a funny thing happens: *Everything cooperates.* You find sales at the supermarket. The cleaning goes faster; there's less gunk. You get coupons at the dry cleaner. A schedule of classes for that dance academy arrives in the mail. A neighbor offers you a slightly-used 12-CD course in classical Sumerian so you can follow your bliss: to study and lecture on the ancient archaeological finds.

Cameron notices that when we make a commitment to doing something, the means begin to show up: "Leap, and the net will appear."[10] What you thought before was impossible becomes a natural event, progression or outcome.

Ponder explains it this way: "As you affirm 'the divine plan,' you begin to draw to yourself the ideas, opportunities, events and people that are meant to be a part of your divine plan."[11]

I have a cherished bookmark with the frequently quoted words of James Dillet Freeman:

> Dare to be what you are meant to be
> and do what you are meant to do,
> and life will provide you the means to do it and be it.[12]

A man told me how he quit his cushy job and finally committed to his longtime love of freelance photography, especially of children. He had some savings, but he often found himself short of grocery funds. As he got established, he found himself invited to dinner almost every night by grateful mothers for photographing their children in the park.

I once read of a woman who sold everything she had to produce her first film. She traveled to the wilds of Wyoming and there met an avid film buff with a 10,000-acre ranch. He was so fired up about her project he handed over his ranch to her, the cast and crew for as long as they wanted it.

Begin!

Despite all the advice in this chapter, and especially the list of "Action Actions," maybe you're still hesitant, overwhelmed, confused, badgered by the naysaying gnats. Afraid? Feel you don't know where or how to begin?

In his classic early 19th-century play *Faust*, Goethe issues this timeless challenge and promise that still speaks directly to us:

Are you in earnest?
Seize this very minute!
What you can do, or dream you can, begin it!
Boldness has genius, power and magic in it.
Only engage, and then the mind grows heated.
BEGIN, and then the work will be completed.[13]

Commit to your Dream, commit to bringing it into your reality. When you do, you'll attract what you need: ideas, the right sequence, material help, money, time, other people's attitudes, stamina, courage, a sense of direction and exhilaration.

What do you need to do to begin? You've gotten clear on the end goal. Next you need to take pointed, definite, sequential actions to reach it.

Start as Small as You Need To

Obviously, if you dream of becoming a college professor and you're currently getting your bachelor's degree, you've got to first earn a master's degree and then a doctorate in your chosen field before you can realize your Dream. If you've been in real estate sales for 10 years and dream of owning your own company, you've already got a lot of experience, so your first step may be to make an appointment with a bank officer for a business loan to get started. A first step toward running an adoption agency might be to visit several in your area and take the director to lunch. To reach your goal of singing, visit a music school and listen in on the chorus rehearsals. For painting full-time, your initial move may be to unearth your oils from the attic. Then you might consider where to set up your studio. If you have no room in your own place, look at the local paper for spaces to rent.

You might barter. Once, when I felt the need to write in a neighborhood place, away from my apartment, I advertised in the local paper offering to type correspondence in exchange for daytime work space. A woman who had a day job but was also getting a home business off the ground answered my ad. She needed letters and envelopes typed, so we struck a great bargain. I used her place in the afternoons for writing, and she left folders of work that I took home to type in the evenings.

One daily small action tells you, "Hey, I'm working toward it!"

Organize Yourself to Act

As you start, make a list of practical needed steps and write out a simple plan. Maybe the earlier model in "Action Actions" works for you. Make your own list and think in sequence, as thoroughly as you can.

You don't have to do everything in sequence, though. Use your self-listening to scan the list daily and see which activity is feasible at a given time. For your dreamed-of catering business, 15 minutes between sales calls could be a good time to scan the paper to see how catering firms are advertising. If you must be home all morning while the furnace gets fixed, that could be a good time to scan the Internet for unusual dessert recipes you could offer in your business and even try out a few.

You can carry out parts of the plan between the daily and weekly ordinaries, or even as part of them. For your catering business, make friends with the catering manager at the local supermarket. You'll pick up a lot of hints and maybe even get a job offer or some referrals.

Do as much as you can comfortably. Other than squeezing in activities between other things, devote an hour, an afternoon, day or week to one or more activities. Visit several catering companies. Travel to another city to interview the best voice teacher.

However much or little you can do, choose one activity every day that contributes *something* toward your ultimate goal. Your list helps you keep track of your progress, see where to go next, recognize the holes in your knowledge, and, most important, feel you are moving in the right direction.

Decide on day-week-month targets for each item on your list. Doing so will give you a sense of structure.

I made nine (!) new commitments to myself for finishing this book. When other things intervened, like client emergencies, in which their goals had to be met so they could finish their degrees within university time limits, or family events that needed attention, I had to put this book aside, sometimes for weeks at a time.

I adjusted my target for finishing—and adjusted it, and adjusted it. It was always there in front of me, and eventually, I met it.

You, too, are in charge of your targets. As a wise business consultant friend says, "No 'What' without a 'When.'"

To help other writers, I wrote an article with over a dozen suggestions for starting, keeping at it, and staying productive.[14] The following steps, adapted from this article, continue to help me, and I trust you, in acting toward realizing your Dream.

12 Steps for Acting

1. Make your work space comfortable. Starting and continuing are hard enough without feeling your work area is out to get you.

   Arrange proper lighting, invest in an ergonomically sensible chair and desk setup, bench, easel or the particular sitting/standing furniture appropriate to your pursuit. You need to be absolutely comfortable working.

2. Make your work space pleasant and nurturing. Think of it as inviting you in.

   Arrange a few things that nourish your eyes and soul—a plant, some polished stones, a model car or plane, pictures of significant others, or framed affirmations (I've got that favorite Wilbur quote taped above my computer screen).

In the background, if it doesn't interfere with your concentration, play music. Classical music soothes me while I work, and I alternate between the lone local classical radio station and CDs.

If you can face a window with a view, do so. Looking out occasionally gives your eyes a welcome break and your brain a noticeable boost. On the other hand, or pane, a view may be distracting. The English novelist Somerset Maugham faced a spectacular London view from his studio but avoided its seduction by facing his desk toward the wall. The choice is yours.

3. Stay neat. Especially if you're chronically haphazard, get as neat as you can. We all fight the battle of the clutter. Set compartmentalized neat-tasks and do one a week—collect all the drafts or sketches in a file, file the rejection letters together, make a list of gallery directors' names and requirements, throw out all the fragments of paper that have multiplied over every surface. It's not artistic or freeing to live in a mess.

A cluttered work area reflects a cluttered mind, and you want to stay clear for your work. When you work in neat surroundings, you'll not only find things quicker, but you'll stop finding excuses to approach your workspace. Instead it will beckon, and you'll love entering it.

4. Decide what project you're working on today. Choose a time for working and put down in your calendar the hours (or minutes) you'll unconditionally devote to your project in the next 12 or 24 hours.

With writers, for example, some can write for an hour a night from 10 to 11, after all household duties are done and the kids are bathed and bedded. Some writers get up religiously before going to work and write from 4 to 6 in the morning (I never had such discipline). Some write only on Saturdays and Sundays, with time out for a pizza with friends.

Whatever your chosen time, decide on it and stick to it. Success and completion come not from how many hours you work but how many you work consistently.

5. Set specific times for project completion by month and day. Do this even if it's a small project. Be realistic; the rest of life, its necessities and necessary respites, can intrude. If, as the days go by, you see there's no way you can make it, change your target and still stay specific. Forgive yourself and keep going.

6. List the tasks involved in completing the project in logical, chronological order. Begin at the beginning, realize that you, like everyone else, can do only one thing at a time. Picture yourself doing one thing after another, and jot down everything that comes to mind. This list takes that earlier one of "Action Actions" to completion. A journalist wrote this list for finishing an article:

   a. Type handwritten notes.

   b. Research background on Internet.

   c. Type rough outline.

   d. Interview Bob, Sandra, Margaret.

   e. Call the guy at Consolidated for an interview.

   f. Type interview notes.

   g. Do rough draft.

   h. Do next draft.

   i. Check all facts.

   j. Send draft to interviewees for approval.

   k. Do final draft

   l. Send to editor!

   This list will not only help organize you but will also show you that the project, contrary to your dismayed assumption, isn't endless and overwhelming. You'll be able to choose one task at a time and focus only on it.

7. Decide, with your list in hand, what you'll work on next. One of the most difficult parts of completing a project is contin-

uing, and we often get waylaid by everything else we can think of to stall. A writing friend, whom I'd always admired for her steady productivity, shared her secret.

She said, "I used to have the worst trouble continuing. Once I got going I was all right, but I'd do anything not to start—you know, clean the house, catch up on newspapers, rearrange the linen closet. Then I read about a great technique: Before ending your current session, decide what you'll do next. Even if it's the smallest thing, like drafting an email, set out what you'll need. Put your notes on top of your desk so they're the first thing you see when you go back to work next time."

Finally I understood her productivity. With this method, she'd eliminated procrastination.

The night before, choose the first and then several more things from your project master list. If you decide to start your research, get out the materials—a list of key words for Internet searching, phone numbers and questions for professionals in your area, or clippings, reports or brochures. Star the first so you see it instantly at your next session. Keep going.

8. Start easy. When you choose a task on your master project list, and despite its chronological logic, start with one that's obvious, easy or short. Some time management gurus advise starting with what's hardest, but I've never found this productive. All I do is sit, gnaw my nails, and agonize, wishing I were someplace else.

Starting easy is warming up. Completing an easy task will give you a great sense of accomplishment, made even sweeter by checking it off your list. At the same time, you'll gain confidence in what you're doing, and you'll start to flow.

A caution: All of us occasionally misjudge what to start with. A novice writer chose to begin with the scene in which his major characters resolve their conflicts. He found himself sitting blankly, getting more anxious as ideas collided in his brain and the idle minutes mounted. If your chosen task is too hard, switch to an easier one. Your fourth-grade teacher isn't holding a ruler to your wrist.

9. Compartmentalize. If the constant sight of all the tasks and piles are giving you heartburn, do what a college freshman English teacher advised me during my first year of teaching: "Take out five term papers and hide the rest under the bed." Translation: arrange your physical environment to reflect your present task. Hide all the stuff you're not using right now in a drawer, file, carton or under a blanket until you need them. Out of sight, out of anxiety attack.

10. Take breaks. It's a well-known fact of learning that attention and focus are greater when you take periodic breaks. If your self-allotted project times are more than fifteen minutes, get to know how long you work best at a time. For some people, a good stint is 45 minutes or an hour. For others, it's two or even three hours. You know you're reaching the limit when you feel headachy, blurry-eyed, mentally fatigued, cranky and slightly depressed.

Take mental breaks: leaf through a magazine, meditate, make a phone call, watch 15 minutes of television (set a loud timer). Take physical breaks: a little cleaning, a short walk, stretching in the living room or walking on the treadmill gathering dust in your bedroom. I have one of those large, air-filled exercise balls and drape myself over it on my back for a few minutes. It's a great tonic for stretching all the computer-cramped shoulder and neck muscles.

A full-time children's book writer friend told me she loves to take cooking breaks. "Cooking is relaxing and creative," she said. "My mind bubbles around with what I'm working on as I keep fixing the dish. I like cooking on all cylinders."

11. Keep your promises to yourself. Whatever your project time for the day, stick to it, whether it's many hours, an hour or

two, or a few minutes. Choose your time and show up. A wise mentor once said, "There are no writing blocks. There are only unkept promises to get to the desk and stay put."

12. Reward yourself. When you finish a task, a section, a day's work, or a whole piece, congratulate and treat yourself. It may be a double brownie fudge cookie, a wallow in a favorite magazine, or a long walk. Or scrub the sink—whatever pleases you. You deserve it.

An often-quoted statement by Napoleon Hill tells us, "A goal is a dream with a deadline."[15] This is why it's so important to set your goal-tasks specifically. *Decide* to be successful at every step. This decision is a prelude to the success and fulfillment you desire and long for. The decision propels your actions, your right actions in the sequence and order that are right for you.

Send Love Ahead

Before you start any action toward your Dream—a call, meeting, class, exam, presentation, creative session, difficult situation—use another visualization technique: Send Love Ahead. I learned this most precious method from a study group in *A Course in Miracles*. Here's how it works.

1. Visualize the event, to the very room, where you'll be working, sitting, talking. If you don't know the details literally, imagine them.

2. Fill the physical space with love. See it shining in light. Picture yourself and each other person involved smiling, extending hands to you, nodding "Yes."

3. Feel the light and peace envelop you and radiate out from you.

4. Gently think about how you want to come out of the situation. When you leave, what do you want to feel? What do you want to have accomplished? What direction do you

want to know you're next going in? If it helps, write down the answers to each of these.

5. If others are involved, see each of them leaving feeling satisfied, fulfilled, happy with the outcome, and ready to take the next action.

6. Repeat these words: "I surrender all to God. I feel only Love here."

I once had to go to a difficult meeting on behalf of a client. Using these principles, beforehand, I made a list of how I wanted to feel afterwards. My adjectives included "peaceful," "strong," "satisfied with the outcome," "understood," "respected," "listened to," "knowing next direction."

On the way home, I looked at my list. To what shouldn't have been my amazement, every one of these feelings had been fulfilled. Besides this, the individuals on the other side had assured me of their complete cooperation to resolve the matter speedily.

As you continue to take the steps in front of you, you may find hills and valleys. That is, your initial enthusiasm and spurt of energy may level off, and you may be tempted to revert or get pulled into the old negatives—"I only took one course and have 42 to go," "What's the use?" "It seems impossible," etc., etc. I like what U.S. space scientist Wernher von Braun observed (he was responsible for inventions that landed our astronauts on the moon): "I have learned to use the word 'impossible' with the greatest caution."[16] And he was only speaking about rocket science!

Take baby steps and reward yourself. Keep your dates with your Inner Self. Believe in the order you placed with the Universe and God's infallible delivery service. Continue to ask, listen and affirm. Here are some fortifying thoughts:

Bolstering Action Affirmations

- God is working in and through me.
- I listen easily and continuously to my inner guidance.
- I exchange impatience for joyous expectation.
- I have what it takes.
- I do what it takes.
- I am what it takes.
- I relax in the certainty of God's promise.
- I have now fulfilled my life dream.

Finally, a wonderful statement from Hay:

> It is a joy and a delight to plant new seeds, for I know these seeds will become my new experiences. I use my affirmative thinking to create exactly what I want.[17]

Go to bed and wake up thinking "Accomplishment! Fulfillment! Success!" If you say nothing else positive to yourself today, repeat these words as often as you can. It's your choice, as it's been your choice in the past not to act. In this present instant, you can make a new choice.

Let these words from *Daily Word* resonate through you: "I choose to be successful and follow divine instruction that leads me to mastery and achievement."[18]

Trust your intuition and inner guidance. Trust your drive and desire. Whatever you haven't done, wished you'd done, and want more than ever to do toward your Dream, just take another step.

You're in control. Every moment is a new opportunity for your success. If you falter momentarily, forgive yourself and get back on the bicycle, or onto the email account.

Keep listening and acting. One day you'll look around, as I did after staring for years at that photograph of the Southwestern living room with the typewriter and computer, and with a gentle shock and heart overflowing, you'll see that you *have* reached your Dream.

CHAPTER 12

Your Dream Is Here:
Start Living It

Now that you've begun to act, it's very important to protect your Dream. Now that you believe it *is* possible, and you can see a glimmer of the final goal, you deserve to have the success of your Dream.

No, it's not too good to be true. Yes, you do deserve it. (Mind those dancing shoes, and feet, of yours.)

In yet another variation of the "If only" habit, people often think, "Oh, if only I were successful. Then, everything would be wonderful!" They get to the edge, cusp, lip, curb of success. What do so many do? They do everything possible to stop short of that final step. They miss the important rehearsals for the play, go to a bachelor party instead of studying for the final exam, get into a fight with the boss who said he'd recommend them for an important promotion, put off sending the requested material for an article, gallery show, and so on.

Once, for an accepted article from a magazine I'd ached to get into since I started writing, I didn't return the signed contract for a whole 12 months! Still can't believe I did, or didn't, do that. The editor, maybe realizing the syndrome or too busy to notice, published the article the following year.

Why all this self-defeating behavior? Usually, without knowing it consciously, they—we—are afraid of success. In Gay

Hendricks' phrase, we've reached our "Upper Limit," the limits of positive feelings or good we can stand.[1]

Success in Our Society

The definitions of success vary with one's culture, upbringing, inclinations and inherent desires. In some societies, success is measured by how many skins, cows, wives or sons one has. In ours, of course, success is wealth, fame, glamour, owning homes, cars, yachts, planes, real jewelry and the fastest computer around that froths your cappuccino and massages your shoulders. Success is being a doctor and having your parents finally approve of you. Success is earning more and having a higher position in the company than your high school rival who beat you to the class presidency. Over a century ago, in a 1906 letter to a friend, William James called it "our national disease."[2] It's still chronic.

Is this really success? Reams have been written about the short-lived satisfactions of our touchstones of success and what happens after we get them. When we don't have them, we console ourselves reading of movie stars' depressions and addictions, billionaires' health problems and broken marriages, idolized athletes' slumps and abusive behaviors.

Yet we still crave these goals and possessions as the ultimate success. These prizes aren't wrong in themselves. Money—or cars or yachts—is not the root of all evil: "For the love of money is the root of all evil" (1 Tim. 6:10). The operative phrase is *love of* money. Maybe you're saying, "What's so bad about loving money, like you love apple pie, breakfast burritos and *American Idol*?" Well, Paul makes sure to explain to Timothy: "For the love of money is the root of all evil; which while some coveted after, they have erred from the faith" (1 Tim. 6:10).

It was the same over 2,000 years ago as it is now: the inordinate, extreme, radical, unbalanced love of money—or anything else—instead of keeping faith with ourselves and our Source is what brings suffering.

When we err from the faith, as Paul puts it, and value insubstantial things above all else, distort ourselves, and maybe even act dishonestly to get them, we pierce ourselves through with many sorrows. We may rationalize that we're doing the right thing, or the only thing under the circumstances, but inside we know we're doing the wrong things and not being true to our Selves.

Success and Fame

After reaching the sought-after thing, as so many attest, too often the recipients feel a huge letdown, a disappointment, a punctured balloon. Attaining the goal may give us joy, satisfaction, fulfillment, gratification, deep pleasure. That's fine. Realize, though, it's only for a while. Maybe that's why it's also said that the most dangerous time is when you reach a cherished goal.

The famous must still wake up the next day after winning the Oscar, Super Bowl, beauty pageant, book contract, Pulitzer, tenured appointment, painting commission, Nobel, National Endowment for the Arts grant, bake-off, or salesperson of the month. They, too, must still wash, shave, and, most important of all, face the next script, camera, empty stadium, mirror, page, classroom, canvas, laboratory, music score, mixing bowls, order blank.

Anne Lamott is wise about the difference between fame and success in her profession, publishing and writing: "[P]ublication is not all it that it is cracked up to be. But writing is ... the actual act of writing ... turns out to be the best part."[3]

Success as fame doesn't stay. If we're looking for a specific *event* to fill us full, we'll inevitably be let down, as Lamott implies. Cameron points out the addictive quality of fame: "When fame is sought for itself, we always will want more, more and more."[4] One remedy is, as she suggests, to make something for someone else, not to be somebody. This is an aspect of the larger remedy: to create another goal by which you measure success.

Another truism you've probably heard applies here. "Success is not a destination but a journey." True, but I never liked this statement because it implies that you shouldn't have goals. What's called for is a fine balance between enjoying the trip, yes, and also creating successive goals that empower and propel you.

What *Is* Success?

Success can be a good day's work, whatever your field. Some mothers see success as raising their children without drugs and delinquency. Other mothers think of it as seeing their children married to stable, good-earning spouses. Success to other people is building a business, building a barn, building a long-term relationship. Sometimes success is landing a decent job and having enough left over to buy pizza and beer on weekends. Sometimes success is not taking a drink for yet one more day.

More takes: Henry Ford pronounces, "The whole secret of a successful life is to find out what it is one's destiny to do, and then do it."[5] In *Walden*, Thoreau sees success in other daily terms: "If the days and the nights are such that you greet them with joy, and life emits a fragrance like flowers and sweet-scented herbs, is more elastic, more starry, more immortal—that is your success."[6] The great psychologist Abraham Maslow recognizes that "a first-rate soup is more creative than a second-rate painting."[7] *Daily Word* suggests we bring joy to whatever we're doing, "whether we are placing flowers in a vase or actually creating a vase on a potter's wheel."[8] Marianne Williamson says, "Success means we go to sleep at night knowing that our talents and abilities were used in a way that served others."[9]

Business writer and journalist Srully Blotnick wrote of a 20-year study of men who became millionaires. Among them were automobile magnates, industrialists, publishers, real estate developers and creative artists. The single thing they all had in common was *not* an overriding desire to make money or gain international reputation, but an overriding love of and determination to do what they loved doing.[10] They practiced the principle embodied in the title of a current classic for reaching one's dreams, Marsha Sinetar's *Do What You Love: The Money Will Follow.*[11]

Writer, poet, journalist and English professor Donald M. Murray confessed that he "lusted after recognition." He continued, "Still, having sipped that wine, I know the most satisfying part of writing is the making meaning when I am alone at my desk with language."[12] Richard Carlson, author of *Don't Sweat the Small Stuff ... and It's All Small Stuff* (there's a lesson!), suggests redefining a "meaningful accomplishment ... the true measure of our success comes not from what we do, but from who we are and how much love we have in our hearts."[13]

I believe, with these wise authors, that success is the realization and actualization of our life purpose, identifying and doing what we love to do, following our bliss. The more we do what we love, the more we'll enrich the quality of our lives, and the less we'll envy others' perceived successes. Then the more we'll experience our own.

Success, in the end, despite the world's, society's, or your Aunt Harriett's wanting to see an engagement ring on your finger, is whatever makes you most fulfilled. Success is what *resonates* in you and, unbidden, wells up, singing in your heart: *"Yes! This is it! This is why I was born!"*

Throw out all the old voices of the past that haunt and stick and listen only to your heart, your Inner Guide, and your God-given desires. These alone will point you to what is success for you.

Fear of Success

Sometimes success is too much. It's unknown, frightening, fraught with further and greater expectations of performance. When we decide to be true to our Self, to pursue our passion, Bottorff notices we stir up "every fear, every self-imposed limitation, every self-doubt, every feeling of inadequacy" that we've got.[14]

This new feeling may be new territory, a scary bend in the road, our self-defined quota of positive feelings we can handle—successful conclusions, good events, great outworkings.[15] How often have we done or gotten what we really want? It's much more comfortable to stick with our complaints, frustrations, grousings and muted life. We torpedo all our good work and effort up to this point. Why? What messages, like tainted baby food, are we feeding ourselves?

An Anti-Success List

- I'm afraid.
- I don't deserve this.
- I'll get punished.
- Robert works harder than I do. He deserves it.
- I'll make a mistake.
- I've got to do it perfectly the first time.
- My friends will hate me.
- My parents will hate me.
- My partner will hate me ... and leave.
- They'll all find out I'm a fraud.

- I can't stand it.
- It won't last.

To unarm this gang of negatives, here's a potent reminder: Your Dream is from God. Your Dream is implanted by God. Your greatest Dream desire is God's desire for you. God is seeking to express through you. Remind yourself of this as much as you need to as you take the steps to making real your Dream.

Patience

On the way, though, certain aspects, phases, outcomes may need time to simmer. Anything worth doing does. Sometimes we lose sight of this necessity. With steady persistence, let God work through you. It is promised: "I am the Lord; in its time I will do this swiftly" (Isa. 60:22). As we put one foot, brushstroke, phone call after another, we will see fruition. Patience is not only waiting interminably, itchily, legs pumping with nervous energy. Patience is "active, joyous expectation … a positive tool that is powered by a deep, abiding faith in God."[16]

All in its right season. The ancient Greek philosopher Epictetus declares, "No great thing is created suddenly. If you tell me that you desire a fig, I answer you that there must be time. Let it first blossom, then bear fruit, then ripen."[17]

Ah, patience! When I was a neophyte writer, I would fume at the rejections of the prevailing editorial powers. "Why," I raged internally, "don't they accept my work? I've got a lot of important things to say! I'm a great writer!"

They had a very good reason for rejecting the work. I hadn't honed my craft enough so it was polished and professional. It took many years before acceptances began to come in, only after I'd taken the necessary steps, kept at it consistently, and grew into deserving the success of publishing.

Not only did I have to practice the art and craft of writing but I also had to grow internally. It wasn't easy and I'm sure it's not easy for you. Moses, after a long married life as a father and shepherd, was called when he was an old man to lead the Israelites from Egyptian enslavement to freedom. He lacked confidence, was afraid to speak in front of people, had a speech defect, and kept reminding God of these shortcomings (Ex. 4:1, 10, 11; Ex. 6:30). After much divine tutelage and tremendous growth (we can bet), only at 80 years old did he lead the Israelites out of Egypt.

Here's a perspective from Ponder about the patience required of the very father of Israel:

> Abraham waited 25 years for the birth of his son Isaac. During that time he realized that God's delays were not denials and that, as promised, God would fulfill in His own time and way. Meanwhile, Abraham had to cleanse his thinking of fear, doubt and bitterness and grow into answered prayer. The birth of Isaac was that answer.[18]

Abraham had to clear out his negatives—his doubts, angers, resentments and feelings of nondeserving. So do we. In the example of my writing, I had to do more than apply pen constantly to paper. I had to let go of my resentment that the publishing powers I deified didn't instantly recognize the great child prodigy (or so my mother told me), and I had to grow up to deserving success, of which I was mightily afraid.

So have patience with yourself, like a tender, small child. Know that a divine plan is at work in your life, whose fullness you cannot possibly see. A sincerely spiritual but wiseguy friend reminds me of the biblical promise, "Every valley shall be exalted" (Isa. 40:4), and he adds with a chuckle, "and every stray sock shall be found."

Just keep doing what's in front of you to do, with diligence and faith. *A Course in Miracles* tells us, and the thought has been repeated by Wayne Dyer and other New Thought writers, that "only infinite patience produces immediate effects."[19]

Enlarging Yourself to Success

We usually ask too little, of ourselves and the Universe. It's superabundant. It was created for us. We're part of it. It's God's good pleasure to give us the kingdom. As Dyer says, if we feel we "are important enough to ask and divine enough to receive," we will receive.[20] Claim all you should have. The Consciousness Abraham directs us with abandon: "Be the spiritual you and create like a physical fiend." [21]

Louise Hay likens the universe to the ocean. Look out at the abundance available to you. If you want some water from it, what kind of container are you holding? "Is it a teaspoon, a thimble with a hole in it, a paper cup, a glass, a tumbler, a pitcher, a bucket, a wash tub, or ... a pipeline?"[22] Whatever you're holding—whatever your consciousness—you can't possibly drain the ocean dry. There's plenty for everyone. Let's practice with Hay's powerful meditation.

Practicing Abundance

Preferably outside, stand up and open your arms wide, palms up, on each side. Say: *I am open and receptive to all the good and abundance in the Universe.*[23]

Do you find it hard to open your arms fully? How much are you willing to receive? The law is this: The Universe can only give us what our consciousness allows: "For unto every one that hath shall be given" (Mt. 25:29). As *A Course in Miracles* says, "We look on what we feel within."[24] That is, again, the outer reflects the inner. Expand your thoughts, increase your ability to create and receive, and the Universe will oblige. The Universe, in fact, will *rush in* to obey your thoughts and images: Open wide your mouth and I will fill it (Ps. 81:10).

If you find it difficult to open your arms, if you feel foolish, if your arms feel stiff, hurt, or any of a hundred other things you call reasons, you're not as ready to receive as you'd like to be. You don't have to accept this limitation.

What's the remedy? *Practice.* Train yourself to a new habit, a habit of greater deserving, greater room, greater space for good. Today, open your arms an inch or two. Then tomorrow, you can try four or five inches. Soon you'll be opening your arms wide and easily, and loving it.

Anxious About Expansion?

When I first started to do this exercise, I got jumpy, anxious, hungry. I wanted to run to the refrigerator and eat blackberry jam with a tablespoon right out of the jar. I was unaccustomed to the expansion, the wonderful feeling that swept over me. How could I stand this feeling? It was strange, uncomfortable and somehow threatening.

I've experienced similar feelings in writing. Writing, so the cliché goes, is supposed to be difficult, hard, torturous. Many writers have suffered from alcoholism, drug addiction and mental illness. The myth is that only through such means can you write decently, much less greatly. It shouldn't be surprising that we feel something is radically wrong when we feel *good*.

Other writers have described similar feelings. One said it's "a crazy, exhilarating anxiety." Another said, "It makes me shake all over. I feel a terrible joy." A third confessed, "When I'm stuck, it's familiar. Sure I get depressed, and I can handle that. But when the writing's flowing, I get nervous, itchy, elated, giggly and panicky, all at once."

Consciously or not, many of us live convinced we must always struggle. We're victims of life, destiny, God. If, contradicting these deep-rooted beliefs, things start to flow, how indeed *can* we stand it?

If your energy level is higher than usual, and you're not accustomed to it, try some of the things my writer friends used. Walk up and down, jump in place, swing your arms (a good thing for opening them wider), dance a little, scrub a counter or a tub. Such actions will discharge some of that unfamiliar energy and help you tolerate it. Eventually, you'll be able to accept more and more. One day, when you feel sad, depressed or in the dumps, *this* will be the strange feeling.

Mysterious Ways

When you open yourself to greater abundance and fulfillment of your Dream, all kinds of things start to happen, expected and unexpected, logical and serendipitous. An ad for the right-priced kiln you need for your budding pottery business catches your eye. You start talking to the person in front of you on the bank line who offers a lead to a promising business contact. You turn the TV on at noon, something you never do, and see the perfect pastry set for your fledgling catering business at half off the store prices.

As you get back to your painting with the Dream of opening your own show, you see a small notice of an art collector and entrepreneur halfway across the globe coming to the United States and opening a gallery—in your city—for new, promising artists.

If you'd known about this gallery when the collector was setting it up, you'd have probably gone into a self-flagellating panic. You'd berate yourself about how much you've stalled, that you've missed yet another opportunity, and that life is indeed passing you by. Following your plan, you will have cleared out the spare room, set up your studio, and be painting on a regular schedule. You'll have even completed several paintings of which you're moderately proud. Everything cooperates.

Accept all the gifts the Universe gives you. You don't always need to know how or why, much as we always want to. Don't be like the man lost in the woods who prayed for deliverance. Toward nightfall, a hunter discovered him. The man cursed. "I asked God for deliverance, and all He did was send me a hunter."

Accept the gifts. Say, "Thank you, thank you, thank you." Then expect more.

Success thinking is a habit. It's almost as simple as replacing your old self-perpetuating messages with new, more nurturing ones. Start with some new messages.

Success Affirmations

- I finish what I start.
- I have the self-discipline to keep acting toward success.
- I keep acting to reach success.
- Nothing can keep my good from me.
- God is with me.
- God is working in and through me for my perfect outcomes.
- I choose to be successful and follow divine instruction that leads me to mastery and achievement.[25]
- I can do it as I believe I can.[26]
- I trust God to provide me the guidance, opportunities, information and energy I require to carry out my dreams at every step.[27]
- This is a time of divine fulfillment.[28]
- I let go and trust now in the divine fulfillment of my life.
- I control my life by yielding to God's Voice.
- I succeed by surrendering to God's Voice.

- I can stand success.
- I can stand the joy and change that comes with success.
- I am now a fulfilled, productive, creative successful
  _____! (Fill in the blank.)

With such soaring thoughts, it's essential to keep yourself mentally on the right track. You can do so by consciously acknowledging and accepting all your successes along the way. No, they're not too good to be true. They're meant to be true. Here are several ways to practice.

Four Exercises to Guarantee Your Success

1. At the end of each day, review your activities and list your successes, from the mundane to the sublime. Sometimes stocking in the groceries is a success. One client, who had a nine-to-five job and whose goal was to establish her own party planning business from home, made this list at the end of the evening: Finished the laundry, made three cold calls to prospects, wrote to two companies about their products, kept on my diet (except for a really small hot fudge sundae), did two miles around the park.

2. Forgive your self-perceived failures. My client had to forgive herself for the sundae (which she loved), for not making four calls, and for watching a TV game show when she felt she could have been making that fourth call.

3. Replay how you'd do it better. As you know by now, our minds don't know the difference between our imagined thoughts and feelings and our physical ones. Go back to the beginning of the day. Rerun what you'd do first, second, third, instead of what you did. Rehearse your will power—say no to the sundae and take an apple instead, stick on the phone for one or two more calls. Then watch TV.

4. Acknowledge yourself. You've identified your mistakes and taken corrective measures, so congratulate yourself for what

253

you *did* do. Each thought, each activity, each addition to a list, each new idea is a step toward your dream.

Accept your progress, recognize it, embrace it. At the risk of redundancy, I declare again that you deserve it.

Endless Bloomin' Success

When I was typing, impatient and frustrated at not moving fast enough, I saw only an unbridgeable gap between where I was then and where I craved to be. The psychic I consulted at that time advised me to accept where I was and love it. The more I loved it, she promised, the more my life would spill over and propel me closer to what I really wanted to do. (In different words, a recent business article advocated the same: "Loving Your Day Job and Your Life" by journalist and professor of religious studies Laura Rowley.[29])

The psychic was suggesting I follow that beautiful axiom, "Bloom where you are planted." Part of the divine plan for our success is to make the absolute best of where we are at a given moment, to approach it positively, give it our all. We have much to learn, as Martha Smock points out in the poem quoted earlier, from the "devious" ways and apparent "wastelands of our life" that we may not fathom for a long time.[30]

As we let go of self-pity, resentment and rage at our present situation, accept it, even love it, and listen inside for guidance, ideas will come. All it takes is trust. When I'm feeling anxious, unsure, unready and don't want to dress for action, I often repeat this prayer from *A Course in* Miracles:

> In You is every choice already made.
> In You has every conflict been resolved.
> In You is Everything I hope to find already given me.
> Your peace is mine.[31]

Quieting our minds and reassuring ourselves, we'll take more steps in the right direction and keep blooming. Bottorff advises, "Bloom where you are planted, yes. But the real key to successful living is to work toward planting yourself where you will bloom biggest and best."[32]

This is important: our God-given, Source-connected creative capacities are endless and exciting. Look at all creativity in Nature—the strains of flowers, species of animals, classes of bugs, shapes of clouds. Look at all the creativity humans express and explode with in music, art, literature, dance, sculpture, architecture, science, design, cooking. The variations are as endless as each individual. If you succumb for an instant to that cry, "I'll never make it!" remember the multitude of rock and cooking stars and repeat after me: There's always room for someone good.

The talents and abilities that flow through you, as Hay says, are unique; they speak to others who are always looking for them.[33] As you listen to your Self, hear the guidance, and carry out the directions with your all, you cannot help but arrive at where you will bloom biggest and best.

When we do this, our blooming cannot help but reflect back on ourselves. It's a law: as we give we receive. This is why withholding ourselves from pursuing our Dream shrinks us and gives us less. The more you invest—develop and use—your talents, the more you'll get in return. What do you do?

Chop Wood, Carry Water

Huh? My house is all electric, and I've had indoor plumbing for three years.

This is a Zen saying, well known in New Age circles, from a poem written more than a thousand years ago by a Chinese Zen master:

Magical power,
Marvelous action!
Chopping wood,
Carrying water.... [34]

As with all New Age philosophy, the meaning of this poem is ancient and timeless. It means that the spiritual and the daily physical material are inextricably intertwined. In doing our "dailies," which are both the necessities and the inspired actions, we find our spiritual truths and our Selves.

Let me tell you about an experience of illumination. It didn't take place in a grand cathedral, by a majestic waterfall, at the feet of an enlightened master, or in the ninth angelic sphere. It was in my kitchen while I was making salad.[35]

Chopping Salad: A Moment

Fixing the salad for any day's dinner, turning from counter to sink, my Time stopped for a moment.

Something, in bare recognition, broke into my day-babbling thoughts. Squinting, I knew it, long hidden but there, like old baby pictures in the back of a drawer.

It spoke as I heard a strong, subtle thread still connected from then to right now: Who would have thought I'd be here, in this time and this place and this life? Who would have known or predicted or seen that I'd reach here and now in this way?

Just for a moment, I saw through this life and making the salad. For a small, fragile moment, something much older broke through the unquestioned surface that makes up this life. I could glimpse, for a moment, like the barely discernible trail of a fawn through the woods, the way traveled.

In this same moment Time shattered, its meaning dissolving in slivers around. I saw in this moment what sharp, cutting edges we make of our lives, the damage we breed by our lauding and cursing, the illness we spread by our grading of status or mud.

Clearer than glass, I saw through what is meant by this time and this life. Slicing tomatoes or signing laws, wrapping garbage or writing books—the threads are all different; the moment is one and the whole.

In this same moment, I was freed of my bindings of judgments and envies, freed of my waste box of striving and hope, and breathing a peace unfamiliar.

I was there, back behind, opening the cupboard for oil for the salad, taking the bottle, loosening the cap. I was watching my self in the reflex of movements, unwinding my thread.

I found, in surprise, that the I who was watching was smiling—a parent, in fondness and awe.

I saw, in this moment, that the steps must be taken in the child's own time. To rush does not hasten the learning. To force does not quicken the pace.

In this same moment, in flitting half-shadows, I tasted a sadness, deeper than dreams born in childhood, older than age. I glimpsed for an instant the length of my thread winding down through the times, and the seemingly endlessly tangled long pathway ahead.

Then I sighed, back behind, washing the lettuce, tearing the greens. I stared at the bowl, with its plans and impatience, its joys and its terrors, its visions and dark disappointments. I sighed at the yearnings and pain of the thread.

Something compelled me to look way beyond, and my sigh in that moment breathed "Ah," like the fawn coming out of the woods to a field.

And in that same moment, I saw how we loosen our knots by doing the movements before us. Doing our movements, more and more open, trusting our nature, our thread leads us out, like the fawn from the woods, into light.

It's Time once again. I look at my salad, and the long, golden Voice echoes sure:

Who would have thought I'd be here, in this time, and this place, and this life?

Do what's in front of you to do. Do it with awareness and love. All activity is a part of the path, and we're here to learn how to chop our wood and carry our water. That is, to chop our woulds into will, the Will, and to carry the waters of our talents and desires to others.

We all thirst. We all end up at the well, craving to drink the water of life.

We are all the Samaritan (read: enemy) woman at the well, offering our water to the Christ within each other (Jn. 4:6-14). This is the water that makes us no longer thirst.

You don't have to try for a big splash, a torrent of awakening, or an ocean of accomplishment. Chop your wood for the warmth of love it will bring others—and thereby yourself—and carry your water to the parched souls you'll meet who look out at you from behind hollow eyes.

The Circle of Blessing

As you most earnestly chop your wood and carry your water, your fire will warm all in your circle and your water will cleanse and nourish the arid ground our souls so often walk on. This is the circle of blessing. Phrase it as you wish—you reap what you sow, you get back what you give, you receive what you give. When you invest yourself fully in what's before you right now, you cannot help but gain. In the process, you cannot help but help others gain. Bottorff emphasizes, "Your heartfelt dreams are the intended means you are to use to externalize your true Self. Therefore, you can render no greater service to God, to yourself, or to your world than to be true to your Self and to follow your dreams."[36]

As you do more for yourself, act on your Dream, you'll be better willing and able to do things for others. You'll do them almost automatically, gladly, willingly, voluntarily. Because of the Law of Attraction (you attract what you are, do, feel, believe), people will come into your life who will help you. As you get more used to the truth that there's enough for everyone, and always room for someone good without threat of taking away from anyone else, you'll also realize the relatedness of all things.

> I rejoice in others' successes, knowing there is plenty for us all.[37]
> Into the hands that give, the gift is given.[38]

I've found this principle blessedly true countless times. It has become a great way to relieve those feelings of low self-worth: "if you've got it, I can't get it." An article called "Conquer Jealousy: Wish Other Writers Well" tells how my giving to other writers gave me several wonderful gifts.[39]

When I learned that a writing colleague had signed a contract to publish her historical novel, I fell into one of those shriveling depressions, couldn't write, and wanted to eat everything in sight. Then I recalled the wise words of a preacher: "If you curse the successful, you'll never be one of them. Bless them instead." Abraham echoes this thought:

> Bless those who are finding abundance. And in your blessing of them and their abundance, you will become abundant too. But in your cursing of their abundance, you hold yourself apart from it. It is a ... powerful law.[40]

I took a deep breath and wrote my friend a congratulatory note. At my desk, I also loudly, if somewhat self-consciously, affirmed, "Deborah, I wish you all the success, fame and wealth you want, and more!"

She not only responded thankfully but offered me a personal referral to her agent. Greatest of all, my jealousy evaporated and depression disappeared. I leapt into a manuscript I'd been avoiding for weeks and did splendid battle for several too-short hours.

This is only one example of the circle of blessing. You have undoubtedly experienced many in your life and will experience more as you keep these principles in mind. As we let God's light shine on us, in us, and from us, all things shine in it. As God's light shines on us and in us, so it shines out from us to all. If biting doubts crop up, remind yourself that before you call you are answered. Turn again to God:

> In You is every choice already made.
> In You has every conflict been resolved.
> In You is everything I hope to find already given me.[41]

As you listen to, act on, and honor the guidance of your best Self, you'll flow toward your Dream. As you wisely, lovingly and willingly forgive yourself, reframe your past, and do what is yours to do, you'll be blessed with the fulfillment of your heart's deepest desires.[42] You'll become happier, more open, joyful, energetic and creative. As the circle of blessing is fulfilled through you, you will be a blessing to others.

* * * * * *

When do you trust? Always.
Ever a condition? Never.
Can you depend on God for every answer? Always.

Can you trust God for all things? Always.

God holds you, keeps you, guides you, comforts you, whispers to you, shouts to you, breathes out from you, breathes into you, and walks close at your side every step of your way to your Dream.

I extend my greatest blessings and joy to you as you go on to fulfill your Dream.

Trust God and trust your life. Trust your life and trust God.

Endnotes

Please note: Second and subsequent references are by author's last name and page number only. If two or more publications by an author or authors appear, they are differentiated by short title.

Introduction

1 Quoted in Dan Zadra, *I Believe in You* (Edmond, WA: Compendium, 1999), 60.

2 Deepak Chopra, *The Seven Spiritual Laws of Success: A Practical Guide to the Fulfillment of Your Dreams* (San Rafael, CA: Amber-Allen; Novato, CA: New World Library, 1994), 22.

3 Brendan Gill, *Late Bloomers* (New York: Artisan, 1996).

4 Charles G. Oakes, *Working the Gray Zone: A Call for Proactive Ministry by and With Older Adults* (Franklin, TN: Providence House, 2000).

5 Jacob White, "Boston's Fastest Great-Grandmother," *Running Times Magazine*, April 2009. http://www.runningtimes.com/Print.aspx?articleID=16086.

6 "82-year-old lands first book deal," *Guardian* (UK), June 28, 2010. http://www.guardian.co.uk/uk/2010/jun/28/teacher-82-first-book-deal.

Chapter 1

1 Quoted in Peter McWilliams, *Do It! Let's Get off Our Buts* (Los Angeles: Prelude Press, 1994), 342.

2 Wallace Terry, "He Refuses to Limit Himself," *Parade Magazine (Miami Herald)*, July 21, 1996, 4.

3 Bruce Wilkinson, *The Dream Giver* (Sisters, OR: Multnomah Books, 2003), 14.

4 Martha Smock, "No Other Way," *Fear Not! Messages of Assurance* (Unity Village, MO: Unity Books, ©1986, 1997), 22-29.

5 Hugh Prather, "Rev. Hugh's Homilies: The Ego-Addicted Dream," *The Holy Encounter* (September/October 2004), 13.

6 James Allen, *As a Man Thinketh* (Marina Del Rey, CA: DeVorss, 1988), 13. Originally published 1902.

7 Ken Keyes, *Handbook to Higher Consciousness* (Berkeley, CA: Living Love Center, 1974), 77.

8 *Daily Word,* March 29, 1991: 43.

9 Catherine Ponder, *Pray and Grow Rich* (West Nyack, NY: Parker, 1982), 92.

Chapter 2

1 Barbara M. Newman and Philip R. Newman, *Development Through Life: A Psychosocial Approach* (Belmont, CA: Wadsworth Cengage, 2008), 604.

2 Newman and Newman, 604.

3 Matt Schudel, "Twilight Picasso," *Fort Lauderdale Sun-Sentinel*, January 28, 2001, 3D.

4 Marvin Glassman, "Randall at His Peak," *Boomer Times and Senior Life* 14.7 (2003): 37. Judith Newman, "The Odd Couple," *Marie Claire*, July 2008. http://www.marieclaire.com/sex-love/relationship-issues/articles/tony-randall-wife.

5 Terry, 4.

6 McNeil-Lehrer Report, Interview with Gordon Parks, interviewed on McNeil-Lehrer Report, PBS-TV, January 7, 1998.

7 Elisa Turner, "His Weapon Against Poverty, Racism was a $7.50 Camera," *Miami Herald*, November 7, 1999, 5M, 7M.

8 "Ageless Vitality," *Delicious! Magazine,* May/June 1992, 12.

9 Alison Flood, "Little-known 90-year-old wins $100,000 poetry award," *Guardian* (UK), April 15, 2010. http://www.guardian.co.uk/books/2010/apr/15/90-year-old-100000-poetry-award.

10 Errol Louis, "Janet Wolfe, 95, Keeps NYCHA Orchestra Humming Along," *New York Daily News*, February 3, 2010. http://www.nydailynews.com/opinnions/2010/02/03/2010-02-03.

11 Prill Boyle, "It's Never Too Late to Follow Your Dreams," *Third Age*, May 19, 2010. http://www.thirdage.com/whats-next/its-never-too-late-to-follow-your-dreams. Robin Finn, "Painting at 99, With No Compromises," *New York Times*, October 26, 2010. http://www.nytimes.com/2010/10/27/nyregion/27artist.html?_src=1&ref=robin_finnmv&ref=nyregion.

12 Lee Bergquist, *Second Wind: The Rise of the Ageless Athlete* (Champaign, IL: Human Kinetics, 2009).

13 David Robson, "An Interview With Bodybuilding Legend Ed Corney," *Body Building.com*. http://www.bodybuilding.com/fun/drobson247.htm.

14 Stuart Elliot, "Looking Back Can Help You Plan Your Future," *Evansville Courier and PressRedding Record Searchlight*, January 6, 2007. http://www.redding.com/news/2007/jan/06/looking-back-can-help-you-plan-your-future/.

15 Humberto Cruz and Georgina Cruz, "Life in a Nursing Home: Retiree's Column Opens Eyes," *Fort Lauderdale Sun-Sentinel*, August 8, 2004, 5D.

16 Connie Goldman and Richard Mahler, *Secrets of Becoming a Late Bloomer: Staying Creative, Aware, and Involved in Midlife and Beyond* (Minneapolis, MN: Fairview Press, 2007), xi.

17 Robert Kraus, *Leo the Late Bloomer* (New York: Windmill/HarperCollins, 1998), 20, 26.

18 Gill, Table of Contents, 6-7.

19 Gill, 10-11.

20 Gill, 11.

21 Gill, 11.

22 Kathleen Kernicky, "Still on Track," *Fort Lauderdale Sun-Sentinel*, February 4, 2001, 3E. Dennis McCarthy, "Getting Their Lives on Track After Heart Surgery, Four Men Run Race for Survival," *Los Angeles Daily News*, March 6, 2005. http://www.thefreelibrary.com/GETTING+THEIR+LIVES+ON+TRACK+AFTER+HEART+SURGERY%2c+FOUR+MEN+RUN+RACE+...-a0129927959.

23 Webster Schott, "Children of Sorrow," *New York Times Book Review*, September 30, 1990, 35. "Belva Plain: Author Bio," www.randomhouse.com, http://www.randomhouse.com/features/belvaplain/author.html. Elsa Dixler, "Belva Plain, Novelist of Jewish-American

Life, Dies at 95." *New York Times*, October 17, 2010. http://www.nytimes.com/2010/10/18/books/18plain.html.

24 "Winners and Losers." *Time Magazine* 149.13 (1997): 23. "Milestones," *Time Magazine* 154.19 (1999), 33.

25 Betsy Blaney, "'Red' Rountree: Bank Robber Launched Crime Career at 86," *Boston Globe*, November 23, 2004. http://www.boston.com/news/globe/obituaries/articles/2004/11/23/red_rountree_bank_robber_launchedcrime_ career_at_86/.

26 Jenna Goudreau, "How to Live to Be 101," *Forbes*, June 8, 2010. http://www.forbes.com/2010/06/08/healthy-living-aging-live-to-be-101-forbes-woman-well-being-longevity.html.

27 Caryl Stern, "Who Is Old?" *Parade (Miami Herald)*, January 21, 1996, 4-5.

28 Thomas T. Perls and Margery Hutter Silver, *Living to 100: Lessons in Living to Your Maximum Potential at Any Age* (New York: Perseus Books, 2000). Glenn Plaskin, "Hope, Health, and Happiness: Secrets of the Centenarians," *Family Circle,* September 2, 2003, 97, 98, 100-103.

29 Stern, 5.

30 Noelle Sterne, "David Johnson: Spotlight." *Black and White Magazine* 9.53 (2007): 76-79. Noelle Sterne, "Octogenarian Photographer Extraordinaire," *Apogee Photography Magazine*, December 14, 2009. http://www.apogeephoto.com/dec2009/nsterne122009.shtml.

31 Julia Cameron, *The Artist's Way: Meeting Your Creative Myths and Monsters,* audiotape (Boulder, CO: Sounds True Recordings, 1993).

32 Perls and Silver, xiii.

33 John Milton, *Paradise Lost: An Authoritative Text, Backgrounds and Sources, Criticism* (New York: W. W. Norton, 1993), 393.

34 Milton, *Paradise Lost*, 393, 676-77.

35 Martha Smock, "It Is Never Too Late," *Always in God's Presence: Stories of Answered Prayer* (Unity Village, MO: Silent Unity, 2003), 5-7.

36 Robert H. Schuller, *Hour of Power*, August 31, 2003.

37 Marianne Williamson, *The Age of Miracles: Embracing the New Midlife* (Carlsbad, CA: Hay House, 2008), x. For those unfamiliar with *A Course in Miracles,* Williamson describes it this way: "The *Course* is a self-study program of spiritual psychotherapy contained in three books. It is not a religion, but rather, a psychological mind-training

based on universal spiritual themes. The practical goal of the *Course* is the attainment of inner peace through the practice of forgiveness" (xx).

38 Deepak Chopra, *Ageless Body, Timeless Mind* (New York: Harmony, 1993), 7.

39 Smock, "It Is Never Too Late," 7.

40 Smock, "It Is Never Too Late," 7.

41 Eckhart Tolle, *The Power of Now: A Guide to Spiritual Enlightenment* (Novato, CA: New World Library; Vancouver, Canada: Namaste Publishing, 2004), 3.

42 Robert H. Schuller, *Putting Your Faith Into Action Today!* (Garden Grove, CA: Crystal Cathedral Ministries, 1993), 51.

43 McWilliams, 411.

44 *Daily Word*, October 5, 2000: 19.

45 *A Course in Miracles (ACIM). Volume Two: Workbook for Students* (Farmingdale, NY: Foundation for Inner Peace, 1975), 65.

Chapter 3

1 Herbert Benson, *The Relaxation Response* (New York: Avon, 1975). Ram Dass, *Be Here Now* (Albuquerque, NM: Lama Foundation, 1971).

2 Marianne Williamson, "Meditation," *O, The Oprah Magazine,* October 2000, 119.

3 Elizabeth Gilbert, *Eat, Pray, Love: One Woman's Search for Everything Across Italy, India and Indonesia* (New York: Penguin Books, 2006).

4 Ponder, 100.

5 Louise L. Hay, *You Can Heal Your Life* (Carson, CA: Hay House, 1987).

6 Diane Benson Harrington, "Pray Away Stress: A Soothing Strategy," *Family Circle,* January 20, 2004, 30, 32-33.

7 Marianne Williamson, *Illuminata* (New York: Berkeley Books, 1994). Thomas Moore, *Care of the Soul* (New York: HarperCollins, 1993).

8 *ACIM, Workbook,* 411.

9 Stephan Bodian, *Meditation for Dummies.* 2nd ed. (Hoboken, NJ: John Wiley, 2006).

10 James Dillet Freeman, "A Drill in the Silence," *Silence: Your Key to the Secret Place* (Unity Village, MO: Unity School of Christianity, 1992), 30.

11 *ACIM, Workbook,* 220.

12 Emmet Fox, *The Golden Key* (Marina Del Rey, CA: DeVorss, 1959), 2.

13 Richard Wilbur, "Walking to Sleep," *Walking to Sleep: New Poems and Translations* (New York: Harcourt Brace & Jovanovich World, 1969), 1, lines 3-4.

14 *ACIM, Workbook,* 455.

15 Barbara Graham, "Tune into Yourself," *O, The Oprah Magazine,* October 2000, 96. See also her *Women Who Run With the Poodles: Myths and Tips for Honoring Your Mood Swings* (New York: Avon, 1994).

16 Maura Lynch, "The-Brain-Stomach-Connection," *Elle,* May 18, 2010. http://www.elle.com/Beauty/Health-Fitness/Emotional-Eating-The-Brain-Stomach-Connection.

17 Martha Beck, "4 Games to Play Before Saying Okay," *Redbook,* November 2000, 32.

18 Martha Beck, "Keeping Your Center," *RealSimple,* October 2000, 145.

19 Graham, "Tune into Yourself," 96.

20 Esther M. Sternberg and Philip Gold, "The Mind-Body Interaction in Disease," *Scientific American* 7.1 (1997): 8-15. http://www.mmu.k12. vt.us/teachers/kefferm/humanbio/nervous/articles/1997%20mind body%20interaction%20disease.pdf. Esther M. Sternberg, *The Balance Within: The Science Connecting Health and Emotions* (New York: W. H. Freeman, 2001). Esther M. Sternberg, *Healing Spaces: The Science of Place and Well-Being* (Cambridge, MA: Belknap/Harvard University Press, 2009).

21 Herbert Benson, *Timeless Healing: The Power and Biology of Belief* (New York: Simon and Schuster, 1997). Larry Dossey, *Healing Words: The Power of Prayer and the Practice of Medicine* (New York: HarperCollins, 1997). Bernie S. Siegel, *Meditations for Enhancing Your Immune System,* audio CD (Carlsbad, CA: Hay House, 1998). Bernie S. Siegel, *365 Prescriptions for the Soul: Daily Messages of Inspiration, Hope, and Love* (Novato, CA: New World Library, 2009). O. Carl Simonton, Stephanie Matthews-Simonton, and James L. Creighton, *Getting Well Again* (New York: Bantam, 1992). Andrew Weil, *Spontaneous Healing* (New York: Fawcett Columbine, 1995).

22 Hay, *You Can Heal Your Life,* 184.

23 Hay, *You Can Heal Your Life,* 184.

24 Gilbert, 53.

25 Ellen Debenport, "How to Recognize God's Voice," *Survival Guide for the Soul* (Unity Village, MO: Unity, 2009), 18. See also her *The Five Principles: A Guide to Practical Spirituality* (Unity Village, MO: Unity House, 2009).

Chapter 4

1 Hay, *You Can Heal Your Life*, 130, 186.

2 Simonton, Matthews-Simonton, and Creighton, 56-72.

3 Louise L. Hay, *The Power Is Within You* (Carson, CA: Hay House, 1991), 117-28.

4 Eva Bell Werber, *The Journey With the Master* (Marina del Rey, CA: DeVorss, 1950), 66-67.

5 Neale Donald Walsch, *Conversations with God: An Uncommon Dialogue: Book 1* (New York: G. P. Putnam, 1996), 210.

6 Esther Hicks and Jerry Hicks, passage excerpted from the workshop in San Antonio, TX, No. 280, April 21, 2001.

7 Cheryl Richardson, *Stand Up for Your Life* (Carlsbad, CA: Hay House, 2010).

8 Wendy Kaufman, "Real Nurturing," *Miracle Journeys* 5.1 (2001): 24-26.

9 Julia Cameron, *The Artist's Way: A Spiritual Path to Higher Creativity* (New York: Tarcher/Putnam, 1992), 18.

10 Cameron, *The Artist's Way: A Spiritual Path*, 19, 20.

11 Tama Kieves, "You''ll Find Your Real Career, When You Discover Your Real Self," *Tama Kieves' Trusting the Journey Times*, May 3, 2010.

12 *Spiritual Preparation for Easter 2000* (Unity Village, MO: Silent Unity), 45. These annuals are marvelously powerful.

13 Noelle Sterne, "The Voice," *Miracle News* 1 (1978): 2. Republished in *11.11 Magazine* 3.5 (September/October 2010), 40-41.

14 *ACIM, Workbook*, 389.

Chapter 5

1 Cameron, *The Artist's Way: A Spiritual Path*, 25.

2 Cameron, *The Artist's Way: A Spiritual Path*, 27.

3 Cybil Wolin and Steven Wolin, "Reframing," *Project Resilience.com.* http://projectresilience.com/framesconcepts.htm, p. 1.

4 "The Most Successful College Dropouts in History," *Retireat21,* February 10, 2009. http://www.retireat21.com/blog/the-most-successful-college-dropouts-in-history. "Success Without a College Degree." *RateItAll,* September 15, 2005. http://www.rateitall.com/t-20542-success-without-a-college-degree.aspx. "10 Famous People Who Didn't Go to College." *Financial Planning,* 2008. http://learn financialplanning.com/famous-people-who-didnt-go-to-college/.

5 Wolin and Wolin, 2.

6 Esther Hicks and Jerry Hicks, *Money and the Law of Attraction: Learning to Attract Health, Wealth and Happiness* (Carlsbad, CA: Hay House, 2008), 72.

7 Wayne W. Dyer, *10 Secrets for Success and Inner Peace* (Carlsbad, CA: Hay House, 2001), 74.

8 Stephen R. Covey, *Principle-Centered Leadership* (New York: Summit Books, 1991), 67.

9 Sharon Boone, "Turn Your Flaws into Advantages," *Mind Body & Spirit Fitness,* October 2003, 86-90.

10 Bruce A. Pasternack and James O'Toole, "Yellow-Light Leadership: How the World's Best Companies Manage Uncertainty," *Strategy + Business* 27, Second Quarter (2002): 81.

11 Joan Borysenko, *Minding the Body, Mending the Mind* (New York: Bantam, 1988), 137.

12 Quoted in Thomas Campbell, *My Big TOE: A Trilogy Unifying Philosophy, Physics, and Metaphysics: Awakening, Discovery, Inner Workings* (Huntsville, AL: Lightning Strike Books, 2007), 779, www.LightningStrikeBooks.com.

13 Allen, 19, 21.

14 Rhonda Byrne, *The Secret* (New York: Atria, 2006). Diane Alquist, *The Complete Idiot's Guide to The Law of Attraction* (New York: Alpha Books/Penguin, 2008).

15 Wayne W. Dyer, *The Power of Intention: Learning to Co-create Your World Your Way* (Carlsbad, CA: Hay House, 2004). See pp. 66, 67, 77, 91.

16 Quoted in Mike Brown, "The Human Heart: The Key to Everything," interview with Gregg Braden, *11.11 Magazine* 2.6 (November/December 2009): 13.

17 Gay Hendricks, *The Big Leap: Conquer Your Hidden Fear and Take Life to the Next Level* (New York: HarperOne, 2010).

18 Dyer, *The Power of Intention*, 173.

19 *ACIM, Workbook*, 447.

Chapter 6

1 Tama Kieves, "Reach for Greatness Instead of Familiarity," *Tama Kieves' Trusting the Journey Times*, September 8, 2010.

2 Hicks and Hicks, *Money and the Law of Attraction*, 105. See also Esther Hicks and Jerry Hicks, *Ask and It Is Given: Learning to Manifest Your Desires* (Carlsbad, CA: Hay House, 2004), 40-41.

3 Dyer, *10 Secrets*, 80, 88.

4 Noelle Sterne, "Trust Your Life," *Miracle Journeys* 5.6 (2001): 22. Noelle Sterne, "Trust Your Life," *Natural Awakenings*, November 2003, 32-33.

5 Although my Voice helped me arrive at this conclusion, Anne Lamott gives similar advice in *Bird by Bird: Some Instructions on Writing and Life* (New York: Anchor Books, 1995). With her title as metaphor, she directs, "That is all we are going to do for now. We are going to take this bird by bird ... we are going to finish this one short assignment" (20).

6 Dyer, *10 Secrets*, 80.

7 *Spiritual Preparation for Easter 1990* (Unity Village, MO: Silent Unity, 1990), 15.

8 *ACIM, Workbook*, 50.

Chapter 7

1 Gerald G. Jampolsky, *Goodbye to Guilt* (New York: Bantam, 1985), 149.

2 Hay, *The Power Is Within You*, 53.

3 Dyer, *10 Secrets*, 71.

4 Hay, *You Can Heal Your Life*, 150, 153, 158, 164, 167.

5 Eric Butterworth, *Discover the Power Within You* (New York: Harper and Row, 1968), 149.

6 Jampolsky, *Goodbye to Guilt*, 153.

7 Quoted in Salley Shannon, "Five Steps That Could Change Your Life," *Woman's Day*, February 1, 2004, 61.

8 Fred Luskin, *Forgive for Good: A Proven Prescription for Health and Happiness* (New York: HarperOne, 2003).

9 Jampolsky, *Goodbye to Guilt*, 149.

10 Butterworth, 153.

11 Jampolsky, *Goodbye to Guilt*, 154.

12 Werber, 70-71.

13 Louise L. Hay, *Love Yourself, Heal Your Life Workbook* (Carson, CA: Hay House, 1990), 91.

14 Hay, *You Can Heal Your Life*, 10, 36.

15 Hay, *The Power Is Within You*, 140.

16 Louise L. Hay, *Morning and Evening Meditations*, audiotape (Carlsbad, CA: Hay House, 1983).

17 Michael E. Kerr and Murray Bowen, *Family Evaluation: An Approach Based on Bowen Theory* (New York: W. W. Norton, 1988).

18 Cameron, *The Artist's Way: A Spiritual Path*, 25.

19 Hay, *Love Yourself, Heal Your Life Workbook*, 97.

20 Jampolsky, *Goodbye to Guilt*, v, 83.

21 Jampolsky, *Goodbye to Guilt*, 90.

22 Hay, *Love Yourself, Heal Your Life Workbook*, 97.

Chapter 8

1 *Daily Word*, January 11, 1992: 25; *Daily Word*, December 16, 1994: 30.

2 Hay, *You Can Heal Your Life*, 104.

3 Terry Morrison and Wayne A. Conaway, *Kiss, Bow, or Shake Hands: The Bestselling Guide to Doing Business in More Than 60 Countries* (Avon, MA: Adams Media, 2006).

4 Hay, *You Can Heal Your Life*, 104.

5 Ponder, 62.

6 Esther Hicks and Jerry Hicks, *The Vortex: Where the Law of Attraction Assembles All Cooperative Relationships* (Carlsbad, CA: Hay House, 2009), 78.

7 Esther Hicks and Jerry Hicks, workshop in Philadelphia, PA, No. 470, April 24, 1998.

8 Harry Douglas Smith, *The Secret of Instantaneous Healing* (West Nyack, NY: Parker Publishing, 1965), 53.

9 Smith, 54.

10 Gerald G. Jampolsky, *Love Is Letting Go of Fear* (Berkeley, CA: Celestial Arts, 1979), 93.

11 Schuller, *Hour of Power,* August 31, 2003.

12 *Daily Word,* December 26, 2001: 40.

13 Butterworth, 153.

14 Dyer, *10 Secrets,* 75.

15 Michael Moran, *Heal the Past, Release the Pain: A Meditation on Forgiveness,* audiotape (Unity Village, MO: Unity, 2001).

16 Fox, 9.

17 Hay, *Love Yourself, Heal Your Life Workbook,* 97.

18 *ACIM, Workbook,* 357.

Chapter 9

1 Neal Zaslaw and William Cowdery, eds., *The Compleat Mozart: A Guide to the Musical Works of Wolfgang Amadeus Mozart* (New York: W. W. Norton, 1991). See also Maynard Solomon, *Mozart: A Life* (New York: Harper Perennial, 2005).

2 "Mr. Everything," Schwarzenegger.com. http://www.schwarzen egger.com/en/athlete/mreverything/index.asp?sec=athlete&subsec= mreverything.

3 Dyer, *The Power of Intention,* 151-52.

4 Many spiritual teachers point out these destructive outcomes. See especially Carmen Harra, *The Eleven Eternal Principles: Accessing the Divine Within* (New York: Crossing Press/Crown, 2009).

5 Quoted in Wayne W. Dyer, *The Shift: Taking Your Life From Ambition to Meaning* (Carlsbad, CA: Hay House, 2010), 94.

6 Esther Hicks and Jerry Hicks, workshop in Asheville, NC, No. 330, May 1, 2005.

7 Norman Vincent Peale, *Enthusiasm Makes the Difference* (New York: Ballantine, 1996).

8 Leonard Roy Frank, *Quotationary* (New York: Random House, 2001), 690.

9 Ponder, 103.

10 Esther Hicks and Jerry Hicks, workshop in Larkspur, CA, No. 373, August 16, 1998.

11 J Douglas Bottorff, *A Practical Guide to Prosperous Living* (Unity Village, MO: Unity Books, 1998), 20.

12 Wilkinson, 23, 74, 91.

13 Quoted in *Quotations Book*. http://www.quotationsbook.com/quote/11435/.

14 Cameron, *The Artist's Way: A Spiritual Path*, 87.

15 Frank, 387.

16 Terry Cole-Whittaker, *How to Have More in a Have-Not World* (New York: Fawcett Crest, 1985).

17 Maurice Sendak, *Higglety Pigglety Pop! Or There Must Be More to Life* (New York: HarperCollins, © 1967, 2001), 5.

18 Quoted in Bottorff, 41.

19 *Spiritual Preparation for Easter 2000* (Unity Village, MO: Silent Unity, 2000), 45.

20 The King James version resonates: "For God hath not given us the spirit of fear; but of power, and of love, and of a sound mind" (1 Tim. 1:7).

21 For example, *Christ in You: Spiritual Preparation for Easter, 2002* (Unity Village, MO: Unity, 2002), 24.

22 *ACIM, Workbook*, 107.

23 Esther Hicks and Jerry Hicks, workshop in North Los Angeles, CA, No. 544, March 22, 2003.

Chapter 10

1 Smith, 111.

2 Ponder, 195.

3 Mary L. Kupferle, *God Will See You Through* (Unity Village, MO: Unity School of Christianity, 1983). Mary L. Kupferle, *Trust in the Goodness of God* (Unity Village, MO: Unity Books, 2000).

4 Noelle Sterne, "Are You Blooming or Wilting Where You Are Planted?" *Pure Inspiration* 13 (2009): 74-77.

5 Walsch, 169.

6 Frank, 837.

7 Napoleon Hill, *Law of Success: The 21st-Century Edition, Revised and Updated* (Los Angeles, CA: Highroads Media, 2003). Napoleon Hill, *Think and Grow Rich: The Landmark Bestseller—Now Revised and Updated for the 21st Century* (New York: Tarcher/Penguin, ©1937, 2005).

8 Christine Brennan, "Florida Athlete Only Needed One Leg to Have a Hall of Fame Career," *USA Today*, April 21, 2009. http://www.usatoday.com/sports/columnist/brennan/2009-04-20-carljoseph_N.htm.

9 United Technologies, *Don't Be Afraid to Fail* (Hartford, CT: United Technologies Corp., 1981). John White, *Rejection* (Reading, MA: Addison Wesley, 1982). See also *Chicken Soup for the Soul.* http://www.chickensoup.com/.

10 William Cox, "Henry Ford Was a Failure!" *ArticlesBase*, July 17, 2007. http://www.articlesbase.com/motivational-articles/henry-ford-was-a-failure-183322.html.

11 James Hillman, *The Soul's Code: In Search of Character and Calling* (New York: Warner Books, 1996), 248.

12 Kieves, "Reach for Greatness Instead of Familiarity."

13 Smith, 111.

14 Ernest Holmes, *Your Invisible Power* (Los Angeles, CA: Science of Mind Publications, 1985), 23-24.

15 Hay, *The Power Is Within You*, 164.

16 Nancy McFadden. http://www.motivationaldepot.com/speakers/authors/k-o/Nancy-McFadden/main/speaker-Nancy.htm.

17 Gilbert, in the first third of *Eat, Pray, Love.*

18 Frank, 257.

19 Cameron, *The Artist's Way: A Spiritual Path*, 3.

20 Butterworth, 143.

21 Bottorff, 2.

22 McWilliams, 65.

23 *Daily Word*, March/April 2010, April 6, 2010: 53.

24 Hicks and Hicks, *Money and the Law of Attraction*, 103-104.

25 U. S. Andersen, *Success Cybernetics: Practical Applications of Human Cybernetics* (North Hollywood, CA: Wilshire, 1972), 29-31.

26 Andersen, 31.

27 Shakti Gawain, *Creative Visualization: Use the Power of Your Imagination to Create What You Want in Your Life* (Novato, CA: New World Library, 2002). Wayne W. Dyer, *You'll See It When You Believe It: The Way to Your Personal Transformation* (New York: Quill/HarperCollins, 2001).

28 Gawain, 16-17.

29 Lee Pulos, *The Power of Visualization: Seeing Is Achieving*, audiobook (Niles, IA: Nightingale-Conant, 1993).

30 Katie Struckel, "Find Identity With Joyce Carol Oates," *Writer's Digest* 81.2 (2001): 23.

31 Joseph Murphy, *Special Meditations for Health, Wealth, Love, and Expression* (Marina del Rey, CA: DeVorss, 1987), 23.

Chapter 11

1 Susan (Sorah) Dubitsky, "Jean Houston: Human Potential Pioneer," *Miracle Journeys* 5.1 (2001): 39.

2 McWilliams, 381.

3 Hay, *The Power Is Within You*, 44-45, 98-101.

4 Esther Hicks and Jerry Hicks, *The Law of Attraction: The Basics of the Teachings of Abraham* (Carlsbad, CA: Hay House, 2006), 24.

5 *Online Etymology Dictionary*. http://www.etymonline.com/index. php? term=talent.

6 Lettie Cottin Pogrebin, "Border's Original Voices," *Inside Borders*, November/December, 2002, 23.

7 Anaïs Nin, *Under a Glass Bell, and Other Stories* (New York: Penguin, © 1948, 1980), 221.

8 Chopra, *The Seven Spiritual Laws of Success*, 22.

9 Robert Busha, "Smooth Out Your Writing Time," *Writers' Journal* 23.3 (2002): 21. See also David Allen, *Getting Things Done: The Art of Stress-Free Productivity* (New York: Penguin, 2001).

10 Cameron, *The Artist's Way: A Spiritual Path*, 2.

11 Ponder, 111.

12 Quoted in Mary Anderson, *Awaken To Your Soul: A Guide to Remembering Who You Really Are* (Bloomington, IN: iUniverse, 2009), 19.

13 Johann Wolfgang von Goethe, *Faust: A Tragedy* (New York: W. W. Norton, 2000), 30. Emphasis in text. Originally published early 19th century.

14 Noelle Sterne, "Fourteen Fundamentals for More Productive Writing," *The Write Place at the Write Time*, Spring 2010. http://www.thewriteplaceatthewritetime.org/writerscraftbox.html.

15 Quoted in Nita Leland, *The New Creative Artist: A Guide to Developing Your Creative Spirit* (Cincinnati: North Light Books, 2006), 160.

16 Quoted in Alan Cohen, *Sanity: A Five-Minute Soul Recharge for Every Day of the Year* (Carlsbad, CA: Hay House, 2010), 23.

17 Hay, *You Can Heal Your Life*, 90.

18 *Daily Word*, March 24, 1991: 38.

Chapter 12

1 Hendricks, 2.

2 William James, *The Selected Letters of William James* (New York: Anchor Books/Doubleday, 1993), 260. See also two more recent books: John de Graff, David Wann, Thomas H. Naylor, and David Horsey, *Affluenza: The All-Consuming Epidemic* (San Francisco: Berrett-Koehler, 2005). Clive Hamilton and Richard Denniss, *Affluenza: When Too Much Is Never Enough* (New South Wales, Australia: Allen and Unwin, 2006).

3 Lamott, xxvi.

4 Julia Cameron, *Walking in This World: The Practical Art of Creativity* (New York: Tarcher/Penguin, 2003), 147.

5 Frank, 834.

6 Frank, 837.

7 Abraham Maslow, *The Maslow Business Reader* (New York: John Wiley, 2000), 22.

8 *Daily Word*, June 4, 2004: 19.

9 Marianne Williamson, *Return to Love: Reflections on the Principles of a Course in Miracles* (New York: HarperCollins, 1992), 179.

10 Srully Blotnick, *Ambitious Men: Their Drives, Dreams, and Delusions* (New York: Viking, 1987).

11 Marsha Sinetar, *Do What You Love: The Money Will Follow* (New York: Dell, 1987).

12 Donald M. Murray, "So You Want to Be a Writer?" *The Writer's Home Companion* (New York: Henry Holt, 1997), 28.

13 Richard Carlson, *Don't Sweat the Small Stuff ... and It's All Small Stuff* (New York: Hyperion, 1997), 216.

14 Bottorff, 51.

15 Hendricks's "Upper Limit," 2, 3, 6, and throughout.

16 *Daily Word*, March 10, 1991: 24.

17 Quoted in Ponder, 22.

18 Ponder, 22.

19 *A Course in Miracles (ACIM). Volume One: Text* (Farmingdale, NY: Foundation for Inner Peace, 1975), 81.

20 Dyer, *10 Secrets*, 157.

21 Esther Hicks and Jerry Hicks, workshop in Virginia Beach, VA, No. 577, April 12, 1997.

22 Hay, *You Can Heal Your Life*, 122.

23 Hay, *You Can Heal Your Life*, 122.

24 *ACIM, Workbook*, 349.

25 *Daily Word*, March 24, 1991: 38.

26 Adapted from Hill, *Law of Success*, 125.

27 *Daily Word*, May 10, 2003: 25.

28 Ponder, 92.

29 Laura Rowley, "Loving Your Day Job and Your Life," *Personal Finance News,* February 15, 2010. http://finance.yahoo.com/career-work/article/108823/loving-your-day-job-and-your-life.

30 Smock, "No Other Way," 29.

31 *ACIM, Workbook*, 430.

32 Bottorff, 45.

33 Hay, *You Can Heal Your Life*, 112.

34 Quoted in Rick Fields, Peggy Taylor, Rex Weyler, Rex, and Rick Ingrasci, *Chop Wood, Carry Water: A Guide to Finding Spiritual Fulfillment in Everyday Life* (New York: Tarcher/Putnam, 1984), xi.

35 Noelle Sterne, "A Moment," *Magical Blend* 8 (1983): 53.

36 Bottorff, 11-12.

37 Hay, *You Can Heal Your Life*, 126.

38 *ACIM, Text*, 394.

39 Noelle Sterne, "Conquer Jealousy: Wish Other Writers Well," *Absolute Write Newsletter*, September 6-20, 2006. http://www.absolute write.com/novels/conquer_jealousy.htmabsolutewrite.com.

40 Esther Hicks and Jerry Hicks, workshop in Boulder, CO, No. 567, June 12, 2004.

41 *ACIM, Workbook*, 430.

42 *Christ in You: Spiritual Preparation for Easter, 2002* (Unity Village, MO: Unity, 2000), 24.

Resources

In addition to the resources in the Endnotes, I find the following website resources helpful, informative, and downright inspiring. They are here for your use.

A Course in Miracles. Books, products, events. Miracles Distribution Center. *http://www.miraclecenter.org/index.html*

A Course in Miracles. Archives. *http://acim-archives.org/index.html*

Aaron Lazar. Author, speaker, engineer. *www.murderby4.blogspot.com* (Not what it sounds like.)

Abraham-Hicks. The teachings of Abraham. *http://www.abrahamhicks.com/lawofattractionsource/index.php*

Carmen Harra. Psychic, psychologist, author. *http://www.carmenharra.com/*

Corinne McLaughlin and Gordon Davidson. Visionaries, authors, speakers. *http://www.visionarylead.org/*

Deepak Chopra. Author, speaker, founder of Chopra Center. *http://www.chopra.com/*

Jill Jepson. Transformative writing coach, author. *www.writingthewhirlwind.net*

Julia Cameron. Author, spiritual teacher. *http://www.theartistsway.com/*

Laura Backes. Publisher, editor, author. *http://write4kids.com/*

Moira Allen. Publisher, editor, author. *http://www.writing-world.com*

Nicole M. Bouchard. Author, editor, *The Write Place at the Write Time*. *http://www.thewriteplaceatthewritetime.org/*

Patricia Wilson-Cone. Pastor, teacher, therapist. *http://www.jhsmiami.org/body.cfm?id=9361*

Simran Singh. Editor, spiritual coach, author, *11.11* magazine. *http://www.1111mag.com/*

Sister Brigid McCarthy. Co-foundress, Well of Mercy spiritual retreat.
   http://www.wellofmercy.org/

Sorah Dubitsky. Spiritual coach, author, lecturer, editor.
   http://drsorah.com/index.html

Tama Kieves. Spiritual teacher, coach, author. *wwwawakeningartistry.com*

Terry Cole-Whittaker. Minister, spiritual teacher, speaker, author.
   http://www.terrycolewhittaker.com/Terry_Cole-Whittaker/Home.html

Tom Zender. Author, speaker, consultant. *www.tomzender.com*

Unity. *http://www.unity.org/*

Valleri Crabtree. Author, speaker, Unity radio host.
   http://universeresponding.com/index.php

Index

Acknowledgements

I am very grateful to many people for their energy, suggestions, support and prayers during the journey of trusting in this book:

- ❖ Phillip Pierson and Tom Zender, for their initial wonderful endorsements that bolstered me to keep going.
- ❖ Joan Williams, psychotherapist and minister, for her constancy of friendship, support and delight in life.
- ❖ Barbara Van, Unity minister and former Lead Development Officer, for her faith, encouragement and powerful prayers.
- ❖ Stephen Barbara, literary agent, for the time and thought he gave to his critique of my early query before rejecting the book; he doesn't know it, but his wise words spurred me to revise and improve the manuscript.
- ❖ Stephanie Stokes Oliver, acquisitions editor of Unity Books, for her editorial guidance, enthusiasm, consistent encouragement and delightful warmth that helped me complete the manuscript in record time.
- ❖ Sharon Sartin, publishing coordinator, for her skill and efficiency.
- ❖ Andrés Rodríguez and Lila Herrmann, copy editors, for their care and thoughtfulness not only with stylistic details but with substance.
- ❖ Mary Earls, manager of Marketing and Media at Unity, for her expertise, unflagging fervor, and always seeing—and acting—beyond limits.
- ❖ Paula Coppel, Unity vice president of Communications, for her understanding and generosity of spirit.
- ❖ My clients, for the lessons in trusting they taught me and continue to teach me.
- ❖ All the spiritual teachers and authors who share their wisdom and echo in infinitely creative ways the threads of Oneness and trust in the Source.

❖ Tx, my husband, for unstintingly and joyfully surrounding me with the environment, freedom and gorgeous salads I needed to keep nurtured and working.

About the Author

Noelle Sterne is the author of articles, essays, stories, poems and novels blending motivational, spiritual and practical aspects of writing and life. She has published more than 250 pieces in print and online venues, including *Children's Book Insider, 11.11, Living Now, Miracle Journeys, Natural Awakenings, Pure Inspiration, Sasee, Soulful Living, 2008 Novel and Short Story Writer's Market, The Write Place at the Write Time, Writer's Digest* special issues, *Writers' Journal, Writing World, The Writer* and several anthologies.

Her book of original riddles, *Tyrannosaurus Wrecks: A Book of Dinosaur Riddles* (HarperCollins), was in print for 18 years, excerpted in many children's magazines, and featured on PBS-TV's *Reading Rainbow*. A columnist for the *Absolute Write Newsletter*, her column "The Starbucks Chronicles" addressed the struggles of writing, bolstered writers with motivational truths, and extolled the joys of latté sipping.

Dr. Sterne holds a Ph.D. in English and Comparative Literature from Columbia University and taught at the college level for several years. She has conducted a coaching, consulting and editing practice for more than 28 years, and with the highest scholarly standards guides doctorate candidates to completion of their dissertations and subsequent articles. In this work, and as a spititual counselor, she gently helps clients apply the principles in *Trust Your Life*, as she continues to do in her own life.

Visit Noelle online at *www.trustyourlifenow.com*.

B0044